FAMILY FIRMS IN LATIN AMERICA

This is one of the first books of its kind to highlight family firms in a Latin American context, helping students to understand the distinctive nature and challenges of Latin American family businesses and how these issues compare to family businesses around the world.

Building on their experience in teaching, research, speaking, and consulting on the subject of family firms in Latin America, the editors explain the need to implement and adapt traditional frameworks in the changing Latin American reality. Each section provides background on the most important topics in the management of family firms, including strategy, entrepreneurship, and performance, followed by illustrative cases and a discussion of how this knowledge is similar to or different from other parts of the world.

The book's clear writing and in-depth approach will appeal to undergraduate and graduate students of international business, business in Latin America, and family business.

Claudio G. Müller is a Professor of Management at the School of Economics and Business at Universidad de Chile, Chile.

Isabel C. Botero is an Assistant Professor of Entrepreneurship and Family Enterprise at Stetson University, USA.

Allan Discua Cruz is a Lecturer in Entrepreneurship at the Department of Entrepreneurship, Strategy, and Innovation (DESI) at Lancaster University Management School, UK.

Ram Subramanian is Professor of Leadership at Stetson University, USA.

"The book captures the voice of experienced professionals who have thoroughly documented the challenges and opportunities facing a sample of influential enterprising families from 13 different Latin countries. Taken together, they add a nuanced depiction of how family companies emerge and adapt to the economic and social context of Latin America. This book is a much welcomed contribution to our field of our understanding and to what it takes to succeed as a family company in the region."

—**Ivan Lansberg,** *Ph.D., Academic Director for Family Enterprise Programs, Kellogg School of Management, USA*

"Few regions of the world are as influenced by family firms as Latin America. *Family Firms in Latin America* is a breakthrough piece of scholarship. The book presents us with case studies of influential families in business and helps us grasp the conditions and environments in which the families and firms interrelate in order to compete and survive. The editors have performed an invaluable service by compiling studies that help us understand the development and status of family businesses with implications for the future of Latin America and beyond. This is an important contribution to the body of knowledge about family-owned enterprises which will prove valuable for researchers, educators and practitioners."

—**Frank Hoy,** *Ph.D., Paul R. Beswick Professor of Entrepreneurship and Director of the Collaborative for Entrepreneurship and Innovation, Worcester Polytechnic Institute, USA*

"The editors are to be congratulated for not only conceiving of the need for this research but also for assembling an impressive team that has delivered an insightful contribution to global family business scholarship."

—**Emeritus Professor Ken Moores,** *Ph.D. D.Bus, Bond University, Australia; Executive Chair, Moores Family Enterprise*

"Take this journey of discovery from Mexico south all the way to Chile, Peru and Uruguay. Until this book, little has been known about what makes family businesses in Latin America different. Seventeen cases provide an immersion into the different cultures and practices. While not the last word on the subject, this pioneering book will encourage future research and is a colorful and important must read."

—**Ernesto Poza,** *Professor Emeritus, Global Entrepreneurship and Family Enterprise, Thunderbird School of Global Management, Arizona, USA; Founder, E. J. Poza; Founding Member, Family Firm Institute*

FAMILY FIRMS IN LATIN AMERICA

*Edited by Claudio G. Müller, Isabel C. Botero,
Allan Discua Cruz, and Ram Subramanian*

Routledge
Taylor & Francis Group

NEW YORK AND LONDON

First published 2019
by Routledge
711 Third Avenue, New York, NY 10017

and by Routledge
2 Park Square, Milton Park, Abingdon, Oxon, OX14 4RN

Routledge is an imprint of the Taylor & Francis Group, an informa business

© 2019 Taylor & Francis

Library of Congress Cataloging-in-Publication Data
A catalog record for this book has been requested

ISBN: 978-1-138-29849-1 (hbk)
ISBN: 978-1-138-29850-7 (pbk)
ISBN: 978-1-315-09863-0 (ebk)

Typeset in Bembo
by Apex CoVantage, LLC

Printed and bound by CPI Group (UK) Ltd, Croydon, CR0 4YY

CONTENTS

NOTES ON CONTRIBUTORS

Cristina Alvarado is an MSC. Systemic Family Therapy (UAB) with a broad experience in family business consulting. She is currently a doctoral candidate in Psychology of Communication and Change Program of UAB. Her research interest in family firms arose from her extensive experience as a family business advisor in issues as family communication, family governance, family constitutions and conflict management. She has been visiting student of Cox Family Enterprise Center at Kennesaw State University where also she attended the module of Sustainable Strategy and Governance which is part of Advising for Continuity Program. She is focused on understanding the interplay between socioemotional wealth, constructive conflict management and innovation in family businesses.

Carlos R. Arias has a Ph.D. in information systems and applications from the National Tsing Hua University in Taiwan. Carlos has worked as research professor and research director at the Universidad Tecnológica Centroamericana (UNITEC). He has taught computer science courses in Honduras and Taiwan since 1999. He is currently assistant professor of computer science at Seattle Pacific University in Seattle, Washington, where he teaches computer science courses. His research interests are eGoverment, eLearning and computer science education.

Eduardo Artavia is an associate consultant at his family business, Roberto Artavia Consultoría Internacional. In addition, he has a degree in public relations specializing on communications and marketing. He co-founded social enterprise La Esquina in San José, Costa Rica, which helps develop young residents of socially excluded communities through education and social support. He currently works in projects related to automotive, health and retail industries.

Rodrigo Basco has always been interested in the nuances of family businesses. He is an associate professor at American University of Sharjah (AUS)–United Arab Emirates and holds the Sheikh Saoud bin Khalid bin Khalid Al-Qassimi Chair in Family Business. His research focuses on entrepreneurship, management, and regional development with special interest in family firms, and he has taught economics, management, and family business courses at universities in Spain, Chile and Germany. His research has been published in international academic journals, including *Family Business Review, European Management Journal, Journal of Management & Organization* and *International Small Business Journal*, among others. Dr. Basco recently edited a special issue of the *Journal of Family Business Strategy* on the topic "Family Business and Regional Development," and he is an editorial board member for several leading journals. Before joining AUS, Dr. Basco was a post-doctoral scholar at the Witten Institute for Family Business at the University of Witten/Herdecke in Germany. He was also a visiting researcher at the University of Edinburgh (Scotland) and at CeFEO at Jonkoping University as well as a visiting professor at Valladolid University (Spain) and at IMT School for Advanced Studies Lucca (Italy). He also blogs actively about family business topics for a general audience on his Family Firm Blog.

Marc-Michael Bergfeld is founder and director at Courage. Prior to founding the firm, he has served in management consulting and a large German family conglomerate. At Courage, he drives the growth of the firm and actively advises our clients on all aspects of succession and long-term planning. He is also professor of Global Family Firms at Munich Business School, and teaches at world-class universities such as the University of Vermont and the Singapore Management University. He is a Member of the Expert Advisory Group on Innovation in SMEs at the European Commission, on numerous Advisory and Owners Boards in family businesses, and author of the book *Global Innovation Leadership* and the MBS blog.

Isabel C. Botero is an educator, researcher and consultant in the areas of management and family enterprise. She is an assistant professor in the Department of Management and a researcher at the Family Enterprise Center at Stetson University. Isabel obtained her Ph.D. from Michigan State University. Her areas of specialty include strategic communication processes, governance processes, and next generation issues in family enterprises.

Illuminada Severino Bueno has a rich curriculum in the field of research and consulting in family businesses, her primary research interests are in the area of entrepreneurial family enterprising, and the contribution of workplace innovations to organizational effectiveness and performance. She received a Ph.D. in Management from Université of Bordeaux, France in 2012 and is Assistant Professor of

Management at Pontificia Univerisidad Catolica Madre y Maestra, she was part of STEP Project Babson College, Latin American Research Group.

Leonardo Centeno Caffarena is founder and director of Centro de Promoción para el Desarrollo de la Empresa Familiar. He was the Executive Director of the Nicaraguan Institute for the Promotion of the Small and Medium Enterprise, and advised the vice-president of Nicaragua and the Nicaraguan Council for Science and Technology in small firm promotion, entrepreneurship and innovation. He created units at the Universidad Nacional de Ingeniería that foster new venture, promotion of small firm, and survival of family business. Leonardo has published in *International Journal of Entrepreneurial Behavior & Research*, *Sociedad y Utopía* and *Entrepreneurship & Regional Development*, and book compilations. He is an international speaker and his current research is on corporate governance, institutional theory and the internationalization of family firm.

Luis Cisneros is currently associate professor and academic director of the Entrepreneurship and Business Families Hub at HEC Montréal (Canada). He also teaches family business management and governance at the Monterrey Tech's Virtual University (Mexico). Dr. Cisneros has been a visiting professor at ESCP Europe (Paris, France) and Monterrey Tech Campus Guadalajara (Jalisco, Mexico). He has been keynote speaker in many countries (France, Mexico, Sweden, Argentina, Brazil, Spain, etc). He has published several books, chapters, articles and study cases about entrepreneurship and small family business management. Dr. Cisneros holds a Masters in Management (University of Aguascalientes, Mexico), an MSc in Management Control (University Paris-Dauphine, France) and a Ph.D. in Family Business Management (Group HEC Paris, France). He was member of Family Enterprise Research Conference (FERC) Board. Luis Cisneros coordinates several continuing education programs and courses on entrepreneurship and family business management at HEC Montréal. He also advises several Canadian and Mexican business families. Additionally, Professor Cisneros has previous professional experience from a Mexican family business and created and managed three small businesses.

Allan Discua Cruz is a faculty member at the Entrepreneurship, Strategy and Innovation Department (ESI) in Lancaster University Management School. He is a founding member of the Centre for Family Business in ESI. He has published in entrepreneurship journals such as *Entrepreneurship Theory and Practice*, *Entrepreneurship & Regional Development*, *Journal of Family Business Strategy* and *Business History*, as well as in book compilations. He has been a visiting professor in ESAN (Peru), UNITEC and EAP Zamorano (Honduras). His current research focuses on entrepreneurial dynamics by families in business, cooperative forms of entrepreneurship and internationalisation of family businesses.

Neus Feliu Costa is an economist and organizational psychologist as well as a senior associate at Lansberg Gersick & Associates where she has developed expertise in corporate and family governance specializing in large family-owned corporations. Neus holds a Ph.D. in Management Science from ESADE Business School with a specialization in the governance of philanthropy in Family Enterprises. She leads research within LGA on Integrated Philanthropy in Complex Families, Family Enterprise Sustainability, and Leading Women on Family Enterprises

Paloma Fernández Pérez is Professor of International Business History and History of Family Businesses at the University of Barcelona and founder and coordinator of the Network of Interdisciplinary Research in Family Firms. She has been a leading researcher of research groups and competitive research projects about the history of innovation, internationalization, and succession of centennial family firms, in an international comparative perspective. She has recently published "Empresas familiares de Europa, América y Asia, una aproximación cuantitativa" (Bogotá, Uniandes, 2017), and coedited with Andrea Lluch Evolution of *Family Businesses. Continuity and Change in Latin America and Spain* (Cheltenham, Edward Elgar, 2016). She is currently writing on healthcare businesses, and how, in times of weak institutional regulations and economic scarcity, family businesses have played and play in the world an strategic role in flexibly using available resources to innovate and internationalize in specialized health care market niches, often contributing to the dissemination and creation of technological and organizational innovations. She has published several articles on this latest stream of research in Business History about family firms in the global plasma industry, and now is preparing articles about family firms in the modernization of labs, clinics and hospitals, in Europe, North America and Latin America, in the 20th century.

Ana C. Gonzalez L. is Assistant Professor of Management and Director of the Family Owned Business Institute (FOBI) at the Seidman College of Business, Grand Valley State University. Ana holds a Ph.D. in Management from Tulane University in New Orleans, has an M.Sc. in Economics and a Bachelor's degree in Industrial Engineering from Universidad de los Andes in Bogotá, Colombia. Her research interests include entrepreneurship, governance and social responsibility in family businesses. Ana has been a member of the STEP Project for Family Enterprising since 2006, a global research initiative about entrepreneurship in family businesses.

Oscar L. Howell-Fernández is an author and researcher. He is a currently a visiting researcher associated with the Business Families Center at the ITESM, Mexico City. Has recently published a book about the history of a Mexican family-owned business (*La Historia de Estafeta*, Planeta, Mexico, 2017) and a book on digital activism and global business (*La Mano Emergente*, BN, Madrid, 2017). Mr. Howell holds a Masters in Liberal Arts from Harvard University and a B.Sc. in chemical engineering from HAW, Hamburg, Germany. Mr. Howell has held C-level executive positions in IT management and innovation in several companies and has led an Incubation Lab that launched four high-tech start-ups. He advises companies on innovation, strategic IT transformation.

Carole Howorth is Chair in Sustainable and Ethical Entrepreneurship at the University of York in England. She was previously Associate Dean for Research and Interim Dean at the Bradford University School of Management and Professor of Entrepreneurship and Family Business at Lancaster University Management School. Carole researches entrepreneurship in family and social contexts and has been Chair of the Global STEP Family Enterprising Project since 2015. She is academic advisor to the Institute for Family Business Research Foundation.

Luis Jimenez-Castillo is a Ph.D. student focusing on Family Business. Before pursuing his degree at Worcester Polytechnic Institute, Luis was a faculty member at Universidad Panamericana in Mexico where he was also a member of the Advisory Board of the Family Business Management Bachelor's Program. As a Family Business practitioner, Luis served as the Chairman of the Board of his family's firm. He has also consulted for other family managed companies. Luis has published articles in local business magazines in Mexico regarding succession and conflict management in family business. His Ph.D. concentration is on entrepreneurship, and the research topics that are most appealing for him are international entrepreneurship, internationalization of family businesses and corporate governance of family businesses.

María Piedad López-Vergara is full-time assistant professor for the General Management Department at INALDE, Business School, University of La Sabana, Colombia. She obtained her Ph.D. in Economics and Business Administration from the University of Jyäskylä, Finland in 2013 and her executive MBA degree from INALDE, Business School in 2007. She received the Matti Koiranen Award in the category to the best doctoral dissertation made in Finland during 2013–2015. Her research interests include strategy and corporate governance in family firms, the role of women in family firms, psychological ownership in family shareholders and family dynamics in family firms. Professor López-Vergara is the head of INALDE Family Business Research Center. She has experience in Teaching, Academic Research and Business Consulting.

Melquicedec Lozano-Posso is a professor-researcher in Entrepreneurship and Family Business at the Center for Entrepreneurship Development, at Universidad Icesi. He has published papers in different journals as well as book chapters in book compilations. He has been a visiting professor in Universidad de Castilla La Mancha and Universidad de Córdoba, Spain. He is co-author of the book "The New Entrepreneurial Face, research on Youth Entrepreneurship" supported by IADB.

He is winner of "Award UDEM Adalberto Viesca Sada 2009" about Latin American Research Family Business, given by Universidad de Monterrey, Mexico. He is national and international speaker and consultant in several countries. His current research focuses on succession, transgenerational entrepreneurship and entrepreneurial family.

Gaia Marchisio, as an academic advisor, educates and assists entrepreneurial families and their advisors navigating the continuity process over time. Her background in family enterprise started with her family's business where she was raised as a 4th generation successor. As Executive Director, she continually drives innovation in content and delivery methods by developing degree and non-degree programs for entrepreneurial families and professional advisors. Marchisio also founded of the CFEC's Family Business Clinic™, the interdisciplinary advisory arm that provides families immediate assistance on relationship and business struggles. A native Italian, US Citizen, consultant in North and Latin America, Caribbean, Asia, Europe, Australia and New Zealand, and fluent in 3 languages, Marchisio has a strong understanding of interacting with and respecting different cultures.

Fabio Matuoka Mizumoto is Professor at the School of Economics of São Paulo's Getulio Vargas Foundation (FGV-EESP), Brazil. He holds a doctorate in Business Administration from University of São Paulo (FEA-USP) and was a visiting Ph.D. scholar at Olin Business School at Washington University in St Louis, USA. He published a chapter book in the *Handbook of Research on Family Business*, Second Edition. His research interests include entrepreneurship, strategy, organization and governance. He was a former advisor of International Finance Corporation (IFC) and founder-partner at Markestrat, an organization that supports the development of family-owned businesses.

Torsten M. Pieper is Associate Professor of Management in the Belk College of Business at The University of North Carolina at Charlotte, and Visiting Professor with the Family Enterprise Center of the Kenan-Flagler Business School at The University of North Carolina at Chapel Hill (USA). Before joining UNC Charlotte, Dr. Pieper was an associate professor at Kennesaw State University where he was Academic Director of the DBA Program and Research Director for the Cox Family Enterprise Center. Dr. Pieper is President of the International Family Enterprise Research Academy (IFERA), the largest network association of family business researchers in the world, and Editor-in-Chief of the *Elsevier title Journal of Family Business Strategy*, one of only two impact-factored journals dedicated entirely to the scientific study of family businesses. An author of more than 20 articles and 9 books on family business, he is a frequent speaker to professional and industry associations on the topics of family business cohesion, strategy and governance. Dr. Pieper earned his two Master of Science degrees from Saarland University (Germany) and EM LYON Business School (France), and a Doctorate from EBS

University of Business and Law in Oestrich-Winkel (Germany). He grew up in a multinational family business (manufacturer of building materials) and is fluent in German, French and English.

Nadina Mazzoni Pizzati is a Ph.D. candidate in business economics at the Universidad Tecnológica Centroamericana (UNITEC) in Honduras. She is the director of Corporate Social Responsibility (CSR) at UNITEC. Nadina currently teaches a graduate course in corporate governance at UNITEC and her research interests are family businesses, social mobility and corporate social business ethics.

Claudio G. Muller is an Adjunct Professor at the School of Business and Economics at the University of Chile. He received his Ph.D. in Business Economics from Universidad Autónoma de Madrid, Spain. Prior to joining the University of Chile, he was the founder of the Family-Owned Business Chair at the Universidad del Desarrollo, Chile. Claudio leads the FERC Spanish Discussion Group, a virtual conversation group with participants from the Americas, Europe and Asia. He is FERC Advisory Board Member and has been committed to FERC for many years, especially when he acted as overall chair for the 9th Conference organized in Chile 2013, which was held in the southern hemisphere for the first time, then Claudio was the co-host of the 2015 conference in Burlington, Vermont, and of the 2016 conference in Nova Lima, Brazil. Currently, he is collaborating with several research teams and is a guest editor for several special issues in journals with high reputations regarding the topic of family businesses and Latin-American region.

Enrique Ogliastri teaches family business, negotiations, strategy, the case method, and non-profit management at INCAE Business School (Costa Rica) and IE Business School (Madrid, España). He has published over 20 book-length manuscripts, and he is the Director of Academia (ARLA) at the ISI ranked journal of CLADEA (the association of graduate schools of management in Latin America). He is a consultant about family business, and how to do a strategic plan; he is preparing a book about intercultural negotiations.

Luz Elena Orozco-Collazos is full time assistant professor at the Universidad de los Andes. Her research focuses on family firms and organizational economic forms. Regarding family firms, her recent work includes the analysis of gender as part of family firm identity, the analysis of lived values as source of non-economic goals. Professor Orozco-Collazos is Industrial Engineer from Universidad del Valle, M.Sc. in Industrial Engineering from Universidad de los Andes, M.Sc. in Management and Ph.D. in Management from Tulane University.

Maria José Parada is a faculty member at the Strategy and General Management Department and Co-director of the MBA Family Business Lab at ESADE Business School. She teaches Family Business Management and Strategy in different programs. She holds a Ph.D. in business administration from Jönköping International Business School and a Ph.D. in Management Sciences from ESADE. She has been Visiting Researcher of the INSEAD Global Leadership Center, France, and at HEC, Paris. Her work has been published in journals, books, book chapters about governance, professionalization, values, transgenerational entrepreneurship, and next-gen leadership in family businesses. FFI Fellow and Advanced Family Business Advising certificate holder from Family Firm Institute. She is currently chair of the STEP European Council.

Cecilia Pérez Estrella is a researcher at Family Business Center in Pontificia Universidad Católica Madre y Maestra. She is a Professor at the Graduate School and the Marketing School in PUCMM. She was Executive Director of the Global Entrepreneurship Monitor in Dominican Republic. Her current research interests focus on corporate social responsibility, emotions and entrepreneurship in family business, as well as consumer behavior towards family firms.

Héctor X. Ramírez-Pérez is the Dean of the School of Economics and Business Administration at Universidad Panamericana, Campus Ciudad de México. He obtained his Doctoral degree in Administration from Dowling College in the United States in 2015, his MBA degree from Western Illinois University in 2006, and his Bachelor degree in Business Administration and Finance from Universidad Panamericana in 2004. His research interests include strategy, entrepreneurship, and family businesses. He has been visiting professor in Germany and France and he has experience in business consulting for small and medium companies.

Johannes Ritz is Director Latin America at Courage and runs the executive education modules at the Courage Center. Prior to joining the firm, he was Marketing Director at the private university "Universidad Internacional del Ecuador", after working on several consulting projects in different industries in Europe and Latin America. Johannes studied International Business in Munich, Miami, Qingdao and San José (CR) gaining a deep understanding of cultural differences and their effects on business. Johannes advises clients on strategic succession and intelligent innovation, and represents Courage in Latin America. He is pursuing his Ph.D. on internationalization of family firms at University of Antwerp. He is also a Research Associate and Lecturer on Family Firms at Munich Business School.

Salvador Rivas-Aceves, Ph.D. in Economic Sciences, is a faculty member and actual Academic Dean as well as Research Dean at the Government and Economics School in the Universidad Panamericana. He is member of the Mexican Mathematics Society and member of the Research National System as level I researcher. He has published in national and international economic journals since 2005, and his current research focuses on Economic Growth and Financial System Regulation.

Belmarys Rodriguez Polanco is professor and the director at the Marketing School in Pontificia Universidad Católica Madre y Maestra. She worked for nineteen years at the Dominican Republic free zone industry. Her current research interest's area is the online consumer behavior, specifically the power of the brand in the impulse purchase.

Fernando Sandoval-Arzaga holds a Ph.D. in Management Sciences from ESADE Business School and a postdoctoral fellow from London Business School. He has been professor at Tec de Monterrey and EGADE Business School for more than 10 years in subjects such as family business and succession management, firm strategy, and organizational learning, among others. He holds a certificate from the Business Family Foundation to teach the Road Map course. He has also taught at Coursera a MOOC on Business Families. He is research member of STEP (Successful Transgenerational Entrepreneurship Practices) studying successful family businesses around the world and involving internationally renowned universities such as Babson College. He is a member of GRACO-ESADE, a research group on knowledge and learning in organizations. He has presented research papers at conferences such as EGOS (European Group for Organizational Studies) in Barcelona 2009 and Gothenburg 2011, and at the international conference FERC (Family Enterprising Research Conference) of 2010 in Mexico and 2012 in Montreal. He has done consulting on family business and firm strategy for 15 years. He has published in the *Development and Learning in Organizations Journal*, in the *Journal of Family Business Management*, in the *INCAE Business Review* and in *America Economía* online. He currently is the Director of the Center for Entrepreneurial Families in the Metropolitan Zone in Mexico City.

Ram Subramanian, Ph.D., is Professor of Leadership at Stetson University in DeLand, Florida, where he teaches courses in strategic management at the undergraduate, MBA and Executive MBA levels. In May–June of 2016, he spent six weeks as a Fulbright Specialist Scholar at Windesheim University of Applied Sciences in Zwolle, The Netherlands. He has published papers in journals such as *Journal of Management, Journal of Business Research* and *Management International Review*. He is on the editorial board of Case Research Journal.

Luz Leyda Vega-Rosado is a faculty member at the Entrepreneurial and Management Sciences Department and at the Graduate Studies Center of the Inter American University of Puerto Rico at San Germán. Has the Price-Babson Certification for Entrepreneurship Educators. She has been visiting researcher at TEC of Monterrey, Mexico and have recent studies on the Cuban economy. Her research has been in countries competitiveness and family businesses. She is the author of the first book on Puerto Rican family businesses. Her work and publications has been presented in different local forums and international conferences.

Marcos A. Vega Solano is full time Associate Professor for the Agribusiness Management Department in Zamorano University, Honduras. At the same time, he is the Director of the Zamorano Innovation and Entrepreneurship Center. Vega get his B.Sc. in Agricultural Economics in Universidad de Costar Rica in 1988, and then his Master Degree in Agribusiness in 2000 in the same university. At this moment, he is doctorate candidate to get a DBA in ADEN Business School. His experience in the teaching, research and outreach activities in Zamorano University involved several aspects of the entrepreneurial family farm firms performance in Central and South America, writing decision cases presented in various symposiums of the International Food Agribusiness Management Association (IFAMA). Other areas Vega specializes in include Cost Analysis, Business Strategic and Technology Based Innovation.

Diego G. Vélez is a family business consultant, researcher and educator in different areas of management of family business. He is a family business professor in the Business School of Universidad de los Andes in Bogotá, Colombia. He obtained his DBA and his MBA in family Business from Kennesaw State University. His areas of specialty include family and business governance, family business succession, and next generation development in family companies.

Alvaro Vilaseca served as faculty member at IEEM, the Business School of the University of Montevideo and as Visiting Professor at IAE (Universidad Austral), in Buenos Aires; INALDE (Universidad de La Sabana), in Bogotá; IPADE (Universidad Panamericana), in Mexico City; ESE (Universidad de los Andes), in Santiago de Chile; PAD (Universidad de Piura), in Lima; ISE, in Sao Paulo; and IDE, in Quito and Guayaquil. Professor Vilaseca received the Professor Emeritus Alden G. Lank Research Award 1999, given by the FBN, for his research in Family Business ownership. He is co-founder and Fellow of IFERA (International Family Enterprise Research Academy). Given his experience as specialized consultant for the International Development Bank (IDB), concerning the design and implementation of projects regarding the Family Business Firms development, his professional interest is focused in the foundation and development of regional Family Business Centers (CEF-Uruguay and IADEF-Argentina).

David E. Wong Cam is Professor at Faculty of Economics and Finance of the Universidad del Pacífico and CIUP researcher. He has a Ph.D. in Economics and Business Management and M.Sc. in Advanced Management by the Universidad Comercial de Deusto (Spain). He also holds a Master's Degree in Business Administration and a Bachelor's Degree in Administration from Universidad del Pacífico. He has done complementary studies on Management at the Catholic University of Leuven (Belgium). He has extensive experience as a teacher and exhibitor. He has earned awards such as Cátedra del Banco Interandino y Cátedra del Banco Santander, as well as the Prize for interdisciplinary research at the Universidad del Pacífico. He has been a member of Interdisciplinary Studies on Management and Accounting (INTEGRES). Wong is president of the Board of Directors of the Cooperativa de Ahorro y Crédito Efide. In addition, he held the position of director of the Board of Directors of the Cooperativa de Ahorro y Crédito Abaco and was secretary of Centro de Promoción de la Pequeña Empresa (PROPYME). He has also undertaken consultancies for savings and credit cooperatives in Peru, among other institutions.

1

INTRODUCTION

1.1 Family Firms in Latin America: Why Are They Important and Why Should We Care?

Isabel C. Botero, Allan Discua Cruz, and Claudio G. Müller

Family businesses play an important role for the economy around the world (FBN, 2008; Mandl, 2008). Even though family businesses are the most common form of enterprise throughout the world (Howorth, Rose, Hamilton, & Westhead, 2010), most of our knowledge is based on examples from North America and Europe (De Massis, Sharma, Chua, & Chrisman, 2012). This is problematic because cultural contexts can play a role in how family businesses behave due to the effects that culture can have on individuals, the relationship between them, and how the family and the business are understood (Gupta & Levenburg, 2010; Sharma & Chua, 2013). The family business is a complex social system that includes dimensions such as family control, commercial entities and individual family members suggesting that any commercial activity undertaken can have effects on the family in business (Marchisio, Mazzola, Sciascia, Miles, & Astrachan, 2010). With this in mind, we designed this case study book to gain an important perspective about family businesses in the Latin American region.

Geographically, the Latin American region extends from Tierra del Fuego in Chile to the country of Mexico, including the Caribbean Islands. This group of countries constitutes a rapidly growing and influential region of the world. They have a combined population that exceeds 600 million people, are major providers of strategic commodities to the world (i.e., iron, copper, and zinc), represent an important market for manufacturers, and are important partners to major players around the world (Nicholson, 2011). Family firms dominate the business landscape in this area of the world (Fernández Pérez & Lluch, 2016).

There are four environmental factors (i.e., economy, social context, the political and legal environment) that influence family firms. Latin America has been influenced by the multiple changes that have occurred in this region since the 1960s. At an economic level, the environment in the 1960s was characterized by regional protectionism and promoted the development of small national markets (Lansberg & Perrow, 1991). However, between 1970 and 2000 there was a big shift toward international trade and open markets that created big market changes and higher instability (Britannica.com). The push toward internationalization also promoted the shift in many countries from state-owned enterprises to privatization (Hoy & Mendoza-Abarca, 2014). Countries like Mexico, Colombia, and Chile saw major changes in their business structures (Britanica.com). At the same time, other countries in the region changed from private to state ownership (Lansberg & Perrow, 1991). Two examples of this are Venezuela and Ecuador, which moved toward a more socialist government since 2000. The combination of these factors has created an economic environment characterized as fragile, volatile, and in constant flux.

At a social level, the changes in the economy have created an environment of social unrest characterized by constant social conflict. These conflicts have led to civil wars that have mobilized most of the population into urban settings where 79% of the population now resides (UNEP, 2010). This shift in where the population is located has resulted in increased levels of unemployment, underdeveloped infrastructures, and poor education systems that make the acquisition of skilled workers a difficult task (Nordqvist, Marzano, Brenes, Jimenez, & Fonseca-Paredes, 2011, Poza, 1995). These social issues are also manifested in political and legal environments that are always in flux and require organizations to constantly adapt to the changing government regulations and policies (Lansberg & Perrow, 1991).

The Civil Law System is used to govern most countries in Latin America. Civil law is characterized by having an explicit set of rules that provide a normative approach to how corporations should work and the responsibilities of those who are in charge of the firm. This is different from common law, which is the legal system prevalent in North America. Common law is based on precedence and does not have a codified system. When applied to corporate governance, having a legal system based on civil law requires that organizations follow specific codes and rules that will determine the different governance structures and procedures that organizations need to implement. Thus, Latin American countries have prescribed characteristics that require specific governance structures that need to be used for an organization to be considered legal.

When taken together, all of these issues create climates of uncertainty. In these contexts businesses need to have adaptive structures. For family enterprises, this uncertainty means that they require governance structures that differ from other regions in the world (Monteferrante & Piñango, 2011). For example, the presence of political corruption requires family enterprises to have structures that enable them to have people with good negotiation skills and with power within the company to negotiate with officials at various levels within the public bureaucracy to facilitate the practice of their business within their industry and country (Lansberg & Perrow, 1991). At the family and ownership levels, these characteristics require that governance choices can protect the family and its property. Thus, family businesses in Latin America provide a great context to explore what we know about family businesses around the world, and the generalizability of these ideas.

A significant challenge that family firms in Latin America face is to remain competitive (Bianchi & Wickramasekera, 2016). Family firms' sources of competitive advantage relate to human and social capital, patient financial capital, and low agency costs (Colli, Canal-García, & Guillén, 2013). In the Latin American context, the ability to remain competitive demands family business owners and managers to appreciate and develop capabilities in these areas, while also being alert of changes in the global business environment. Such an outlook opens a diverse set of opportunities and challenges for family firms born in Latin America (Parada, Müller, & Gimeno, 2016).

In this book, **Understanding Family Businesses in Latin America**, we have put together a high-caliber case compilation drawing from family businesses researchers who have close interaction with business families across Latin America. This book is based on a collaborative research framework involving authors from 20 countries and representing the growing amount of family business studies in Latin America. The authors explore diverse themes and processes within family businesses across Latin America. The cases in this book showcase that creating and developing a family business is in itself a monumental undertaking—drawing on the skills, resources, and moral support from family members for generations in contexts that range from supporting to hostile toward family enterprises. This book invites readers to take a closer multidisciplinary look at family businesses in Latin America.

Our goal was to compile a set of cases that show the growing strengths and challenges of family businesses in this region. From humble origins, some Latin American family businesses showcased in this book became leading firms in their countries and regions. Some have become, over one or more generations, successful beacons of enterprise in their home countries behind everyday products and services. This book also highlights that while the long-term survival of family businesses in Latin America is fragile, those businesses which have thrived over generations appear to draw on the key element that lead to their genesis: family. This is a particularly relevant book for instructors who teach about managerial principles in established firms owned and controlled by families in Latin America.

We want to provide a detailed description of potential approaches to investigating both young and long-standing family businesses, and direct instructors to accommodate their own cultural and contextual knowledge when approaching the cases of business families participating in this book. The reader will find that the case method used allows the variation that exists in family businesses in Latin America to be appreciated while adhering to core characteristics sought in the family businesses selected. Some chapters provide a rich description of single cases, which allows instructors to teach students about the overlap of family businesses dynamics with multiple academic disciplines.

The cases and the teaching notes included highlight the varied misconceptions often found in literature about family businesses in Latin America and the efforts by researchers to challenge such views. The cases put forward family business in dynamic and competitive economies, with institutional conditions that foster and challenge the prevalence of family firms.

Essential concepts, theories, and themes are discussed in every case, with authors arguing strongly for the relevance of multidisciplinary lenses when approaching the key decisions faced by every business family represented in this book. Instructors will find that the book comprises chapters relying on rich historical analysis, quantitative data, and comprehensive literature review. This approach helps to provide a meaningful balance to deepening understanding of family businesses across Latin America.

In this first section we introduce the Latin American Region, and highlight its importance in the economy of the world. From a practitioner side we discuss the role that family firms from this part of the world have as global competitors. In this section we highlight the unique characteristics that become sources of competitive advantage, and those factors that can inhibit the success of the firm. We finalize the section by summarizing how regional development continues to have an influence in the entrepreneurial development of Latin American family firms.

The second section focuses on ownership and governance structures in Latin American family firms. In this section we introduce the Family Business group as a unique ownership structure that provides opportunities for business, but also brings challenges for the governance of the family enterprise. The cases in this section illustrate how the governance structures that are used in Latin American firms should not always be rigid, and need to provide flexibility to enable families to accommodate all the demands of the different stakeholders of the firm. Cases in this section also show how young these family enterprises are, and the challenges that they face when younger generations leave their countries to study abroad, and then return to be part of a business that is very different from what they learned in the countries that they were educated in. Showing the entrepreneurial initiative that younger generations need to have to be successful in the family firm when they return from their time abroad.

The third section focuses on strategy and entrepreneurship. Cases in this section emphasize the entrepreneurial and strategic dynamics behind family multinationals and draw from family accounts from Chile, Puerto Rico and The Dominican Republic. The cases showcase the way in which families negotiate and adapt to diverse contextual challenges when expanding their businesses. It shows that the family system and its life cycle, alongside inherent processes, influence the way in which businesses expand operations locally and the way such growth goes hand in hand with addressing societal concerns. Cases showcase that emotions, skills, knowledge, and tradition often blend into the way families cope with establishing and strategically developing their firms. Every generation involved had an opportunity to elevate the scope of their businesses, challenged to engage continuously in entrepreneurial activities to ensure the survival of their business in often rapidly changing contexts. The cases showcase that while entrepreneurship practices were strongly associated with founding generations, succeeding generations had to emulate, in their own unique approach, such formidable entrepreneurial action amidst changes in strategy, family culture and managerial techniques. For these businesses to survive the test of time is an achievement in itself.

The fourth section talks about family dynamics and how they affect the family firm and the business family. A strong theme in this chapter is the influence that family dynamics can have in the choices that business families and next generation members make throughout their careers. The cases in this chapter draw on the strong connections that Latin American families have, and how enmeshed they are. The cases illustrate how the high levels of interdependence and sense of commitment and obligation that family members have toward each other influence the types of choices that family members are likely to make in relation to their career, the decisions that they need to make about family, and the commitment toward the business. This chapter identifies the family system as an important source of differentiation for Latin American family firms that can challenge decision-making processes at the individual, group, and organizational level.

The fifth section focuses on organizational performance. Organizational performance is influenced by family goals which have a major effect on competitiveness and market position. This section focuses on cases from Brazil, Chile, and Ecuador. The cases in this section deal with the importance of family ties and agency perspectives. Agency premises are relevant in organizational performance as they deal with managerial costs related to the alignment of goals in the absence (or presence) of family ties, inherent risks and executive management behavior. The families in this section are leading firms in diverse sectors where organizational performance is measured in the responses to financial needs, global competition and resource efficiency. Such responses are often evaluated against family goals and motivations for incumbent and future generations. The different cases offer unique organizational performance challenges that suggest a consensus to find a solution is often difficult to reach as both business and family objectives have to be achieved.

The sixth section focuses on internationalization pathways and innovation. A strong theme is the challenge to the misconception that family firms will be reluctant to internationalize. Drawing on research from family businesses in El Salvador, Mexico, Honduras, Venezuela, and Chile, cases explore the various ways by which family firms and the families behind them are able to develop diverse mechanisms to steer their companies while expanding operations across nations. The innovative mechanisms showcased suggest the unique responses to adverse situations often faced in Latin America. A robust notion within this section is the relevance of institutional support and the advantage that contextual aspects provide to family firms aiming to internationalize and develop innovative responses. This support may allow such firms to challenge and often change standards within the sectors in which they operate. In this section, the family firms showcased demonstrate a gradual, yet not necessarily slow, approach to business expansion overseas and a strong emphasis in developing innovative mechanisms for their firms to survive. It challenges the common perception that family firms in this region are mostly local players hesitant to participate in the international arena. Hard-to-imitate resources and capabilities, nurtured over a period of time, allow family firms to leap outside familiar territory and challenge the way things are done.

Overall, these sections provide relevant cases and perspectives that challenge long-standing misconceptions in studies about Latin American family businesses. The findings emerging from studying family businesses in this book provide a fresh perspective by drawing on businesses that challenge and extend the dominant approaches in family businesses.

References

Bianchi, C., & Wickramasekera, R. (2016). Antecedents of SME export intensity in a Latin American Market. *Journal of Business Research, 69*(10), 4368–4376.

Britannica.com. Retrieved February 17, 2018, from www.britannica.com/place/Latin-America

Colli, A., Canal-García, E., & Guillén, M. (2013). Family character and international entrepreneurship: A historical comparison of Italian and Spanish new multinationals. *Business History, 55*(1), 119–138.

De Massis, A., Sharma, P., Chua, J., & Chrisman, J. (2012). *Family business studies an annotated bibliography.* Northhampton, UK: Edward Elgar Publishing.

FBN. (2008). *Family business international monitor.* Retrieved from www.fbn.ua/downloads/monitor2008.pdf

Fernández Pérez, P., & Lluch, A. (2016). *Evolution of family business: Continuity and change in Latin America and Spain.* Chelteham UK – Northampton, MA, USA: Edward Elgar Publishing.

Gupta, V., & Levenburg, N. (2010). A thematic analysis of cultural variations in family businesses: The CASE project. *Family Business Review, 23*(2), 155–169.

Howorth, C., Rose, M., Hamilton, E., & Westhead, P. (2010). Family firm diversity and development: An introduction. *International Small Business Journal, 28*(5), 437–451.

Hoy, F., & Mendoza-Abarca, K. (2014). Latin America. In S. M. Carraher & D. H. B. Welsh (Eds.), *Global entrepreneurship* (2nd ed., pp. 293–312). Des Moines, IA: Kendall Hunt Publishing.

Lansberg, I., & Perrow, E. (1991). Understanding and working with leading family businesses in Latin America. *Family Business Review, 4*(2), 127–147.

Mandl, I. (2008). *Overview of family business relevant issues: Final report.* Retrieved from http://ec.europa.eu/enterprise/policies/sme/files/craft/family_business/doc/familybusiness_study_en.pdf

Marchisio, G., Mazzola, P., Sciascia, S., Miles, M., & Astrachan, J. (2010). Corporate venturing in family business: The effects on the family and its members. *Entrepreneurship and Regional Development, 22*(3–4), 349–377.

Monteferrante, P., & Piñango, R. (2011). Governance structures and entrepreneurial performance in family firms: An exploratory study of Latin American family firms. In M. Nordqvist, G. Marzano, E. R. Brenes, G. Jimenez, & M. Fonseca-Paredes (Eds.), *Understanding entrepreneurial family businesses in uncertain environments: Opportunities and research in Latin America* (pp. 91–124). Cheltenham, UK: Edward Elgar Publishing.

Nicholson, E. (2011). Discovering Latin America and its family businesses. *Tharawat Magazine.* Retrieved from www.tharawat-magazine.com/en/family-business-articles/1888-discovering-latin-america-and-its-family-businesses-3.html

Nordqvist, M., Marzano, G., Brenes, E. R., Jimenez, G., & Fonseca-Paredes, M. (2011). Understanding entrepreneurial family businesses in uncertain environments: The case of Latin America. In M. Nordqvist, G. Marzano, E. R. Brenes, G. Jimenez, & M. Fonseca-Paredes (Eds.), *Understanding entrepreneurial family businesses in uncertain environments: Opportunities and research in Latin America* (pp. 1–28). Cheltenham, UK: Edward Elgar Publishing.

Parada, M. J., Müller, C., & Gimeno, A. (2016). Family businesses in Ibero-America: An introduction. *Academia Revista Latinoamericana de Administración, 29*(3), 216–221.

Poza, E. J. (1995). Global competition and the family owned business in Latin America. *Family Business Review, 8*(4), 301–311.

Sharma, P., & Chua, J. H. (2013). Asian family enterprises and family business research. *Asian Pacific Journal of Management, 30,* 641–656.

UNEP. (2010). Latin America and the Caribbean environment outlook. *UNEP, Panama, GEO LAC, 3.*

1.2 Latin American Family Businesses and Their Role as New Global Competitors

Neus Feliu Costa

To understand the role that Latin American business families and their businesses play in the world today we need to address four questions that help us differentiate between them and their counterparts in the rest of the world, analyze challenges and opportunities, and explain their competitiveness. In this introductory chapter I aim to illustrate and summarize what I have learned throughout my career as an advisor to business families and family businesses in this region. At the end of this paper, I want to highlight the factors that I believe make the family groups in Latin America competitive and unique.

What Is Unique About Family Businesses in Latin America?

To understand the role that Latin American family businesses play in the global economy we first need to understand what makes them unique. Historically, we know that by the 1700s, Spanish and Portuguese sailors had discovered and colonized most of Latin America. They were later joined by individuals from Western, Central, and Eastern Europe, Africa, Japan, and the Middle East who were looking for opportunities in the New World. By the 1800s the mixture of all of these cultures with the natives of the region had created a new group of people with a system that reflected a combination of many cultures. Thus, even though we use the term "Latin America" to refer globally to the regions of America that extend from the northern part of Mexico to the southern part of Chile, we have to recognize the large diversity of cultures present in this extensive territory. Each region of Latin America has different traditions and norms that are influenced by the type of settlers that initially came to the specific area. For example, Germans have influenced Chile and Argentina; similarly, the Japanese have influenced Brazil and Peru, and descendants of people from the Middle East have influenced parts of El Salvador, Colombia, and Venezuela. In each of these cases, immigrants brought skills, drive, and resilience that complemented the unique knowledge held by indigenous people to create a different type of entrepreneur. At the same time, it created commonalities between the regions; for example, hard work, the spirit of innovation, and resilience that emerged from starting again in a new world. These commonalities and differences represent some of the main competitive advantages and pressures that affect family enterprises of Latin America nowadays.

In today's Latin America, most of the big family business conglomerates are one of three types:

1. Descendants of European settlers. This group has a strong influence from European religious tradition, particularly the Roman Catholic religion.

2. Successful entrepreneurs who are either immigrants from Europe and the Middle East, or extremely competent individuals who have managed to succeed in highly rigid societies.
3. Native entrepreneurs who have exploited the creativity of their ideas and seized opportunities through their determination and hard work.

Families from this part of the world tend to be socially responsible and active citizens contributing in visible ways to the social development of their countries. This is an expression of their values but also a way to protect themselves from an environment that can be hostile. The families' strong religious beliefs promote the need to take care of others in these countries which are characterized by social and economic inequality as well as corruption. Through their social responsibility initiatives, families are able to balance their advantages that come from economic success.

Leaders in these families share remarkable features: confidence, resilience, and high tolerance for environmental uncertainty and risk. They are used to managing the enterprise and leading the family in an environment which is politically, economically, and socially unstable. Power and authority rely on a single individual, the Patriarch, who is the founding entrepreneur or his successor in following generations. Patriarchs have an elevated stature in their family and in their business, but also in the community as a whole. This model of centralized authority poses one of the main challenges of Latin American families: leadership transition to the next generation.

Another characteristic that makes family businesses unique in Latin America is the strong sense of connection between the family and its identity that entrepreneurial families have. These connections are more than those we see in families in business in other regions, such as Europe. For Latin American family members who are involved in the business, family identity is closely intertwined with business identity. This is a positive aspect for those families, as it fosters loyalty and commitment to the family, and the desire in young generations to work and contribute to the enterprise after years of being trained abroad. However, it can also become a challenge. In some families, ownership is an integral part of family membership, thus increasing the number of family shareholders that hold on to ownership for emotional reasons rather than for economic ones. In addition, loyalty and a close and tight-knit family structure can restrain the capacity of the family to disagree, to debate, and have different points of view, promoting groupthink and "consensus at any cost". This can entail governance challenges in large families with different groups of shareholders who have different understandings about the vision and management of the business, and who may, at a particular time, benefit from the consolidation of ownership that could provide new opportunities for the future of the family enterprise.

What Are the Challenges That They Go Through That Are Different Than Those in Other Areas of the World?

To understand the role of Latin American Family businesses in the global economy we also need to understand the challenges that they face. From my experience, the main challenge of business families in this region is continuity. Even though this challenge is not unique to the family businesses in the region, what is distinctive in these families is how this challenge can be successfully managed. As mentioned previously, leaders of prominent Latin American families have unique characteristics (e.g., strong patriarchal beliefs, tendency for control, and attachment to power). Thus, processes like succession of leadership roles and transfer of ownership control to the next generation represent a gigantic venture that requires working together with their increasingly large family, fragmented ownership, and the management of a shared enterprise.

Family entrepreneurs in this region of the world are likely to be business-centered, single-minded, and highly confident in their own judgment. They are used to leading the business by creating a highly controlled and centralized system of governance. However, as families grow they require a configuration of ownership and control that demands a more "democratic" structure for governing the enterprise. This shift in control depends on collaboration, and a change in how families select or become representatives in the firm. For example, it may require the development of a system that objectively selects and develops family members so they can be competent at fulfilling governance roles, and can be good stewards for other shareholders. Additionally, it may require the development of better systems of transparency and accountability for the family, to enhance trust between individuals so they will effectively perform as a family and as business.

Moving to a collaborative and formal governance system that is institutionalized and structured is the crucial and most difficult step faced by Latin American family enterprises. This is particularly true in the transition to the second and, especially, to the third generation of the business. Collaborative governance requires more time and effort. Governance is an investment in which entrepreneurs do not always see the benefits right away. They enjoy their role running the enterprise and have a tendency to focus on management rather than governance.

Leadership transition is also a sensitive task in Latin American families. For some, respect is deeply embedded in their individual psychology, which makes it difficult to make decisions without consulting present and past leaders of the business. This sense of respect is enhanced by the prevalence of hierarchical systems that are characterized by patriarchal authority and centralized decision-making. Thus, the attempt to begin planning for the succession of the leader is considered an irreverent provocation to them as the established authority. Moreover, when planning for leadership succession, many Latin American families aim to find the new charismatic leader and to replicate this previous leadership model, failing to recognize that continuity will come through shared authority and a participative governance system.

Another challenge faced by leading family businesses in the region is political participation. It is not unusual that families are invited to support a particular party or that family executives are offered political positions. This is due to their social stature within their own country, first because they are considered managerially competent and, second, in some families they are encouraged by the family sense of responsibility and commitment to their country. Political visibility entails different dilemmas, especially in countries where political instability is a constant. While no participation can be seen as unpatriotic, active involvement in politics by any member of the family, on the other hand, exposes the entire family and business, and it can also create significant conflicts of interest. These choices can affect the capacity of the business to respond to government policies, the role that politically engaged family members can have in the business (i.e., in management or in ownership), and the harmony in the family. As families become larger, not everyone necessarily holds the same political views, creating tensions among them.

What Are the Positive Aspects of Latin American Family Firms?

Among the many positive characteristics of Latin American family firms we must highlight the following:

1. The importance that they give to the education of their younger generations. This includes academic education, business knowledge, in addition to the transferring of values, such as social responsibility, innovation, loyalty to the family, and respect for the authority of senior members of the family.
2. Many business families in Latin American show an entrepreneurial and cosmopolitan character. This is manifested through the opportunities that they give to their younger generations incentivizing entrepreneurship and education (in many cases abroad), resulting in these young family members bringing new business opportunities and new management methodologies to the family enterprise that can be adapted to the conditions of their business and their markets. Successful families use entrepreneurial action as a strategy for growth. This is not without its own challenges, when the worldview and the vision and aspirations about the business of the seniors and younger generation grow apart.
3. Diversification of most of these enterprises occurs with the entry of the second generation, developing multibusiness structures. These are typically controlled by a holding structure, with several interrelated family holding companies, which serves to focus on the strategy and coordinates the finances of the group.

4. Undertaking new ventures allows families to train their next generation. This is very important for society, as younger generations from leading family businesses do not have many opportunities to develop in other companies within the country, regardless of their expertise or training, as it is expected that they will return to their own family enterprise.

How Competitive Are They in the Global Market Place?

Since the 1990s, most Latin American economies have reopened to foreign companies. Local companies have had to face competition, which was lacking in the past. This has forced family enterprises to test their resilience. The fact that many leading families place great importance on entrepreneurship and quality education has led to the development of highly talented family managers. Newer generations bring change to the business by adapting what they learn abroad into their own context. The combination of new management capacity with a high tolerance to environmental uncertainty and the dedication to work shown by Latin American entrepreneurs has increased executive competence. Families are also very inclined to promote their members' entrepreneurial spirit from an early age by encouraging younger generations to bring in new ideas for business development, and providing financial support to help add these new ventures to the family conglomerate umbrella.

Family businesses in the region are well diversified and internationalized. Their larger size relative to their economies allows economies of scale that increase their productive capacity and efficiency. In some respect, diversification protects them from the economic threats that characterize the Latin American environment.

Leading families in the region have dealt with the challenge of succession by institutionalizing formal governance structures and processes that actively address the generational transition pressures and the increasingly complex dynamics within the family and the business. By doing this, they have embraced a more diverse shareholder group. Changes in governance include creating a formal family council to provide a forum in which family members can articulate their values, needs, and expectations in relation to the enterprise. They also develop policies that guard the long-term interests of the family. Additionally, it entails the creation of an independent board of directors that can help balance the institutional polarities that family enterprises face (i.e., open inclusion versus merit selection; forgiveness versus accountability; patience versus decisiveness). Other changes include planning for the retirement of senior family executives, selecting and preparing their successors, and developing training programs to acquire the process skills necessary to function effectively in a more democratized governance system. In these structures, collaboration, compromise, and trust are key.

When taken together, I believe that there are several characteristics that make Latin American business families and family businesses competitive and unique:

1. The characteristics of their people. Latin American families and businesses are characterized by having individuals who are hard workers, resilient, flexible, creative, concerned about social relationships, with strong ties within the local business network, and able to navigate uncertain and dynamic environments. This helps them in their entrepreneurial ventures.
2. Their sense of responsibility toward others, especially their family. This helps them in finding ways to work together and align their interests, even when there are conflicts within the family.
3. Their entrepreneurial spirit. The need to continue the business process, also driven by the increasing demand for creation of wealth for future generations as the family grows.
4. Their capability to adjust and thrive in high risk and volatile environments.
5. Their reputation (some families describe it as credibility and prestige) also plays a critical role in the competitiveness of Latin American family businesses.

As the readers will see in the cases in this book, these strengths can work in favor of the family and the business. However, they can also create challenges that require family business experts to find new ways to help these distinctive family enterprises.

1.3 Family Firms and Local Development in Latin America

Rodrigo Basco

Latin America is neither a homogeneous group of counties nor a mosaic of different political and cultural regions. If we remove the bureaucratic boundaries that divide and segregate Latin American people, the vast geographical area has a diverse, rich, and unique pre-Hispanic evolution and a common social and economic trajectory after European colonization. Since the beginning of the 19th century, boundaries have fragmented the Latin American map, and each country has economically and socially evolved in particular directions. This is the reason why it is necessary to contextualize the study of family firms and regional development in Latin America.

Part of the economic and social evolution of Latin America has been determined by families involved in economic activities to exploit local or international opportunities. It is estimated that 85% of the firms in Latin America are family owned businesses generating more than 60% of Latin America's GDP and employing around 70% of the workforce (EY, 2017). Families have mobilized economic, social, and human resources to exploit opportunities and execute their entrepreneurial role (e.g., the family coffee farm in Guatemala described by Vega Solano and Discua Cruz [2017]). On the other hand, this positive view of the family as an economic actor for developing wealth fades when family firms play the political rent-seeker role without adding value to the economy (e.g., the case of Odebrecht—"it's a Brazilian construction company that became an international giant over years of using bribery and corruption to secure around 100 projects in 12 countries, generating ill-gotten gains of about $3.3 billion" [Lopez, 2017]). Therefore, the following question emerges: Are family businesses good or bad for local Latin America economies?

To explore the aforementioned question, my intention is to contextualize the Regional Familiness Model (Basco, 2015) in Latin America. The model postulates that the presence of family firms, a priori, is not good or bad for local economies but that to disentangle the effect of these firms, it is necessary to see how family firms behave and interact in geographical space. The Regional Familiness Model attempts to understand the embeddedness of family firms in local productive structures by considering two levels through which family firms affect regional development and local economies: 1) the micro-channel—firm productivity as a consequence of resource allocation and 2) the macro-channel—regional productivity as a consequence of regional economic processes.

First, the Regional Familiness Model suggests that the microchannel in the relationship between family firms and regional development comes from the role family firms play in creating, transforming, and allocating resources (i.e., productive factors, human capital, social capital, and creative/entrepreneurial capital) within the region. Differences in the way family and nonfamily firms allocate resources basically come from the meaning—namely, the goals (Basco, 2017b)—owners and managers assign to the firm. While family firms focus on economic and noneconomic (family-oriented) goals (Aparicio, Basco, Iturralde, & Maseda, 2017), nonfamily firms, shaped by market logic, are more focused on business-oriented goals. This has consequences for the reference points these firms use to make decisions and, consequently, for firm performance and productivity (Basco, 2013). Second, the macrochannel in the relationship between family firms and regional development comes from the effects of proximity on regional processes. Regional processes, such as spillovers, information exchange, learning processes, social interactions, and competition and institutional dynamics, are mechanisms that can accelerate or slow the endogenous and exogenous factors that contribute to external agglomeration effects (i.e., those economies of scale that go beyond individual agents and depend on the collective action of agents). Family firms alter the proximity dimensions that serve as a source for regional processes (Adjei, Eriksson, & Lindgren, 2016). However, geographical proximity cannot be considered in isolation, and other facets of proximity have to be used to interpret the coordination problem of economic activities (economic activities that are organized within organizations to create products and services or economic activities that emerge among organizations) at the regional level.

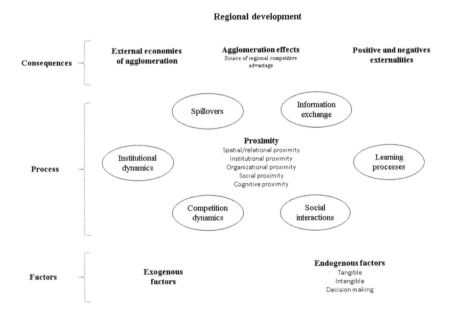

FIGURE 1.1 Regional Familiness Model

Source: Basco (2015)

Specifically, because family firms are locally embedded, thus creating historical, emotional, social, and economic relationships with their context, they may alter the depth and quality of the five proximity dimensions: geographical proximity, cognitive proximity, social proximity, organizational proximity, and institutional proximity.

The aforementioned conceptual model is useful to disentangle the connections between family firms and regional development by connecting the firm and regional levels of analysis. The model itself, however, is contextless. Context is interpreted as "what is beyond the phenomenon itself and it is composed of both physical and cognitive demarcations" (Basco, 2017a). Context matters because economic activities and economic interactions happen within a geographical space that is encapsulated by a macro-context, meso-context, and micro-context. Therefore, I propose that to fully understand the Regional Familiness Model that links the phenomena of family firms and regional development, it is important to consider the industrial, social, economic, geographical, and temporal-historical contexts.

First, the macro-context is characterized by formal (i.e., law, regulations, and written codes) and informal (i.e., cultural) institutional dimensions (North, 1990). While the formal institutional context creates the economic incentives to do business and mobilize resources, the informal institutional context comprises the basic values that individuals and corporations use to discover and exploit opportunities. Second, the meso-context is made up of the particular environment that wraps the link between family firms and regional development. It involves the industry, the region's economic structure, and the social environment in which economic activities are embedded. While the macro-context defines general economic incentives and entrepreneurial opportunities, the meso-context refers to how economic and social actors (formal and informal) are collectively organized around these economic opportunities. Finally, the micro-context is the particular environment of the family that owns, controls, and manages the firm (i.e., the economic resources allocated to exploit opportunities). Business families have their own culture and mechanisms through which resources are mobilized and opportunities are exploited under the macro- and meso-contexts.

The Latin American context is unique (Parada, Müller, & Gimeno, 2016) in terms of its macro-, meso-, and micro-contexts. The macro-context is adapted from the French system of civil law, traditionally recognized by its low protection of minority shareholders and the high ownership concentration in organizations (Faccio & Lang, 2002; La Porta, Lopez-De-Silanes, & Shleifer, 1999). An additional element in the formal context is the weak legal system, a factor that may be behind the large presence of family firms with high levels of family ownership concentration as a mechanism to protect control from external shareholders and to impose their vision within the boundaries of the firm. Beyond the formal context, the importance of family participation in economic activities could be related to the informal institutional (i.e., cultural) context. In general, the

Latin American culture is recognized—using Hofstede's dimensions (Hofstede, 1980)—as a collectivist society with high levels of power distance and uncer tainty avoidance, both of which enhance the relevance of the family in economic activities. While families act as emotional welfare institutions for family members, family firms serve as economic welfare institutions providing economic resources, employment, and security. That is, the family replaces the functions of the state. The result of these formal and informal institutional contexts is often manifested in the immense number of subsistence micro-firms organized through informal flea markets, such as La Salada in Buenos Aires (Argentina) (Beckert & Dewey, 2017); small and medium family businesses that capture economic opportunities, such as in natural resource-based clusters (Basco & Calabrò, 2016); and large family-controlled conglomerates (Robles, Wiese, & Torres-Baumgarten, 2015) that emerge as a diversification tactic to exploit opportunities across industries as a consequence of political rent-seeking strategies (Morck & Yeung, 2003).

The meso-context is greatly affected by Latin America's uneven geographical distribution of natural resources and its urban-rural demographics (i.e., highly populated country capitals are sources of opportunities and wealth but are, paradoxically, where most countries' inequality emerges). Such characteristics determine the existence and types of family firms. For instance, Basco and Cal-abrò (2016) describe the importance of family firms in natural resource-based clusters, where large firms (most of them international corporations) exploit natural resources using local micro-firms (most of them family firms) (Arias, Atienza, & Cademartori, 2014) to supply basic services at very low costs. The uneven economic distribution of resources (i.e., natural, human, social, and political) and industries' regional structures determine the type and quality of relationship between family firms and regional development.

Finally, the micro-context is important because the business family context serves as an economic, social, and emotional support for nuclear and extended family members. In unequal counties like those in Latin America, the economic activities developed by families represent their source of income, their social sta-tus, and the instrument connecting family members. Therefore, the way business families interpret economic activities and the meaning they perceive from those activities determines how family firms behave when looking for, discovering, and exploiting productive (entrepreneurial) and unproductive (political) opportunities. Consequently, family context is the basic source defining family firms' attitudes toward resource allocation and the quality of proximity dimensions.

The Regional Familiness Model and its contextualization are relevant for analyzing and interpreting the trajectory of individual private family firms (case studies), firm groups and conglomerates, the evolution of an industry, and the dynamics of local development. Additionally, the model is a useful tool for poli-cymakers to tailor regional public policy to specific types of economic structures by formally acknowledging that the variety of firms in a region, such as family and nonfamily firms, matters for the local economy (Basco & Bartkevičiūtė, 2016).

References

Adjei, E. K., Eriksson, R. H., & Lindgren, U. (2016). Social proximity and firm performance: The importance of family member ties in workplaces. *Regional Studies, Regional Science, 3*(1), 304 320.

Aparicio, G., Basco, R., Iturralde, T., & Maseda, A. (2017). An exploratory study of firm goals in the context of family firms: An institutional logics perspective. *Journal of Family Business Strategy, 8*(3), 157–169.

Arias, M., Atienza, M., & Cademartori, J. (2014). Large mining enterprises and regional development in Chile: Between the enclave and cluster. *Journal of Economic Geography, 14*(1), 73–95.

Basco, R. (2013). The family's effect on family firm performance: A model testing the demographic and essence approaches. *Journal of Family Business Strategy, 4*(1), 42–66.

Basco, R. (2015). Family business and regional development: A theoretical model of regional familiness. *Journal of Family Business Strategy, 6*(4), 259–271.

Basco, R. (2017a). Epilogue: Multiple embeddedness contexts for entrepreneurship. In M. Ramírez-Pasillas, E. Brundin, & M. Markowska (Eds.), *Contextualizing entrepreneurship in developing and emerging economies* (pp. 329–336). London: Edward Elgar Publishing.

Basco, R. (2017b). Where do you want to take your family firm? A theoretical and empirical exploratory study of family business goals. *BRQ Business Research Quarterly, 20*(1), 28–44.

Basco, R., & Bartkevičiūtė, I. (2016). Is there any room for family business into European Union 2020 Strategy? Family business and regional public policy. *Local Economy, 31*(6), 709–732.

Basco, R., & Calabrò, A. (2016). Open innovation search strategies in family and nonfamily SMEs: Evidence from a natural resource-based cluster in Chile. *Academia Revista Latinoamericana de Administracion, 29*(3), 279–302.

Beckert, J., & Dewey, M. (2017). *The architecture of illegal markets: Toward an economic sociology of illegality in the economy.* Oxford: Oxford University Press.

EY. (2017). *Family business in Latin America.* Retrieved from http://familybusiness.ey.com/pdfs/page-55-56.pdf

Faccio, M., & Lang, L. H. P. (2002). The ultimate ownership of Western European corporations. *Journal of Financial Economics, 65*(3), 365–395.

Hofstede, G. (1980). *Culture's consequences: International differences in work-related values.* Beverly Hills, CA: Sage Publications.

La Porta, R., Lopez-De-Silanes, F., & Shleifer, A. (1999). Corporate ownership around the world. *The Journal of Finance, 54*(2), 471–517.

Lopez, L. (2017). One company has thrown politics in the Western Hemisphere completelly off-kilter. *Business Insider.* Retrieved from www.businessinsider.com/what-is-the-odebrecht-corruption-scandal-2017-5

Morck, R. K., & Yeung, B. (2003). Agency problems in large family business groups. *Entrepreneurship Theory and Practice, 27*(4), 367–382.

North, D. C. (1990). *Institutions, institutional change and economic performance.* Cambridge: Cambridge University Press.

Parada, M. J., Müller, C., & Gimeno, A. (2016). Family firms in Ibero-America: An introduction. *Academia Revista Latinoamericana de Administración, 29*(3), 219–230.

Robles, F., Wiese, N., & Torres-Baumgarten, G. (2015). *Business in emerging Latin America.* New York: Routledge.

Vega Solano, M., & Discua Cruz, A. (2017). Daring to be different: A case study of entrepreneurial stewardship in a Guatemalan family's coffee farm. In M. Ramirez Pasillas, E. Brundin, & M. Markowska (Eds.), *Contextualizing entrepreneurship* (pp. 274–287). Cheltenham, UK: Edward Elgar Publishing.

2

MANAGEMENT AND OWNERSHIP

2.1 Ownership Structure and Governance in Latin American Family Firms

Isabel C. Botero and Diego G. Velez

Family firms represent an important percentage of firms in countries like Argentina (65%), Brasil (90%), Chile (75%), Colombia (70%) and Mexico (95%) and have significant impact in their economies (Poza, 2010; Tàpies, 2011; Superintendencia de Sociedades, 2012). However, we have very limited understanding of how family businesses work in Latin American countries given that most of our knowledge is based on family firms from North America and Europe (De Massis, Sharma, Chua, & Chrisman, 2012). Latin America is one of the fastest growing economies in the world and, with a population of more than 600 million people, can be very influential. Given the important role family businesses play in the world's economy and the limited knowledge that we have about these firms in Latin America, in this section we are going to talk about the unique characteristics of the ownership and governance structures that are used by family firms from this section of the world. Our goal is to provide a basic understanding that can help in the analysis of the three cases presented in this chapter.

Family businesses in Latin America are very young (i.e., most likely to be in their first or second generation) in comparison to Europe and North America. They have high concentration of ownership in the family (Poza, 2010), and are born from the entrepreneur's need to support themselves or their families (Nordqvist, Marzano, Brenes, Jimenez, & Fonseca-Paredes, 2011). One of the unique characteristics of the structure of family businesses in this part of the world is that, as the family businesses grow, they are likely to be organized using a multi-business portfolio structure called "grupo" (Brenes, Madrigal, & Molina-Navarro, 2006; Lansberg & Perrow, 1991; Nicholson, 2011). "Grupos" are holding companies that are structured to include several businesses that are owned by a business family or group of families. The advantage of the "Grupo" structure is that it allows for the involvement of more family members in the business and promotes the diversification of family capital. Additionally, having this structure promotes the entrepreneurial orientation of family members and allows for multiple generations of the family to work in the business at the same time, having power and autonomy over their decisions. As younger generations create spinoffs that are related to the family enterprise (Lansberg & Perrow, 1991), they enter the family business as a company, and are able to retain their independence while having the benefits of the family enterprise (i.e., access to capital, resources, and connections). By having multiple organizations, the family has access to more family capital and can use this capital to fund the new ventures that complement the family portfolio. An important benefit of the "Grupo" structure is that it allows diversifying when the core business has too much cash flow and it is not able to expand within the current market. Thus, by having multiple types of businesses, the family diminishes the investment risk and provides new opportunities for the younger generations. Grupo structures also facilitate the operational management of the firms through the shared resources that they may provide, and can help with financial issues too by reducing the costs and risks for the business family.

However, this business structure can also create interesting challenges to the way family enterprises are governed and managed. For example, having a grupo structure is likely to require a different governance structure. This can be difficult to create because the majority of the governance models discussed in the family business literature assume a single family and single-business structure and do not explain how multiple governance structures can be developed and aligned with the different goals of all of the companies in the group (Steier, Chrisman, & Chua, 2017). Thus, thinking about governance structures and practices in Latin American family firms requires family business practitioners and scholars to be creative and extrapolate ideas from single company structures, to multicompany structures.

In its most general form, corporate governance refers to the study of structures and processes that affect power and influence during corporate decision-making (Aguilera & Jackson, 2010). Within family firms, the study of corporate governance includes the understanding of structures and processes used to ensure that the actions of organizational stakeholders are consistent with the goals of the dominant coalition (Chua, Chrisman, & Sharma, 1999; Gallo & Kenyon-Rouvinez, 2006). However, the family's involvement in a business introduces important considerations to understanding corporate governance (Pieper, 2003). For example, having family involvement in a firm requires structures and processes that allow for parallel family and business thinking that supports, integrates, and balances interests from the family and the business (Carlock & Ward, 2001). Several researchers argue that cultural contexts influence the governance structure that companies elect and the number of structures they use (Aguilera & Jackson, 2003; Li & Harrison, 2008). For example, Suáre and Santana-Martín (2004) suggests that governance practices in Spain are influenced by the characteristics of the legal system. Researchers also argue that a family's involvement in a firm can affect the governance structures that they use. For example, Ward (2001) argues that family firms have a long-term view of their actions and have highly interrelated relationships with other members in the firm. Thus, they use governance structures that help address concerns of the family and the business. Additionally, family businesses are driven by both economic and noneconomic goals. These goals affect how owners decide to structure their governance and other strategic decisions that they make. Thus, family businesses require governance systems that facilitate the development of structures and processes that will help the family, the ownership (i.e., stockholders), and the business (i.e., control/management of the business) systems in their planning, decision-making, and problem solving (Carlock & Ward, 2001).

Therefore, corporate governance in family firms is better described as a system that includes structures and processes that describe how elements from the family, ownership, and business systems interact with each other (Pieper, 2003). In family businesses, governance structures and processes include business components (i.e., Board of Directors, CEO, and top management team), ownership components (i.e., ownership council, shareholder meeting, and family office), and family components (i.e., family meeting, family assembly, and family council) (see Figure 2.1). In the *business* system, corporate governance structures and

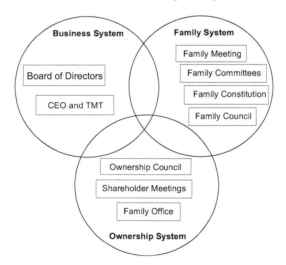

FIGURE 2.1 Family Business Governance Structures by System

(Adapted from Suess, 2014)

processes help outline the practices that managers need to engage in to help the organization achieve its goals (Gersick & Feliu, 2014). In the *ownership* system, the role of governance is to help maintain equity for the owners. This is done by establishing structures and procedures that will help owners with the legal and accounting requirements, setting risk and return parameters, tracking all data on performance to ensure that owners maintain their equity in the firm, and preventing the possibility to take advantage of minority shareholders (Gersick & Feliu, 2014). Finally, in the *family* circle, the governance structures and procedures help the family organize and manage the relationships between family and business (Berent-Braun & Uhlaner, 2012), family and ownership (Montemerlo & Ward, 2011), and family and management (Mustakallio, Autio, & Zahra, 2002). The purpose of governance structures and procedures in the family system is to explicitly articulate and clearly outline the rewards and demands that are linked to being part of the family business, to clearly identify the opportunities for family members to be involved in the business, and to ease the flow of information that is trustworthy between family members (Gersick & Feliu, 2014).

At the practical level, the governance of Latin American family firms can be distinguished based on the generation responsible for control of the business. When the founding generation is in control, it is unlikely that the company or the group will have clearly defined governance structures. During this stage, owners do not believe that others should have a say in their decisions and most of the founders are uncomfortable with being too structured. If the company has any governance structure on the business or ownership side, they are likely to include their friends or friends of the family who would not question their actions. As new generations enter the business, governance becomes more formal because of the need to manage the relationships between members. As the second generation enters the business, organizations need to adapt to a more collective decision-making style. Thus, decision-making is likely to move from autocratic, to consensus to a more participative and democratic style as more generations enter the business. An example of this process can be seen in the role that boards have in the governance of the business and ownership system. As mentioned earlier, it is very unlikely that a founder-led firm will have a board. However, when the second generation joins the firm, Latin American family businesses are more likely to incorporate advisory boards with members external to their families. When siblings are responsible for the business they are likely to rely on their relationship for the management of the business and are likely to consult others on decision, but they will make the final choice. These advisory boards can include the founding generation to keep their ideas and support.

One aspect that is interesting to note about the inclusion of boards of advisors and boards of directors is that when the company moves toward a "grupo" structure the structure of boards changes greatly. Some business families choose to have board structures within every company of the firm, naming one representative from each board to sit on the board for the holding company. This approach is problematic because it leads to conflicts of interests between members and between companies, making the strategic planning for the holding group a very difficult task. A more successful approach that companies have used is to have one board for the holding group with external members, and specific committees that work within each of the companies. The committees consist of the CEO, CFO, and members of the holding company as well as the manager of the subsidiary company. The purpose of these committees is to oversee the strategic and financial direction of the company, and to help the company in contributing the strategy of the holding group. This committee structure helps to prevent conflicts of interest between the different components of the holding group.

One aspect that is unique to family business governance in the Latin American context is family governance. Families in Latin America are more enmeshed, in comparison to other parts of the world. Thus, life is more likely to be centered on the family. Given that most family members are likely to live in the same city, weekly family gatherings are common. Thus, family governance is more informal and done while the family shares time together. In this context, structures like family council, family assembly, or family meetings are less structured because they occur naturally. In some of these cases, a more formal structure for the family governance can be problematic because the family structure tends to become very powerful and wants to control all of the other governance structures including the ownership and business governance. Thus, early on, Mom and Dad manage the conflicts and help maintain harmony in the family. As new generations become involved in the business they start formalizing processes to help the larger family manage the conflicts that can emerge within the family, and between the family, ownership, and business. Finally, structures in the ownership system are likely to become more prevalent with increases in the size of the family and the size of the business.

To conclude we want to highlight three important considerations when thinking about governance in Latin American Family firms:

1. Rigid structures and processes are less likely to work in Latin America. Individuals from these countries like flexibility and are more likely to focus on the relationship between them rather than on the structure of business.
2. The development of governance structures needs to be linked to the relationship of the family and others who are important for the family.
3. Family culture is what makes family businesses in this part of the world different. Thus, family respect, virtues and values need to be considered when thinking about the business family and the family firm.

References

Aguilera, R. V., & Jackson, G. (2003). The cross-national diversity of corporate governance: Dimensions and determinants. *Academy of management Review, 28*(3), 447–465.
Berent-Braun, M. M., & Uhlaner, L. M. (2012). Family governance practices and team building: Paradox of the enterprising family. *Small Business Economics, 38*(1), 103–119.

Brenes, E. R., Madrigal, K., & Molina-Navarro, G. E. (2006). Family business structure and succession: Critical topics in Latin American experience. *Journal of Business Research, 59*(3), 372–374.

Carlock, R. S., & Ward, J. L. (2001). *Strategic planning for the family businesses: Parallel planning to unify the family business.* New York: Palgrave Macmillan.

Chua, J. H., Chrisman, J. J., & Sharma, P. (1999). Defining the family business by behavior. *Entrepreneurship Theory and Practice, 23*(4), 19–39.

De Massis, A., Sharma, P., Chua, J., & Chrisman, J. (2012). *Family business studies an annotated bibliography.* Northhampton, UK: Edward Elgar Publishing.

Gallo, M. A., & Kenyon-Rouvinez, D. (2006). The importance of family and business governance. In D. Kenyon-Rouvinez & J. L. Ward (Eds.), *Family business: Key issues* (pp. 45–57). New York: Palgrave Macmillan.

Gersick, K. E., & Feliu, N. (2014). Governing the family enterprise: Practices, performance, and research. In L. Melin, M. Nordqvist, & P. Sharma (Eds.), *The Sage handbook of family business* (pp. 196–225). London, UK: Sage Publications.

Lansberg, I., & Perrow, E. (1991). Understanding and working with leading family businesses in Latin America. *Family Business Review, 4*(2), 127–147.

Li, J., & Harrison, R. (2008). Corporate governance and national culture: A multi-country study. *Corporate Governance, 8*(5), 607–621.

Montemerlo, D., & Ward, J. L. (2011). *The family constitution: Agreements to secure and perpetuate your family and your business.* New York: Palgrave Macmillan.

Mustakallio, M., Autio, E., & Zahra, S. A. (2002). Relational and contractual governance in family firms: Effects on Strategic decision making. *Family Business Review, 15*(3), 205–222.

Nicholson, E. (2011). Discovering Latin America and its family businesses. *Tharawat Magazine.* Retrieved from www.tharawat-magazine.com/en/family-business-articles/1888-discovering-latin-america-and-its-family-businesses-3.html

Nordqvist, M., Marzano, G., Brenes, E. R., Jimenez, G., & Fonseca-Paredes, M. (2011). Understanding entrepreneurial family businesses in uncertain environments: The case of Latin America. In M. Nordqvist, G. Marzano, E. R. Brenes, G. Jimenez, & M. Fonseca-Paredes (Eds.), *Understanding entrepreneurial family businesses in uncertain environments: Opportunities and research in Latin America* (pp. 1–28). Cheltenham, UK: Edward Elgar Publishing.

Pieper, T. (2003). 'Corporate governance in family firms: A literature review,' Working paper series, INSEAD 2003/97/IIFE.

Poza, E. (2010). *Family business* (3rd ed.). Mason, OH: South Western Cengage Learning.

Steier, L. P., Chrisman, J. J., & Chua, J. H. (2017). Governance challenges in family businesses and business families. *Entrepreneurship Theory and Practice.* Published On-line first.

Suáre, K. C., & Santana-Martín, D. J. (2004). Governance in Spanish family business. *International Journal of Entrepreneurial Behavior and Research, 10*(1/2), 141–163.

Suess, J. (2014). Family governance-literature review and the development of a conceptual model. *Journal of Family Business Strategy, 5*(2), 138–155.

Superintendencia de Sociedades. (2012). *Análisis de gobierno corporativo.* Retrieved de octubre de 12, 2014, from www.supersociedades.gov.co/inspeccion-vigilancia-y-control/gobierno-corporativo-y-rse/documentos/Documentos%20RSE/INFORME%20GOBIERNO%20CORPORATIVO%202012%20(6).pdf

Tàpies, J. (2011). Empresa familiar: un enfoque multidisciplinar. *Universia Business Review,* (32), 12–25.

Ward, J. L. (2001). 'The roles of owners, directors, and managers in family governance', Research Note 10/05/2011.

Case 2.1 JAGA Group: The Difficult Task to Pass from a Serial Entrepreneur to a Family Board

Leonardo Centeno-Caffarena

Don José was looking out the window of his ranch at the flowing river. He thought about how easy the water followed the force of gravity, and how easy it would be if the problems he faced would follow the same pattern. He was facing several problems with his family business group. The JAGA group included 20 firms in different sectors (See Appendix 1), with the most important ones being drug distribution, insurance, valuation of properties, parcels, and an important presence in a hospital, clinical laboratories, farms, and education (a university). Combined, these companies employed more than 700 employees, with sales of US$30 million at the end of 2016. Until now, Don José had managed the JAGA group very informally. This had created an environment that promoted competition between his children, who had different visions for the future of the business, and wanted the best for themselves. Don José had four children who managed different companies within the group. The companies in the group had been their only place of work, and they constantly wanted to show how good they were at their jobs.

Don José was getting ready to hand over control to the next generation. And, as part of this process, he had looked for help from a family business group to plan this process. In conjunction with this group, he had decided to professionalize governance. This offered him two competing opportunities. On one hand, he could name all of his children as members of a board that was responsible for the strategic direction of the group. If he chose this option, it would require his children to leave their positions in the different companies within the group, and work exclusively as directors of the board. This would require them to collaborate and avoid destructive conflict between them. On the other hand, he could hire a professional board and leave all of his children in their current roles. Until now, his children perceived favoritism, unequal load of responsibilities, and were constantly competing with each other to be the best. Thus, if he chose this option it could enhance the current tensions that existed in the family.

Today was the day. His kids were coming to the ranch and he was going to present his ideas and the dilemma weighing on him. What should he do? Should he hire external board members and maintain harmony in the family, or should he persuade his children to work as one in their role as board members? He needed to figure this out soon because his wife wanted him to move on to a new stage . . . one in which he retired.

Background of the JAGA Group

Origins of Don José

The origins of the JAGA Group go back to the entrepreneurial initiatives of Don José. As a young child, he always wanted to make extra money and was always devising different ways to show his entrepreneurial spirit. His brother had always been by his side creating new business ventures with him. Don José was born in Jinotepe, Nicaragua, in 1948. When he was four, his family moved to a small town called La Virgen where he finished primary school and became the best student of the Escuela Superior de Varones and of the Department of Rivas. He had always been an entrepreneur. Some of the economic activities he launched as a child included fishing, commercializing fish and crabs, shoe polishing, account collecting for a funeral home, gloves-production for baseball, organizing baseball teams with all their gear, selling newspapers, and setting up a convenience store in La Virgen along with his mother. Other activities he did later during his college vacations included setting up beauty pageant competitions to select the winner for the yearly beauty pageant for a radio station (Ondas del Sur), selling tickets for dances, and selling commercials for baseball matches.

Back then, Don José was a shy boy, a good student, and focused on working for his future success. When he turned 13, he moved to another city, Jinotepe, to finish his high school degree and study education. After graduating college, he became one of the best teachers in his state and got a full-time position as primary school teacher. This job paid very little, which further encouraged his entrepreneurial spirit, and provided the perfect venue for the development of his "new ventures".

When he was 22 years old, he married Miss Jeanina Gago and had his first and only daughter, followed by three sons. His wife and all of his children were the center of his world, and became his partners as each child would later join the business, and become active members of the JAGA group (see Appendix 2).

In 1973, he moved to the city of Diriamba where he registered his first firm, PROCASA, a hardware store. He obtained a degree in business administration in 1974 in UNAN and a degree in "insurance" at UPOLI in 1979. Studying insurance changed his life, giving him the opportunity to reinvent himself as an account executive focusing on selling and managing insurance claims.

Country Background

Nicaragua is located in Central America, bordering on the north with Honduras, south with Costa Rica, east with the Atlantic Ocean and west with the Pacific Ocean (see map in Figure 2.2).

Throughout the 1980s, Nicaragua was dominated by a war between two main political powers fighting to exert the political supremacy in the Latin American

FIGURE 2.2 Map of Nicaragua

region. This time was characterized by hyperinflation (e.g., up to 43,000%) which was the highest ever in Latin America and one of the highest in world history (Ocampo, 1991). This created a difficult time for doing business and raising a family. The country's population at this time was very divided. Much of the youth was unemployed and/or leaving the country; those in power tormented the Catholic Church; there was a strong dependence on the socialist block; and business owners were being killed and harrassed. However, the beginning of the 1990s brought democracy, and new opportunities for economic growth. During this time the private sector developed and grew, which introduced new drivers to the economy. The country started to grow production and exports, and laid out the bases of the democratic government. However, the Sandinista government won the elections in 2007 with Daniel Ortega who ruled the country following a Christian and pro-entrepreneur approach, mirroring the style from previous Sandinista governments.

Among the milestones achieved by President Ortega are:

1. High levels of growth (i.e., between 4.5% and 5.1%), which are higher than the Latin American average in the last 8 years (BCN, 2016, p. 3).
2. High levels of security (P14GM, 2014, p. 7).
3. Efficient customs service, above the average of the Latin American and the Caribbean (World Bank, 2011, p. 7).

These achievements are the result of the political agreement between the government and the private sector (COSEP, 2017a).

These are some of the challenges faced by the country today:

1. Poorest country in the Americas (Stampini, Robles, Sáenz, Ibarrarán, & Medellín, 2015, p. 8), with a per capita of less than US$3,000 (Forbes, 2016).
2. Strong migration with 20,000 to 30,000 people leaving the country every year, and 10% of the population living either in Costa Rica or the USA (WB, 2008, p. 16).
3. Deterioration of democracy and concentration of power in one family (Economist The, 2014; Magowan, 2016).
4. Control of all the so-called independent institutions, and of the means of communications (La Nación, 2009).
5. High dependence on the international community.
6. High institutional corruption, especially from the electoral power, which is common for the police, the judicial system, and the customs office (Álvarez & Duarte-Pérez, 2017).

The Saga of JAGA

In 1979 the Sandinista Revolution government, following the Cuban model, confiscated most of the insurance businesses of the country. Thus, Don José had to change jobs and become an insurance seller for INISER (the government insurance company). He soon became the best salesperson of that company. During this time, Don José saw many entrepreneurial opportunities. For example, during his frequent visits to drug stores (his kids were small and got sick often), he realized that they sold almost everything: from medical products from Cuba, to beauty items, fruits, and food, and he assessed the huge potential in importing medicines. Thus, through a friend of a friend, he made an appointment with Laboratorios PIZA from Guadalajara Mexico, and dressed in his best suit, met the owners to become their sales representative in Nicaragua. This enabled him to later bring to the country several laboratories: Laboratorios López, ROEME Central America, and Laboratorios Soperquimia from El Salvador.

During the '80s, Nicaragua had scarcity for almost every product due to the "economy of war" imposed by the Sandinista's leaders. To try to help his clients, he started to import different products against all existing restrictions. An existing law determined that exporters could only import and export equal amounts. Given that Don José did not export anything, he bought the "export declaration" from pineapple producers who exported to Costa Rica, allowing him to import different products and supplies. This is how "Importaciones Jeanina Gago", was born.

Once the government started to promote "import substitutions", Don José created a firm named Químicas Maya. From Guatemala, he imported materials to produce beauty products (e.g., perfumes and shampoos), other materials from Miami, and colorants from New York. Under the brand "Jean" he started manufacturing shampoo and conditioner. He later moved to the production of degreaser, floor wax, and other industrial products. He also imported small kitchen appliances (e.g., coffee makers, toasters) from Panama, supplying private companies and the government. Even though all of his products had great acceptance from the local market, the economic blockade imposed by the USA prevented him from bringing more materials, and forced closing the company "Quimicas Maya".

After came the national war (from 1987 to 1989), and when Don José was looking for dollars in the black market to pay his providers, the police stopped him and took him to jail. Being behind bars, he realized that the officer who was taking his declaration did not even have a piece of paper to write on, due to the scarcity in the country. Once freed, he bought a press from a client, and began "Imprenta San Jose", a printing company. With this company he started providing paper materials for the private and government sectors. A partner ran the press, but on one occasion when Don José was in Mexico buying medicines, his associate sold the equipment, and terminated the company.

Those were very difficult times because being an entrepreneur or a business-person was a persona non-grata, a declared enemy of the Revolution, or a "contra revolutionary" for the gang who ruled the country. Those years tanned Don José's skin, and were the best school he ever had, as someone used to working against all odds with very little resources, and being able to build a small empire from the ground up.

Democracy Enters Nicaragua

After democracy returned to the country in 1990, the private insurance broker-age was again a viable option. Don José, who now had 17 years of experience selling insurance and a formidable survival spirit, created "JDC Corredores de Seguros & Cia. Ltda." This company later became the first firm of the JAGA Group. In these first years, he also created "Importaciones Farmacéuticas S. A." (IMFARSA) and "Visión Médica S. A." (VIMESA), and started to forge himself as a successful business owner in the medical field. In the same period ('90s) he started to import used vehicles from South Korea and sell them to cab drivers for US$3,000. He was able to offer comfortable payments of US$10 per day to his buyers. This led to the creation of "Vehículos de Centroamérica S. A." (VECASA). However, given that he did not have experience or the right person-nel to survive in this sector, he decided to close the car company.

Once the economy improved, and the insurance activity was growing, Don José realized the opportunity to develop a company that focused on valuing properties for those applying for credit. Based on this idea, he created "CAPISA", which is today the most prestigious valuing company in the country. During this same period, he also created "Super Desarrollo S. A." (SUDESA) a firm dedicated to the distribution of drugs for humans and animals. Don José also detected the existing difficulties when sending medicines to different cities, and this is how the created CARGO TRAN S.A., a company specialized in transporting parcels, packages, goods, and documents, which is now a referential company in its field.

Today, Nicaragua has a stimulating economic activity with about 20 business groups leading it, most of them family owned. Some of these groups are highly diversified, and are either local or come from the Central American region. These groups have activities in banking, insurance, importation of vehicles, exploitation and export of agricultural products, building, development of infrastructure, customs zone, and commerce, among others. However, only 3.5% of all the firms are considered large (WB, 2011, p. 4).

The most recognized local groups are Pellas, Promérica, Lafise, Lacayo, Cohen, Baltodano, and IPSM (army). Among the foreign-owned groups with local presence are: Poma (Excel Automotriz and Hotel Real Intercontinental Metrocentro), Siman and Q from El Salvador, and Robles (CC Metrocentro), Terra, and Gallo más Gallo, among others from El Salvador, Honduras, Costa Rica, Guatemala, and Taiwán with investments in Mall as Galerías, Metro Centro, and Plaza Inter/ Crowne Plaza (Dinero, 2010). All business groups are members of the Consejo Superior de la Empresa Privada (COSEP), which is the higher representative for business owners, and is an important ally of the government, giving a strong economic and social stability to the country (COSEP, 2017b).

The JAGA Family

The JAGA family includes Don José, Doña Jeannina, and four children: the eldest daughter Jeannina (born in 1971), and the three sons: Geovanny (born in 1972), Carlos (born in 1978), and Jorge (born in 1983). Each of them entered the business at the request of their dad, as he acquired companies and started to grow. They entered the business as soon as they finished college, and had only worked for the family business. However, they brought great energy and purpose to the group as the businesses grew. The family had good relationships and communication; however, they were each responsible for a different company in the JAGA group and had never worked together.

In the last few years, the family had worked together to create several companies: "Agropecuaria Jarquín-Gago", "Warehouse Suply", "J.G. Logistic", Constructora Jarquín-Gago, and Biofarma Laboratorios. By 2008, the JAGA group had acquired many companies, and Don José had become a stockholder and director of other firms (i.e., ALMESA, Porcina San Benito, and Ganadera San Ignacio, Financia Capital, and Hispano-American University). The group was big and Don José believed that he was prepared to face any challenges in the economy, the country, politics, and even natural disasters. Don José believed that the variety of industries in the group gave them an advantage over others.

Don José was a practical man, a visionary, a fighter, frugal, and continuously striving for success. Although he was "retired" in his mind, he was a member of several boards, and was responsible for running an agro-tourism project in the town of Cardenas that provided Walmart with different fruits (e.g., avocado, pineapples, passion fruit, and lemon), and is still very involved in the operations of the group. However, he had not begun to professionalize his company. Right now he was using a "tropical business model" that was informal and allowed him to control all decisions, as he had done for the last 50 years. The JAGA group had more than 20 formal ventures (see Appendix 1). However, what would happen if he died, how could his children manage it all?

Making Decisions About Changes

As the group grew, it became evident that Don José needed to change the way he managed and provided strategic decisions for the group. Until now, the group was accustomed to:

- Working without plans
- Having successors with different visions
- Unequal responsibilities between successors
- Constant friction between successors
- Successors that had doubts regarding their participation in the business
- Successors that were competing to head the most profitable firms in the group, and
- Board meetings that were disorganized, ineffective, and a place for siblings to compete with each other.

To manage these challenges, Don José had looked for the services of an organization specialized in corporate governance for family firms. He had participated in several group meetings and listened to several family business talks. This encouraged him to find the support of a consulting group that would help him create a structure that he needed to achieve continuity in the group.

He had recently finished talking to the consultants, and they had suggested that he needed to create governance structures that that would enable him to strategically plan the role of all of the companies in the group, and to obtain the best benefits for the group. To do this he would need to be able to:

- Develop and schedule planned meetings for the planning and creation of the governance structure
- Create the mission, vision, and values of Grupo JAGA
- Create an organizational structure for a holding company that could help with the management of operations and strategic decision of Grupo JAGA

- Provide a clear description of roles the owners, managers, employees, and family members
- Develop a family protocol to clarify the relationship between the family and the business.

The consultants had suggested that the first step to start this process was the development of a professional board of directors. This board could be composed by completely independent nonfamily members or by a combination of family and nonfamily members. He needed to make a choice as to which option would work best. His wife was asking for more time for her, and he could not reduce his work until he knew that the right structure was in place to make decisions, and to keep growing. This is what the meeting was all about. Would his children want to work together or would he need to hire an independent board to keep the harmony of the family?

References

Álvarez, L., & Duarte-Pérez, J. (2017). Europeos condenan a Daniel Ortega. *La Prensa*, Febrero 17.

BCN. (2016). "Estado de la Economía y Perspectívas 2017", Managua, Nicaragua, Diciembre.

COSEP. (2017a). *Presentan beneficios de las Asociaciones Público Privadas*. Retrieved from www.cosep.org.ni

COSEP. (2017b). *El modelo COSEP: Una Nicaragua próspera y democrática*. Retrieved from www.cosep.org.ni

Dinero. (2010). "Diez grandes de Centroamérica", noviembre 26.

Economist, The (2014). Nicaragua: Democracy weakened. *Politics*, May 15.

Forbes. (2016). Best countries for business.Retrieved from www.forbes.com/places/nicaragua/

La Nación. (2009). "Grupos repudian cierre de radio en Nicaragua", Mundo, San José, Costa Rica.

Magowan, R. (2016). In beautiful, beleaguered Nicaragua, a democracy lies dormant. *Open Democracy*, May 6.

Ocampo, J. A. (1991). Collapse and (incomplete) stabilization of the Nicaraguan economy. Chapter 10 of the book In R. Dornbusch & S. Edwards (Eds.), *The macroeconomics of populism in Latin America*. Chicago: University of Chicago Press.

P14GM. (2014). "Mission trip guide", Project 14 Global Missions, North Caroline, USA, p. 21.

Stampini, M., Robles, M., Sáenz, M., Ibarrarán, P., & Medellín, N. (2015). 'Poverty, vulnerability and the middle class in Latin America,' Inter-American Development Bank, Social Protection and Health Division, IDB Working paper series Nº 591, May.

World Bank. (2008). "Nicaragua Informe sobre la Pobreza 1993-2005", Informe Principal, Informe No. 39736-NI, May 30.

World Bank. (2011). "Enterprise Surveys/Enterprise Note No. 23 Series: Productivity."

Appendix 1

Firms Created

I.   Before or during the Revolution

- Proveedora de Carazo (PROCASA) (1973)
- Importaciones Jeannina Gago Arias
- Químicas Maya, S. A. (QUIMASA)
- Imprenta San José

II. Post-revolution

- JDC Corredores de Seguros Cia y Ltda
- Centro Americana de Protección Industrial S. A. (CAPISA)
- Importaciones Farmacéuticas S. A. (IMFARSA)
- Vehículos de Centroamérica S. A. (VECASA)
- Super Desarrollo S. A. (SUDESA)
- Latin American Cargotrans Logistics S.A. (CARGO TRAN S.A.)
- Visitas Médicas Internacionales (VIMESA)
- Agropecuaria Jarquín-Gago, S.A.
- Warehouse Supply Nicaragua
- J & G. Logistic
- Inmobiliaria Jarquín-Gago
- Constructora Jarquín-Gago (2001)
- Biofarma Laboratorios
- FARMAGO S. A.
- Yeguada Jarquín-Gago
- Proyecto Agro-Turístico (Cárdenas)

Investing as Director/Stockowner

In the 1970s
- Alimentos Mejorados S. A. (ALMESA)
- Porcina San Benito
- Ganadera San Ignacio

In the 2000s
- Financia Capital
- Universidad Hispanoamericana
- Hospital Antonio Roman In Memorian

Appendix 2

FIGURE 2.A1 First, second, and third generation along with political relatives

Case 2.2 Estafeta: Leadership in the Transition to a Family Business

Oscar L. Howell-Fernández, Luis Cisneros, and Fernando Sandoval-Arzaga

Gerd Grimm was an energetic person, determined and independent. He understood the need to make difficult decisions. However, he was not ready for the upcoming meeting. Many questions lurked in his mind about the future. That day in 2011 he was at the doctor because he had not been feeling well in the last few months. After many tests, the doctor was finally ready to talk about what he had.

Dr. Hernandez came that day prepared to explain to Mr. Grimm what he had found. It was not good news. Gerd had a terminal disease. The timing of this news was particularly bad because the market was just recovering from the 2008 financial meltdown, which had hit Estafeta, his company, particularly hard.

Estafeta is a parcel service and express delivery company in Mexico that Mr. Grimm founded. The company started in 1979 by introducing the first door-to-door delivery service in the country, and is now the largest delivery company in Mexico, with over 6,000 employees and 2,500 routes.[1] This company was an important part of his legacy that now faced a continuity challenge. Since he knew that he would not be able to remain at the helm of his company for much longer, many questions about strategy, continuity, legacy, and ownership structure swirled around his mind. Most importantly now, he had to make decisions about the company's future: Should he create a succession plan linking his wife and children, who had never been involved in the business? Or what should he do with his legacy?

Industry Background

The specialized logistics and express delivery service, where Estafeta is a player, is a globalized industry dominated by big transnational corporations and national postal services. Those organizations are active within the global supply chains of major corporations and governments, and are significant in the on-time delivery of everything from industrial parts, supplies, and machines, to the sales of most e-commerce enterprises.

They also provide delivery services for individuals and small companies at competitive prices.[2] One could say, without undue exaggeration, that the modern express delivery company has made the integration of small enterprises into the global trade operation feasible and cost-effective. They do this by operating highly complex multimodal logistics service networks with multiple locations, supported by state of the art information and automation technologies.

Today the size of the sector is close to $150 billion dollars in global revenues.[3] The most important companies worldwide include: FedEx, UPS, TNT

Express, USPS, La Poste Groupe, Royal Mail, China Post, Deutsche Post DHL, Japan Post Group and Sagawa, among others. Over the last decades, the public postal services have adapted to compete on the same terms with private logistics service providers. Some have even been privatized and divested. However, the express delivery sector as we know it today is a recent development. Major companies like FedEx and DHL were created in the United States in 1969 and 1973; FedEx did not start providing international services until the mid-80s. Even though UPS was founded much earlier (in 1907), its business model was originally centered on slow truck delivery. UPS switched only with the arrival of companies like FedEx that developed the express market using airplanes and a new hub-and-spoke logistic model.

Gerd Grimm had been involved from the start in the worldwide development of the express delivery industry. He formed a joint venture in 1974 with World Courier Corporation (WCC), the first company ever to offer international express delivery services. The joint venture, WCI,[4] opened and operated over 50 offices worldwide. Soon after, upcoming competitors like DHL and FedEx lowered prices and pushed WCC out of the mass-market over time, and conquered the international delivery market. In 1978, Gerd Grimm decided to scale down his involvement with WCC and start out on his own in Mexico with the aim of becoming the dominant player in the nascent domestic market for door-to-door express delivery.[5]

The Mexican Context

The express delivery market in Mexico, just like the international market, developed quickly after 1982. New developments in transportation technology and digital communications helped propel the new companies to provide more time-efficient and innovative services. Estafeta would benefit from these changes and would reach its peak of explosive growth around 1998.[6]

NAFTA and the gradual opening of the Mexican economy after 1994 was relevant for the development of the domestic express delivery industry. New infrastructure projects with innovative private/public partnerships models were launched to update the lagging road density in Mexico. New foreign investment flowed into the country to develop new airport facilities and to support a burgeoning *maquila* industry that would require new world-class logistics services.

By 2005 the Mexican domestic express delivery market was a thriving 1-billion-dollar sector, of which Estafeta held the dominant position with an estimated 25–30% of market share, ahead of main competitors like DHL, Multipack, Mexpost, and FedEx.[7] After 2005, foreign companies that specialized in transportation services started to make Mexico a top priority for business development. New companies entered the market and a healthy competitive environment was created, although certain imbalances in NAFTA regulations hamper the sector until today.

Estafeta Background

Estafeta is the market leader for domestic parcel service and express delivery in Mexico. Founded in 1979, the company has been able hold its ground domestically against all the major players, and has remained independent, innovative, and privately held. In 1979, Gerd Grimm and two associates founded "Estafeta Mexicana", the company that would introduce to the market an unknown service: guaranteed overnight door-to-door express delivery. Its first product, called the *Facilito* ("Easily"), was a highly successful disruptive innovation in the Mexican market. At the time, express delivery was already established in the US and Canada, but in Mexico companies had to rely on their own fleet of vehicles or ship using the cargo service of the dominant bus lines. The bus service was deficient and the options were limited. For example, a package sent from Tijuana to Merida could take up to 7 days to arrive, with no guarantees. Customers had to pick up packages at the bus stations. The Facilito was a product that offered a better service and higher pricing, and had to compete against an established service provided by the dominant transportation companies. But in time Facilito succeeded and disrupted the bus companies. Estafeta became immediately a recognized name and a business model to copy.

After the introduction of the first generation of Facilito branded services, the company moved on to create new services that catered to a wider demographic of clients with different needs and in different geographical locations. They started to offer products like: *Económico, Esporádico*, and *Paquetería*.[8] These new products were highly successful in the market. By 1985, Estafeta had expanded and built a network of over 400 representatives spread all over the country.[9]

Building on its initial success, Estafeta decided to integrate the network of independent offices (franchises) into the organization, and create a unified management, sales, and operational structure. The growing company was now organized into several semi-independent regional divisions, which enabled them to better serve client needs. The 5,000-employee mark was broken in 1995, the year after Gerd Grimm stepped down as CEO.[10]

The new CEO, Jose A. Armendariz, steered the company into a new era of specialized IT development, growing the logistical sophistication of the business and launching a wholly owned airline dedicated to cargo transport. He remained as CEO until 2007 when an executive was promoted with the aim of recentralizing the structure and putting an emphasis on operational excellence and quality. This new CEO, who in 2011 still held the position, was successful in the professionalization and institutionalization of the company. He implemented policies that reduced bureaucracy, and created a flatter, more agile organization.

The 2008 financial crisis hit Estafeta and slowed down growth until 2011. In 2011, Gerd Grimm was the majority owner of the company, and had a small number of nonfamily partners as minority shareholders. These included the retired cofounder and a semi-retired owner. The three of them were joined by two outside directors, with limited responsibilities, to form the board and decide the strategic future of the firm.

The Family Leader

Gerd Peter Grimm, born in Germany in 1937 just before the war, had arrived in Mexico in 1961 with $100 in his pocket to work in the import-export business under contract with Fr. Meyer's Sohn, a German freight forwarding company. He soon created his own freight forwarding company (Tratasa, founded in 1964), and continued to expand in the import-export business until several changes in the Mexican economy and legislation forced him to leave this sector and concentrate on a new opportunity: express courier service. Grimm was a self-made man. The hard times during the Second World War and its aftermath prevented him from pursuing a full-fledged education or university degree, and his training was just basic management and fundamental port logistics. But he learned that imagination, hard work, and a straightforward attitude could carry you a long way. Practically on his own, he succeeded in creating a big logistics company: Estafeta.

True to his roots, he instituted a culture of innovation, conservative management practices, financial stability, respect for employees, and founder-centered ownership, very much like the *Mittelstand*[11] model he absorbed as a trainee in Germany. A logistics visionary, Gerd Grimm anticipated changes in the market and adapted the company to new challenges. Thus, Estafeta was always close to the persona of the founder. It was the leadership of Gerd Grimm that gave the business its impetus, its culture and the will to grow and prevail. He was equally as successful in motivating people and crafting a close-knit culture.

The culture of the company gave the employees ample opportunities to try new approaches and make their own decisions. But nobody doubted that Grimm was the person that made all final strategy decisions and his feedback weighed in on all important hires and organizational changes.[12] Even after stepping down as CEO in 1995, his presence was still felt overall in the company. He was the man behind the company. The buck stopped with him.

Mr. Grimm's immediate family has never played a major role in the management of the business or any strategic decision-making. He has always supported and enforced a strong separation of family and business. Thus, in 2011, when Mr. Grimm was faced with a terminal illness and the need for securing his legacy and continuity for the company, he was confronted with three alternatives in ownership changes that could be implemented:

1.   He could craft a so-called "external opportunity". The possibilities included first the launching of an Initial Public Offering (IPO) to take the company public, and second the design of a program for a leveraged buy-in (LBI), or a combination of both. The external option would have allowed him, his

family and his partners to structure an interesting cash-out plan and subsequently relinquish control of the company. This plan could lead to the sale of the company in the future. Global competitors were eager to buy the company, and had submitted unrequested tenders for takeover in the past, which Mr. Grimm had turned down. Moreover, FedEx had recently succeeded in acquiring one of the main competitors, Multipack, and sector consolidation was advancing.

2. The second option was an "internal strategy". This option would not involve the admission of new owners into the company, but would have allowed for the current minority partners and/or managers to augment their ownership interest in the company (MBO). Mr. Grimm and his family would retain a smaller participation in the business. The minority partners would assume control of the company. The older minority partners could be also planning an exit strategy, and the financial burden of the MBO could impact the bottom line of the business.

3. The third option was an "organic change" strategy. Under this approach, Mr. Grimm would establish a way for his whole family (spouse and children) to succeed him in the ownership of the company. The company would then become a family owned business, and the family would have the responsibility for the management, strategy, and growth of the company into the future. However, a large company "morphing" into a family business was fraught with complications, including governance, power, and identity issues. The family was never a part of the business to start with, especially not active in a senior managerial role, and were therefore largely strangers for the professional managers in charge of day-to-day operations.

Mr. Grimm's mind was set on the continuity, independence, and growth of the company. But he was also thinking about possible ways of creating a family legacy. However, given the earlier company history, it was not clear in 2011 if the young CEO or the minority shareholders would welcome the new role of proprietors and directors for Mr. Grimm's wife and four children. It was not certain if the heirs themselves identified with the company or would welcome

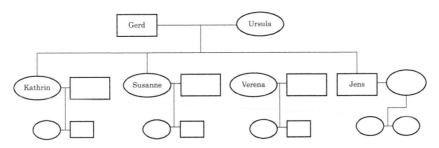

FIGURE 2.3 Grimm family genogram

the ownership, or if a crisis would ensue where the family may be moved to sell the company to avoid strife.

The Decision

Gerd Grimm had built his legacy together with his wife Ursula, with whom he raised four children, three girls and a boy. His view was always that his family should not participate in the business.

Therefore, only his son, Jens, the youngest of the siblings, had worked regularly for the company, starting in operational roles in fleet supervision and later promoted to managerial functions, but was himself never a part of senior management or the board. Gerd's three daughters (Kathrin, Susanne, and Verena) had developed successful professional careers unrelated to the core business or its strategic direction. One son-in-law was briefly hired as a senior manager in charge of IT and innovation, but had long left the company to pursue other career interests. (See genogram for family structure). All siblings are in the 40- to 50-year age bracket, were married, and had children of their own. Even though three of them had not been professionally involved in the firm, they had a strong emotional relationship with the company. For them, Estafeta represented the family's heritage and a source of family wealth. The siblings had formed a strong family core, united and trusting. However, they had never thought about a shared entrepreneurial project.

Mr. Grimm needed to decide how to ensure the continuity, and the proper transfer of power and ownership within a big, successful, and complex company that had remained for all its history closely tied with the founder and his personal style. He needed to make sure that his legacy could continue. But could Estafeta become a family business after such efforts to keep the company out of bounds for the family? Should Mr. Grimm sell and distribute the wealth between his children and wife? What could he do?

Notes

1. As of 2011.
2. Next day delivery of an envelope to almost anywhere in the world costs between 50–70 US dollars.
3. CISION PR Newswire "Global Parcel Delivery Market Insight Report 2015 – Combined Revenues of Carriers Covered in This Report Amounts to US$150 Billion", November 27, 2015, www.prnewswire.com/news-releases/global-parcel-delivery-market-insight-report-2015-combined-revenues-of-carriers-covered-in-this-report-amounts-to-us150-billion-555524051.html, page retrieved June 21, 2018.
4. WCI: World Courier International, a subsidiary of WCC co-owned by Gerd Grimm and headquartered in Mexico City.
5. Five years later the joint venture with WCC was dissolved and Grimm's company retained only the Mexican operations.
6. For a complete account see: Howell-Fernández, Oscar. *La Historia de Estafeta. Un recorrido excepional*. Grupo Editorial Planeta: Mexico City, 2017.

7. According to figures provided by Estafeta.
8. "Económico" is a low-priced variant with no pick-up service, "Esporádico" is a service sold to walk-in customers in a Point of Sale (POS), and "Paquetería" is a service designed for packages weighting 1 kg and over.
9. Howell, *Historia*.
10. Ibid.
11. "Mittelstand: can be used to describe an individual organisation or a type of specialist SME. It has a strong stakeholder commitment, and a focused product-service, usually in industrial sector niches, involvement. The term Mittelstand (strong specialist small enterprise) was coined in Germany and describes companies with 50 to 500 employees and up to 50m annual turnover" (Financial Times, Lexicon).
12. Like the creation of a Board of Directors in 2004, that allowed Gerd to transition into new position with a lower profile.

Case 2.3 What Do They Need to Do If They Want to Belong to This Group? Preparing for the Sixth Generation to Enter the Family Business Group

Melquicedec Lozano-Posso and Isabel C. Botero

Harold Enrique Eder is the fifth generation of the Eder Family that has worked for Grupo Manuelita, a family business group started in Palmira Colombia by Santiago Eder, an American citizen of Russian descent. Manuelita started as a sugar plantation, but now focuses on sugar, oils, ethanol, food, and other products. They have operations in four countries, and are known for their focus on innovation and sustainability. Harold Enrique Eder had joined the group in 2008, to succeed his father and take the reins of the now large corporation. When he entered the business there had not been a clear procedure to determine the characteristics that family members needed to have so they could be active participants in the group. However, he was the only family member who had been interested at the time, which had prevented the potential problems that could have occurred.

As the sixth generation was growing older, there were already five members that had expressed a strong interest in being part of the group at a professional level. They all loved the legacy that the family was developing and wanted to be an active part of it. Harold Enrique was very happy to see this. However, he was also very nervous because the family did not have clear procedures to manage a situation in which multiple members of the family would be interested in joining the business.

In an attempt to prevent future problems, Harold Enrique had started talking with the different members of the fifth generation so they could work together on developing a more formalized structure that could help them manage a situation like this. The family was divided. Some of them thought that this was a futile exercise. They said: "Why do we need this now? We have figured this out for the last five generations, so why do we need to change?" Another group thought it was a great idea. This group believed that a formal structure would give all family members an equal chance of being the director of the firm one day. A third set of members was totally indifferent. They all lived abroad and could not care less what happened in the business as long as they received their dividends.

For Harold Enrique this was a big opportunity to leave his mark in the family side of the business. The family had an annual family owners meeting and he wanted to present this idea. The meeting was three weeks away, and he needed to have a plan so he could include the item in the discussion part of the meeting.

The Origin of Manuellta and Its Initial Transition

Santiago Eder was born in Russia in 1838. At the age of 13 he immigrated to the United States, where many of his siblings resided. He later studied law at Harvard Business School, and, in 1861, right after graduation he moved to San Francisco to practice law. He started working as a lawyer and commercial representative for Panamanian Trading firm, and moved to Buenaventura, Colombia as a representative of the company. In 1864, shortly after moving to Colombia, Mr. Eder found a great opportunity to invest his money . . . a farm close to the city of Palmira called "La Manuelita". He bought the property in a public auction and decided to plant several crops, including coffee and sugarcane.

Due to the strategic location of the plantation (River Valley), sugarcane became the primary product for the farm. Don Santiago had a bigger vision. He wanted to become the primary sugar producer in the country. To achieve this goal he developed the first sugar mill in 1867. Initially it was powered by animal energy. However by 1874, they had changed to hydraulic based power. The production of sugar kept increasing, and by 1901, Don Santiago introduced the first steam engine into Colombia. This engine was the second one in South America, and allowed for a production of 50 tons of sugar per day.

As the business grew, the Eder family began to buy the properties around them to incorporate them into the business. In the beginning of the 20th century, these lands were concentrated in three big farms located in three districts: Miranda (Hacienda "Guengue"), Zarzal (Hacienda "el Guavito"), and Palmira (Hacienda La Manuelita, Hacienda La Rita, and Hacienda Oriente). As the business grew, the Eder family bought and added.

In the beginning, the company focused on the production of bread, honey, aguardiente, and other products that were needed by people in the region. However, when sugarcane became the main focus and the production of sugar increased, they had to rely on the creativity of their employees to overcome the transportation and mass production challenges. Back then, this region of Colombia had no electricity, train, and limited capability to transport products. Thus, Don Santiago developed a mini railway system to move the products around, and to facilitate transportation of the sugar products. This system used wagons to transport the sugarcane. Here the bagasse (i.e., the leftover of the sugarcane after it is processed) was used instead of firewood.

The beginnings required a lot of innovation and adaptation of technology into a different environment. During this time, Manuelita was an important source of progress for the industry and for the country. The Eder Family became associated with hard work and success, and became the pioneers of the Colombian sugar industry.

Don Santiago was a true entrepreneur that led the company through its first stages of development. However, by 1903 he decided to relocate back to the US with his wife. At this time his two eldest sons, Henry and Charles, took over the management and control of the business. The other siblings decided to leave Colombia and start their lives abroad; however, they retained ownership in the business.

The Sugar Sector in Colombia

Sugarcane was brought into Colombia in the 1540s as part of the Spanish Culture. It entered through the port of Cartagena, but expanded through the Cauca River as Spanish conquistadores started using the river to explore other parts of Colombia. Once planted, sugarcane expanded throughout the riverbanks and valleys of the Rio Cauca, where today most of the industry is located, and includes more than five different provinces: Cauca, Caldas, Risaralda, Valle del Cauca, and Cesar.

FIGURE 2.4 Rio Cauca

The sugarcane sector is one of the major driving forces the agricultural industry in Colombia. The country has the capability to produce 76,000 tons of sugar per day and works 330 days per year. In 2016, sugar was one of the top ten exports of Colombia (#8). Almost 80% of the annual sugar production is exported to Peru, Chile, United States, Haiti, and Ecuador. The sugar sector is an important contributor to the agricultural industry (3.4% of agricultural sales in Colombia), and .05% of Colombia's GDP.

Although most of the sugarcane market related to the food and beverage industry, sugarcane plantations from the southwestern region of Colombia have been diversifying their production to include the construction and installation of alcohol distilleries for alternative uses for sugarcane. This has generated the emergence of other industries that are highly connected to the sugar business, and provide new opportunities in internal and external markets. For example, there are several sugarcane plantations that have used the plant for the production of rum, and others have started to produce ethanol.

The Eder Family

In 1867, Don Santiago traveled to London on one of his business engagements. During this trip he met and married Elizabeth Benjamin. Seven children were born from this marriage: Henry, Charles, Luisa, Walter, Phanor, Fanny, and Edith. All of his children were born in Colombia, and were educated outside of the country.

Henry and Charles were the two children that showed interest in the business from early on. Thus, after studying in the US, they returned to Colombia to work and develop the business. They worked very well together, and never involved the other members of the family into the planning of the business. Under their leadership, several important innovations were introduced like the steam engine to power the mills and grew the production from 50 to 300 tons per day.

Henry's son, Harold Henry Eder, took the reins as the third generation in the business. He entered the business in 1930 and worked in the company until 1965, when he left after being the president for several decades. Henry James Eder was the fourth generation who was involved in the business. He directed and was the first to hire a professional president external to the family. His son, Harold Enrique Eder represents the fifth generation, and is the one that currently runs the business. By now the company has grown to include ventures in other industries (i.e., oil, energy, ethanol, fish, food, etc).

Ownership and Business Governance

Manuelita has transformed into an economic group that generates close to 6,000 jobs related to the operations controlled in Colombia, and more than 2,000 jobs in Brazil, Peru, and Chile. Indirectly they also represent an important player for the local economy. For example, in Colombia they have more than 1,000 suppliers, 80% of which are small ventures.

As the group has grown, the family has done a very good job creating a governance system that is well defined in the ownership and the business side at the group level. They have a clearly defined shareholder structure, with a general meeting held every year. This was necessary after a member of the third generation sold part of their shares in 1965. At that time, the company was traded on the stock exchange and another business group purchased shares, gradually achieving up to 30% of ownership. Afterward, another of the larger conglomerates purchased that 30%, and offered to buy other shares from family members, gradually owning 49% of the group. At this point, the Eder family decided to partition the group, with half of the companies going to the outsider group and the other half (Manuelita) to the Eder Family. After this occurred, the family became more organized in their ownership structure.

They also have an Independent Board of Directors, with no directors belonging to any of the companies. Directors serve for a two-year term that is renewable after a successful individual and group evaluation. The president of the group has a voice but not a vote in the decisions of the board.

To assist with the general functioning of the group, there are also:

- Human resources and sustainability
- An auditing committee
- General Business Units
- Corporate office

These areas help in the management and decision-making process related to the economic, social, and environmental affairs of the group. They have helped in the development of the core values for the group (i.e., integrity; respect for people and commitment with their development; social and environmental responsibility; entrepreneurial spirit; austerity; and customer orientation). They have also helped in the development of their code of conduct to ensure the integrity and the future of the organization.

On the family side, the governance is not very formal. This is problematic given that nowadays, the family group, including wives and children, has more than 200 living relatives. Half of these are family members who live abroad and have a very small percentage of ownership in the firm. However, as more members of the sixth generation grow up in Colombia, they also want to be involved in the business in some capacity. So now, they need to start formalizing this part of the governance.

Harold Enrique and His Decision

Harold Enrique Eder had been the president of Manuelita since 2008. After studying economics at Brown University and completing his MBA at Stanford, he worked for Procter & Gamble, Corporación Financiera del Valle, and the

Organización Corona. Later he had been part of the commercial office at the US Embassy in Colombia. He had come to Manuelita with a lot of managerial experience, and with no contention from any other members. Up to now he had focused on the business side, strengthening the strategy of diversification and internationalization, and preserving the family legacy through the creation of their family foundation.

Although it had been clear from the beginning that the Eder last name would not automatically get him a position in the company, there had never been a clear outline of what type of process family members would need to follow if they were interested in joining the firm. The sixth generation was now at the age when they were starting to express their interest in the joining the family group. However, they did not have a clear structure for what to do. He believed that the family should start thinking about this now, and have a clear plan of what to do so they could guide those in the sixth generation that were interested in joining the firm.

Harold had heard from several of the members of the fifth generation and had seen three positions:

1. The "No need for change" group—The members in this group had suggested that everything had worked well until now so, why change?
2. The "Yes" group—The members of this group were ready to start the process.
3. The "Who cares" group—The members of this group were indifferent. They all lived abroad and could not care less what happened in the business as long as they received their dividends.

Harold Enrique was preparing for the annual family owners meeting and wanted to bring this up. He wanted to explain why this change would be beneficial, and provide an idea of what could be included as part of these policies. He only had 3 weeks and was struggling on how to do this . . . what should he do?

3

STRATEGY AND ENTREPRENEURSHIP

3.1 Families in Business: Entrepreneurs and Relations

Carole Howorth

There are many books on entrepreneurship but the majority ignores family influences, which is surprising because family businesses are the dominant business ownership model. Entrepreneurship in a family business context can take a variety of forms and many families have multiple businesses. To really understand entrepreneurship in a family business context, we should therefore shift the emphasis from individual family businesses to the family in business and examine how family members act entrepreneurially together.

At the simplest level, nascent entrepreneurs frequently look first to their family when they are seeking support, resources and employees or partners for their business (Alsos, Carter, & Ljunggren, 2014). In some families, this becomes a norm and more experienced family members might be offended if they were not approached by their offspring or siblings for advice on and support for a new business. For other families, and particularly many Latin American business families, entrepreneurship goes beyond offering support, advice and resources, and becomes a way of working together. In a study of family businesses in Honduras, Discua Cruz, Howorth, and Hamilton (2013) showed how family members from different generations come together as family entrepreneurial teams to found and develop portfolios of family owned businesses. Rosa, Howorth, and Discua Cruz (2014) demonstrate that such portfolio entrepreneurship is a widespread phenomenon among families in business globally.

The case studies in this section examine families in businesses that are active entrepreneurially. It is important therefore that we consider what drivers enable family members to act entrepreneurially in partnership. Three interconnected theories help our understanding: social capital, stewardship, and trust.

Social capital enables the sharing of resources, networks, and knowledge necessary for entrepreneurial activities. All entrepreneurs will employ social capital to a greater or lesser extent, looking to who they know or should get to know to help them access particular resources or markets. Business contacts come and go but family relationships are enduring, so families in business retain a distinctive social capital in relationships between family members. Indeed, social capital could underpin the very familiness that makes family businesses distinct from other types of businesses (Pearson, Carr, & Shaw, 2008). Family members are bound together by a shared past and expectations of a shared future. Relationships among various family members, who may or may not have a formal role in the business, introduce a complexity that nonfamily businesses do not face. Social capital can be extended through family members.

However, the complex social interactions and relationship dynamics of families in business have been labeled 'bivalent' because they have both positive and negative implications (Tagiuri & Davis, 1996). Unique to families in business, family members without a formal role as owners or employees can be influential in the business, some of which may be enhancing and some may be detrimental. Strong bonds between family members create shared understandings on their view of the world and enable them to make speedier decisions about entrepreneurial opportunities and direction, because explanations between family members are not required. The flip-side is that nonfamily managers may feel excluded and peripheral and this can constrain the families' ability to exploit entrepreneurial opportunities.

Stewardship theory complements social capital in that it relates to commitment and shared vision. A stewardship perspective would influence family members to focus on strategies that protect or build their shared assets rather than pursuing their individual interests (Donaldson & Davis, 1991). Thus, family members will provide access to their social capital to further the entrepreneurial efforts and interests of the collective. Stewardship explains commitment to one family business that is served by generation after generation of the same family as well as commitment to support entrepreneurial opportunities throughout the family. Stewardship might constrain entrepreneurship if it leads to risk adverse strategies aiming only to protect the family's wealth. This is more likely when family owners are more distant and focus on short-term financial rewards, i.e. dividends from their shares, rather than long-term investment. In such cases, some families "prune the family tree" to restrict ownership to a smaller group of family members who are more entrepreneurially focused.

It should be noted that the etymological roots of stewardship emphasize that good stewards aim to grow the assets they have, not just protect them in a caretaker role. A stewardship perspective that is true to these roots would be entrepreneurial, not protective, and family members will act entrepreneurially to expand the wealth, assets, and opportunities of the family.

However, families in business are not internally consistent nor externally homogeneous (Westhead & Howorth, 2007). Not all families will adopt a stewardship perspective and those that do may find that there are pockets characterized by self-interested attitudes and behaviors that destroy rather than build value. If some family members indulge in self-serving behaviors, others may feel betrayed and less motivated to contribute toward the general good. Discua Cruz, Howorth, and Hamilton (2013) indicated that where individual family members are self-serving rather than collective-serving, there is likely to be more fragmentation of entrepreneurship within the family and expansion of the original family business may be constrained as individual family members found their own businesses independently or small groups of family members join in founding new businesses together.

In such circumstances, stewardship is undermined by a breakdown in trust. Höhmann and Welter (2005, p. 4) argue that "entrepreneurial behavior cannot be understood without taking into account the phenomenon of trust." Social capital is threaded through with trust, norms, obligations and identity, and trust probably underpins many of the theories that are used to explain behavior in family businesses (Eddlestone, Chrisman, Steier, & Chua, 2010).

A widely used definition of trust is "the willingness of a party to be vulnerable to the actions of another party [who] . . . will perform a particular action important to the trustor, irrespective of the ability to monitor and control that other party" (Mayer, Davis, & Schoorman, 1995, p. 712). When you trust someone you are willing to open yourself up to their actions; if their actions have to be monitored or controlled, this suggests a low level of trust. In entrepreneurial families in business, different individuals or "parties" (e.g. family members, owners, managers) depend on each other and puts themselves at risk, i.e. make themselves "vulnerable to the actions" of the other party. Trust is therefore vital for successful entrepreneurial endeavors. Within families, trust is more likely to be the strongest form, based on identification, as family members identify with each other and frequently share values and behaviors they would understand as normal (Discua Cruz et al., 2013).

Perceptions of trustworthiness vary with context. Mayer et al. (1995) break trust down into trust in another's ability, their benevolence and their integrity. In practical terms, we might trust that our parents will be kind to us (benevolence) and that they will be honest in their dealings with us (integrity) but we may not trust that they will be good at a particular task (ability). Conversely, we may trust that someone is very skilled and capable of doing the task but we might not trust their integrity.

Entrepreneurship in a family business context then is as much about relationships as it is about economic decision-making. We need to consider a broad family context rather than an individual business. As you read the cases in this book, I challenge you to consider the theories discussed here and explore how they provide insights into the entrepreneurial behaviors of these families in business.

References

Alsos, G. A., Carter, S., & Ljunggren, E. (2014). Kinship and business: How entrepreneurial households facilitate business growth. *Entrepreneurship & Regional Development*, *26*(1–2), 97–122.

Discua Cruz, A., Howorth, C., & Hamilton, E. (2013). Intrafamily entrepreneurship: The formation and membership of family entrepreneurial teams. *Entrepreneurship Theory and Practice*, *37*(1), 17–46.

Donaldson, L., & Davis, J. H. (1991). Stewardship theory or agency theory: CEO governance and shareholder returns. *Australian Journal of Management*, *16*(1), 49–64.

Eddleston, K. A., Chrisman, J. J., Steier, L. P., & Chua, J. H. (2010). Governance and trust in family firms: An introduction. *Entrepreneurship Theory and Practice*, *34*(6), 1043–1056.

Höhmann, H. H., & Welter, F. (2005). *Trust and entrepreneurship: A West-East perspective*. Cheltenham, UK: Edward Elgar Publishing.

Katz, J. (2001). Structural reforms and technological behaviour: The sources and nature of technological change in Latin America in the 1990s. *Research Policy*, 30(1), 1–19.

Mayer, R. C., Davis, J. H., & Schoorman, F. D. (1995). An integrative model of organizational trust. *Academy of Management Review*, *20*(3), 709–734.

Pearson, A. W., Carr, J. C., & Shaw, J. C. (2008). Toward a theory of familiness: A social capital perspective. *Entrepreneurship Theory and Practice*, *32*(6), 949–969.

Rosa, P., Howorth, C., & Discua Cruz, A. (2014). Habitual and portfolio entrepreneurship and the family in business. In M. Nordqvist, L. Melin, & P. Sharma (Eds.), *The Sage handbook of family business* (pp. 364–382). London: Sage Publications.

Tagiuri, R., & Davis, J. (1996). Bivalent attributes of the family firm. *Family Business Review*, *9*(2), 199–208.

Westhead, P., & Howorth, C. (2007). "Types" of private family firms: An exploratory conceptual and empirical analysis. *Entrepreneurship & Regional Development*, *19*(5), 405–431.

Case 3.1 El Meson Sandwiches: The First Puerto Rican Fast Food Chain[1]

Luz Leyda Vega-Rosado

Introduction

El Mesón Sandwiches (commercial name for El Mesón de Felipe, LLC) is a family business founded in 1972 by the Pérez-Grajales family in Puerto Rico, a country of the Caribbean. This is the first fast food chain born at the island. They have 39 restaurants in Puerto Rico and three in Florida, United States of America (USA). Three generations of the family have been involved in the business, with the current leaders of the company being members of the second and third generations of the family. This family business is experiencing an important point in its growth strategy due to the challenges of the internal and external environment of the business. One of its challenges is to test that the strategies and the business model are viable outside of its domestic country. Another challenge is to continue growing domestically in a country that is in a deep economic crisis made worse after two hurricanes whipped the island in 2017. A third challenge is how to keep the business growing in the best appropriate way while keeping the ownership in the hands of the family. How do you recommend to the Pérez-Grajales family to meet these challenges?

El Mesón Sandwiches was founded in 1972 by Mr. Felipe Pérez-Valentín. He established a sole proprietorship as a way of self-employment, with the help of his wife, Mrs. Estela Grajales-López. Previously, Mr. Pérez-Valentín was a policeman and Mrs. Grajales-López,a teacher. They had three children: Felipe, Stella Maris and Gil. Felipe and Gil started working very young in the family business when they had vacations from school. Now, the two brothers are the owners of the business founded by their father. Felipe (son) has three children: Felipe Hamílcar, Iraida María, and Lucía. All of them are in their twenties and studying bachelor's degrees related to business. Stella Maris has two girls; one is pursuing studies in law and the other is still a child. Gil has two boys: Franco and Marcos, both pre-teens.

The company is the first fast food chain born in the country (El Mesón Sandwiches, 2017). It was started in the town of Aguadilla, on the western coast of the island (see Figure 3.1). This town has around 2% of the total population of the country with a territory of 1% of the island. The business initially was a small cafeteria, established at the Marbella Shopping Center, a small local shopping center. The main products of this family business are sandwiches prepared with different local ingredients of the highest quality.

In 1987 the oldest son, Mr. Felipe Pérez-Grajales, entered the business as the president and changed it from an individual proprietorship into a regular

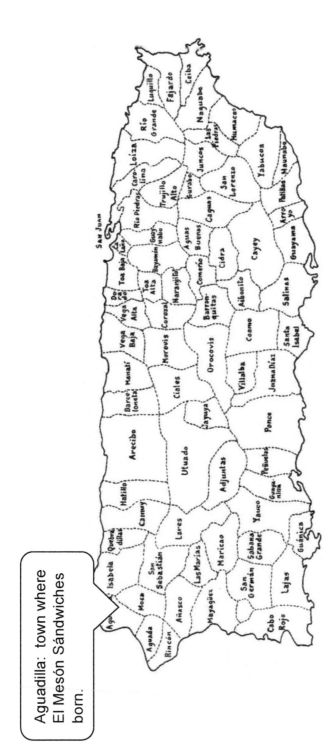

Aguadilla: town where El Mesón Sándwiches born.

FIGURE 3.1 Map of Puerto Rico

Source: Google images. Puerto Rico map. Retrieved from www.google.com.pr/search?q=Puerto+Rico+map&tbm=isch&tbo=u&source=univ&sa=X&ved=0ahUKEw iL_Oznr_rUAhVCSSYKHRThCqQQsAQIJA&biw=1366&bih=622#imgrc=IC8jx-X6_-Cs8M:&spf=14995405409140n July 8, 2017.

corporation. He standardized processes and infrastructure. In 1992, Mr. Gil Pérez-Grajales, the youngest of the three children of Mr. Pérez-Valentín, entered the family business to manage one of the main restaurants in the capital city of the country and is now the vice-president and oversees the supply chain of the firm. The expansion period of the family firm began with the entry of the second generation of the family, opening 37 stores around Puerto Rico and most recently, three in USA. Since 2015, the company is testing its model, for the first time, outside the country. They began in Central Florida, very close to Orlando, using the same strategies that have been successful in the domestic market.

Context of the Country

Puerto Rico (PR) is a country in the Caribbean region located between North and South America (see Figure 3.2). It is the smallest of the Greater Antilles Islands with a territory that covers an area of 100 miles by 35 miles. It is a territory of the United States of America (USA) since 1898 when the USA won the Spanish American War against Spain, the country that colonized the island in 1493 in a trip led by Christopher Columbus. Since 1952, Puerto Rico has been known as the Commonwealth of Puerto Rico. Its population is 3.4 million. Its annual per capita income is US$11,394 (US Census Bureau, 2017). Due to its historical cultural heritage and its geographical location, Puerto Rico has its own idiosyncrasies with a mix of Latin and American manners and mores.

Puerto Rico has been going through an economic crisis since 2006 when the economists officially declared a recession. The crisis has become ever deeper. On June 30, 2016, former US President Barack Obama approved a law called Puerto

FIGURE 3.2 Puerto Rico in the World

Source: www.geology.com. Retrieved from http://geology.com/world/puerto-rico-satellite-image. shtml on July 7, 2017.

Rico Oversight, Management, and Economic Stability Act (PROMESA). That law allows the establishment of an Oversight Board over the local government of Puerto Rico. Many austerity measures have been imposed at the government level to pay off the country's debts. These measures affect the entire population and the businesses. Some measures or laws have been aimed at favoring the business sector such as a labor reform that was effective in January 2017.

At present, entrepreneurship is the main alternative to improve the economy of Puerto Rico. The local market is too small due to different demographic variables that have declined, and economic constraints have stopped the expenditures of the consumers. The business sector must be very creative and proactive in developing strategies of growth that contribute to the national accounts.

Context of the Industry

El Mesón Sandwiches is part of the service sector which is very important to Puerto Rico. It is part of the "accommodation and food services" industry. It is a company that operates as a "restaurants and other eating places" which is classified under code 72251 of the North American Industrial Classification System (NAICS). The restaurant industry supports other industries in Puerto Rico, such as agriculture and food manufacture, which, in turn, produce added employment.

The food and beverage sector comprise 15% (10.7% less than in 2012) of total consumer spending. The restaurant industry controls 36% (7% less than in 2012) of the food and beverage market. Sales in restaurants and cafeterias total over US$3.9 million annually. (Puerto Rico Trade and Export Company cited by ASORE, 2015 with data from 2014).

The main competitors for El Mesón Sandwiches are Subway, Quizno's and the other fast food restaurants that have added sandwiches to their menu such as Burger King and Church's. All of them are American franchises. These last two restaurants present a challenge because they offer lower prices. The average price for a meal at El Mesón Sandwiches is US$6, while Burger King's is around US$4. However, quality and service remain a priority at El Mesón Sandwiches.

Microenvironment of the Family Business

Don Felipe (father) initially prepared his own sandwiches at his restaurant located on Marbella Street in Aguadilla, very close to his home. He also sold ham and cheese by the pound, as done in New York delicatessens and in European shops that he had visited. In her nearby home kitchen, his wife prepared soups, meats, and cakes, which were sold at the restaurant. The decisions were simple, fast and made only by Don Felipe (Vega-Rosado, 2009).

Aguadilla is a town very close to main beaches on the western coast of the country and close to the Rafael Hernández International Airport. It is an important place for the tourism that the island receives from other countries, especially from USA. To appeal to both tourists and locals, the name El Mesón Sandwiches was crafted from two words: one in Spanish, and one in English. The original menu in its first restaurant in Aguadilla was written only in English to service the tourists who visited the area. Customers would read the menu in English, while the restaurant staff addressed them in Spanish (Vega-Rosado, 2009).

Growth and Development of the Family Business

The oldest son of the founder, Felipe, returned to Puerto Rico in 1987 after having obtained a bachelor's degree in management and marketing from The University of Jacksonville in Florida, USA. He returned with knowledge, energy, and motivation to make real the dream that he had since his youth about the potential of his father's business. The same year, the father and son opened a second store in the Mayagüez Mall, the biggest shopping center in the west side of the country. They also incorporated the business that year under the laws of the Commonwealth of Puerto Rico under the corporate name of El Mesón de Felipe, Inc. (alluding to the founder's name). The new corporation would grant 50% of its profit to Felipe (father), to pay him back his original investment; the other 50% would be equally distributed (25% each) between the father and son. The following year, Felipe's (father) original investment in the second store had been paid back in full (Vega-Rosado, 2009).

In 1988, Felipe (son) opened El Mesón Sandwiches at Plaza Las Américas, the biggest mall in the Caribbean located in the capital city of San Juan, Puerto Rico. One of the company's most important achievements from this phase has been its expansion from the western corner of the island to the northern capital, as well as the standardization of procedures and business operations and the purchase of the equipment necessary for it. Gil joined the business full-time in 1992 to head the El Mesón Sandwiches store that was opening in Old San Juan, the historic capital of the country. Besides the siblings of the family, external managers have been incorporated into the business in all the main functional areas, most of them people that begin working at El Mesón Sandwiches making sandwiches. Most of them are still working for the company (Vega-Rosado, 2009).

In 2003, due to the company's expansion throughout the island a new legal and administrative structure that would facilitate a better organized and more efficient operation became necessary. A new corporation, incorporated under the laws of Puerto Rico, was created under the name of Quick Service Restaurant Champs (QSR Champs) a nonfamily business because it has five stockholders, two from the Pérez family and three external. It now administers the 41 restaurants of El Mesón Sandwiches, two Meso Express restaurants (small version of El Mesón Sandwiches) and Western Meat Processor. QSR Champs also oversees the following exclusive suppliers: LMM Food Distributors and El Trigal Bakery.

QSR Champs is considering administering other businesses outside the Pérez-Grajales' family businesses (Vega-Rosado, 2009 and Pérez-Grajales, 2017).

El Mesón Sandwiches, led by Felipe Pérez-Grajales, his brother, a team of managers including Felipe Hamílcar from the third generation of the family, and 1,300 *mesoneros*, as they call their employees, used many strategies to develop the expansion. As Felipe (son) says "we make non-paternalistic decisions". However, one of their internal strengths is the retention rate of their employees and the benefits that they provide to them beyond what the law requires, such as extra bonuses sharing their revenues. Appendix 1 includes information on each of the 41 restaurants that have been opened (QSR Champs, LLC, 2017). Only two of them were closed, the first due to relocation and the other due to closure of the food court where it operates.

To guarantee product quality El Mesón Sandwiches has established close partnerships with local suppliers, or in some cases, has created its own companies that supply restaurant provisions. El Trigal Bakery, a family business owned by Rosa's family from Aguada, PR, is the exclusive producer of the bread used by El Mesón Sandwiches. Western Meat Processor (WMP), another business of the Pérez-Grajales family, led by Gil, purchases, processes, and packages all the meat, sauces, and dressings that are delivered weekly to the restaurants. WMP's facilities meet the highest quality standards in terms of equipment and hygiene that is required by state and USA federal agencies that regulate this type of operation in Puerto Rico. El Mesón Sandwiches developed a partnership with the producers of its coffee. LMM Food Distributors in Arecibo, PR produces an exclusive coffee bean blend developed for the El Mesón Sandwiches' coffee brand. Pérez-Grajales are 50% stockholders of LMM (Vega-Rosado, 2009).

El Mesón Sandwiches use different formats for its restaurants. One format type is the independent store or "freestanding" format and has access through a drive-in window. Each of these independent stores requires an approximate investment of US$700,000 and occupies about 2,000 square feet. Other restaurants in the chain, requiring an average US$350,000 investment, are in strip malls or food courts, along with other businesses. The third restaurant format, known as "combo stores", started in 2000 as a partnership with Baskin-Robbins and Dunkin Donuts, American franchises. Under this agreement, El Mesón Sandwiches shares the same location with these shops, which do not compete with it, but rather complement its menu. Dunkin Donuts is an American chain that sells donuts and coffee. It closed its establishments in Puerto Rico in 2014. Baskin-Robbins is the world's largest chain of ice cream specialty shops, providing one special ice cream for each day of the month. They have 21 stores in Puerto Rico and still one restaurant from El Mesón Sandwiches is in the "combo" format with Baskin-Robbins (Vega-Rosado, 2009).

El Mesón Sandwiches has proven to be a successful business model that has integrated its value chain with its suppliers to provide a product and service of high quality. During the first 41 years of this family business, they opened 39 restaurants in the local market. They have presence in 20 of the 78 municipalities of Puerto Rico. For 43 years the Pérez-Grajales family proved that this business is successful in Puerto Rico. In the last ten years they had failed attempts to open restaurants in Dominican Republic and Panama; due to permits and public policy constraints in those countries they gave up.

After five years of reflection, study, analysis, advice from seniors in the industry and a separate budget of US$5 million, the Pérez-Grajales family decided in 2015 to expand its business to the United States using the same business model they use in Puerto Rico. As the president says, "this was a proactive decision and not a reactive decision to the economic situation of the country". The third generation of the family, represented by Mr. Felipe Hamílcar Pérez-Rodríguez (oldest grandson of the founder), joined the business full-time that year. He wanted to "do his things" and contribute to the family business and not to be "the shadow of the previous generations". He oversees the operations of the family business in Florida, by merit and by his own decision. He knew the business very early in his life because he worked there during the summers when he was a K-12[2] student and after that, he began at the managerial level working in a restaurant in Puerto Rico (Pérez-Grajales, 2017).

In 2015 they opened the first restaurant in Orlando, Florida, USA and in 2016 they opened two more stores in the same state. The sales have been growing in the three restaurants. The main customers are Puerto Rican residents in that area of Florida. They are trying to use these stores as a test of their business model in the Anglo-Saxon market. Now, only in one of the three stores they have 95% of customers from abroad and 5% from Puerto Rican diaspora. They need a better sample of stores in the continental USA with mostly Anglo-Saxon customers and with the appropriate financial numbers to grow that market (Pérez-Grajales, 2017).

At this point, all the restaurants are property of the Pérez-Grajales family under the actual legal entity of Limited Liability Company (LLC).[3] They have external managers for each restaurant including those in the United States. They have developed some partnerships with suppliers in Orlando, but most of the raw material is supplied from Puerto Rico (Pérez-Grajales, 2017).

As a family business that feels responsible for their inheritance and entrepreneurial legacy for next generations, they are considering what their strategy of continuous expansion should be. The second generation is considering not just financial matters but also the sense of identity and commitment to the business of nonfamily owners. They are discussing the possibility of selling franchises and analyzing the experience of potential buyers for their business model. The third generation is growing and the children of the current president have demonstrated interest in the business founded by their grandfather; all of them work full- or part-time in the firm. What strategies do you recommend to the Pérez-Grajales family to continue growing and developing its company, to test its business model outside of the domestic market (for example in North America, Latin America and Europe), and to incorporate next generations of the family into the business?

References

Asociación de Restaurantes de Puerto Rico (ASORE). (2012 & 2015). *Information sheet, 2012 and 2015*. San Juan, Puerto Rico. Asociación de Restaurantes de Puerto Rico.

El Mesón Sandwiches. Retrieved June 30, 2017, from www.elmesonsandwiches.com/

Pérez-Grajales, F. Interview on July 13, 2017. El Mesón Sandwiches administrative offices. Mayagüez, Puerto Rico.

QSR Champs, LLC. (2017). *El Mesón Sandwiches administrative offices*. Mayagüez, Puerto Rico: QSR Champs, LLC.

Vega-Rosado, L. L. (2009). El Mesón Sandwiches. In *Successful Transgenerational Entrepreneurship Practices (STEP project for family enterprising)*. Boston, MA: Babson College.

United States Census Bureau. (2017). *Quick Facts for Puerto Rico*. Retrieved June 30, 2017, from www.census.gov/quickfacts/PR. United States Department of Commerce.

Appendix 1

El Mesón Sandwiches Restaurants, 1972–2017

TABLE 3.A1

Year	Location	Restaurant format
1972	Marbella, Aguadilla	In line (closed)
1987	Mayagüez Mall	In line (no drive-in)
1988	Plaza las Américas, San Juan	Food court
1991	Mayagüez Town Center	Food court (closed)
1992	El Viejo San Juan	In-line (no drive-in)
1992	Plaza del Caribe, Ponce	Food court
1992	Plaza del Norte, Hatillo	Food court
1994	Plaza Carolina	Food court
1996	Plaza del Oeste, San Germán	Freestanding
1996	Plaza Palma Real, Humacao	Food court
1998	Las Catalinas Mall, Caguas	Food court
1999	Carr. 107, Aguadilla Borinquen	Food court
1999	Western Plaza, Mayagüez	In line (no drive-in)
1999	Sierra Bayamón	In line (with drive-in)
1999	Aguadilla Mall	In line (no drive-in)
2000	Hatillo II Carr. #2, Hatillo	Freestanding
2000	Plaza Escorial, Carolina	Freestanding
2000	Ponce II, El Tuque (C-Store)[4]	"Convenience store" freestanding
2000	Yauco Plaza	Freestanding: combo (with Baskin-Robbins)
2001	Belz Factory Outlet World, Canóvanas	Food court
2002	Rexville Towne Center en Bayamón	Freestanding: triple combo (with Baskin-Robbins and Dunkin' Donuts)
2003	Plaza del Sol, Bayamón (Meso Express)	Food court

(Continued)

TABLE 3.A1 (*Continued*)

Year	Location	Restaurant format
2003	Fajardo Shopping Center	Freestanding
2005	Plaza Jauca, Santa Isabel	Freestanding
2006	Plaza El Trigal, Manatí	Freestanding
2006	Mesolite, Plaza Las Américas[5]	Food court
2005	Plaza Río Hondo, Bayamón (Meso Express)	Food court
2007	International Airport Luis Muñoz Marín, Carolina	In line
2007	El Monte Town Center, Ponce	Free standing—combo (with Baskin-Robbins)
2008	Mayagüez Terrace	Freestanding
2008	Centro Comercial Galería 100, Cabo Rojo	In line (with drive-in)
2009	Villa Humacao	Freestanding
2010	Montehiedra	In line
2011	Cayey	Freestanding
2011	Dorado	Freestanding
2012	Guaynabo (Carr 199)	Freestanding
2012	Santurce	In line
2013	San Sebastián	Freestanding
2015	Florida Mall, Orlando, Florida	Food court
2016	Osceola Parkway, Orlando, Florida	Freestanding
2016	Vineland Premium Outlets, Orlando, Florida	Food court
2017	Galería San Patricio	Freestanding

Source: QSR Champs, LLC. (2017). El Mesón Sandwiches administrative offices. Mayagüez, Puerto Rico.

Appendix 2

El Mesón Sandwiches (Commercial Name for El Mesón de Felipe, LLC) 2006–2016

TABLE 3.A2

Year	Revenue	Restaurants in Puerto Rico	Employees
2006	$40,000,000	25	500
2007	$42,000,000	27	600
2008	$43,000,000	29	712
2009	$48,000,000	30	700
2010	$52,000,000	31	910
2011	$57,000,000	33	840

Year	Revenue	Restaurants in Puerto Rico	Employees
2012	$65,000,000	35	1,200
2013	$67,000,000	36	1,400
2014	$70,000,000	36	1,400
2015	$75,000,000	36	1,600
2016	$78,000,000	36	1,600

Source: QSR Champs, LLC. (2017). El Mesón Sandwiches administrative offices. Mayagüez, Puerto Rico.

Appendix 3

El Mesón Sandwiches in Florida

TABLE 3.A3

Year	Revenue	Restaurants in Florida	Employees
2015	$1,467,275.00	1	35
2016	$3,837,701.00	3	65
2017	$3,983,097.00	3	80

Source: QSR Champs, LLC. (2017). El Mesón Sandwiches administrative offices. Mayagüez, Puerto Rico.

Case 3.2 Challenging the Status Quo: Family Entrepreneurship in Chile's Grupo Kaufmann

Johannes Ritz, Marc-Michael Bergfeld, and Claudio G. Müller

Introduction

Lionel Kaufmann was behind the wheel of his shiny Mercedes sports car driving on the highway on his way back from a visit to one of the dealerships of Grupo Kaufmann. As the beautiful countryside of Chile was passing by, his thoughts were circling around what to do next with his life. For the last couple of years he had followed the path cut out for him by his family. As a third-generation member of the Kaufmann family he has been preparing for a leadership role in the family's business in the Auto Industry in Chile all along. After university he did not want to work immediately for the family business because he wanted to gain a broad international experience;so Lionel moved to Germany and gained experience working for Porsche and Daimler respectively from 2004 to 2006. He actually liked living and working in Germany a lot and was about to start a very attractive and exciting job at a consulting company. However in a lengthy phone call his father, the son of the company's founder Walter Kaufmann, had persuaded him to come home. He wanted him to take on a major project, implementing SAP in companies operations in Chile and Peru. Reluctantly he gave up the consulting opportunity and followed his family's call of duty and moved back to Chile to join the family business. After successfully implementing SAP, an intense project Lionel once described as his "military service", he took over the responsibility for one of the sales regions in Chile. As designated successor his great performance since joining the family business had him on the fast track toward being the future CEO of the Group.

In 2010 Lionel traveled to San Francisco to join an executive program in Silicon Valley's Singularity University. The program turned out to be a life changing experience for young Lionel. He had a moment of truth right away at the start of the course during the introduction round as his fellow students presented themselves: From innovative entrepreneurs to NASA scientist, they all had fascinating stories and seemed to have a lasting impact on the world's development. When it was his turn to introduce himself he just said: "I'm Lionel from Chile and I sell cars." This key experience or moment of serendipity together with the content of Singularities program made him realize that there was much more out there that he wanted could achieve. Ever since his return to Chile he was looking for a way to do something more impactful with his life and had started to talk to the company's board about fostering innovation within Grupo Kaufmann.

However, as he was approaching the group's headquarters for a meeting with his father he was tightening the grip around his Mercedes' steering wheel: He was more and more convinced that "selling cars" just was not enough . . .

Chile and the Influence of Migration

Chile is one of the most peculiar countries in the world due to its shape and geographic location. It is more than 2,700 miles long and only 110 miles wide on average, and it also has a wide variety of climates, which is a geographical feature. In addition, it has one of the driest deserts in the world and the beautiful Patagonia region in the South. Due to these characteristics, much of the growth of Chile's population has occurred through the immigration of different groups and citizens mainly from Europe. One of the most important colonies was established by Germans in the Southern region between 1850 and 1925, where more than 10,000 families traveled from various regions of the German Confederation (Germany began to exist as a country in 1871) to settle in Chile contributing with their culture, customs, and industrial experience.

Eventually, at the end of the Second World War, Chile began to transform itself with an unprecedented industrial revolution, with the creation of large companies. A petroleum refinery, a copper smelter, and the Huachipato steelworks were created along with the construction of large hydroelectric plants. This development was promoted by the strategy of "import substitution", an experiment in political economy that sought to achieve self-sufficiency.[6]

Grupo Kaufman—the Beginning

In this social context of the 1950s with high immigration led by European countries which saw Chile as an opportunity for development, and in this economic scenario of import substitution, marked with hyperinflation of more than 84%, Mr. Walter Kaufmann with his family headed from Germany to Chile to find a suitable representative for Daimler-Benz AG. However the conclusion was that nobody was more qualified than Don Walter himself so in 1952 he looked for the adequate facilities to install a workshop and a warehouse of spare parts as he was named Daimler's official representative for Chile. The opportunity to rent a property located at Av. Pajaritos came along and the back of the large building was occupied for the warehousing of spare parts. One year later, Walter achieved a major breakthrough with the sale of the first bus type O321H to the group of Ursulines. The vehicle caused a sensation and generated a high demand, allowing to demonstrate in practice the technical and economic superiority of these vehicles. In 1956, the approximately 10,000-square-meter industrial property located in Av. Pajaritos was bought, of which the possibility to acquire the adjoining properties existed.

This possibility materialized, so at present, the Company operates in a property of 45,000 square meters. In 1958, Kaufmann sold 250 small buses to the city, contributing to decongest the traffic of passengers in Santiago. Subsequently,

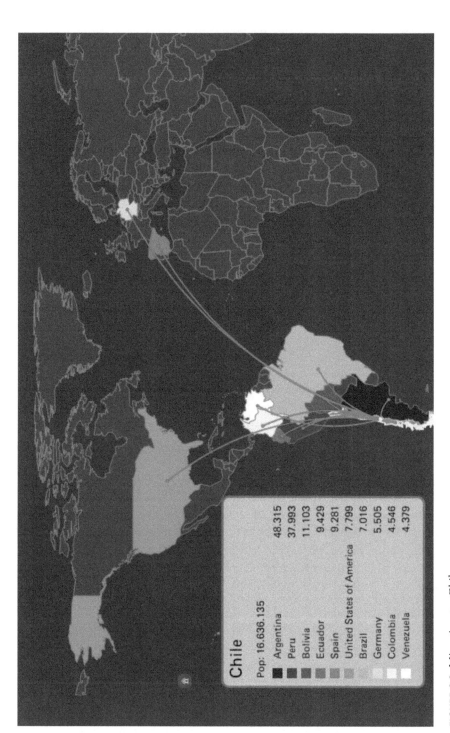

FIGURE 3.3 Migration to Chile

Source: http://migrationsmap.net/#/CHL/arrivals

Walter Kaufmann made great efforts to weave a cohesive network of representatives throughout the country, facilitating the penetration of the "Mercedes-Benz" brand. Between the years 1960 and 1970 positive development continued in the sale of all types of vehicles and in the improvement of its customer service.

The Kaufmann Family

On October 14, 1950, the Kaufmann family arrived in Valparaíso. They had left behind a Germany devastated by war, although they only left after the war was over and they had already contributed to the country's reconstruction. Don Walter Kaufmann had started working with Mercedes-Benz in Germany at age 26 before the war started. He was a skilled mechanical engineer and despite many job offers he came to Chile in search of a representative for Mercedes-Benz, a role that eventually he ended up taking on himself.

Walter and his wife came to Chile with their two sons, Miguel and Cristobal. Both grew up to join the family business and start their own families. Miguel married Brigitte Ritschka and had two boys, Alex and Max, and two girls, Vera and Tamara. Cristobal on the other hand married Annette Vogt, also member of a Business Family, and had two children, Lionel and Melanie. In addition Lionel and Melanie have an older half-brother, Philipp, from a prior relationship of Cristobal. Despite having seven members in the third generation, in 2012 only Lionel was working in Grupo Kaufman.

Grupo Kaufman—Growth With the Second Generation

In 1968 Miguel came back to Chile after 8 years in Zurich to join the family business, and his brother joined four years later. Between 1980 and 1990 the company began its growth at the national level with the opening of branches in the main cities of the country. Quickly after that Kaufmann acquired the representation of the North American brand of trucks, Freightliner. With this alliance, the company took a major turn at the market level, incorporating the line of heavy trucks. With the closing of this business, the After Sales service was extended, professionalizing and raising its quality standards, differentiating them within the market. In 1993, mainly promoted by the second generation already active in the business, Kaufmann began its expansion in Latin America with its arrival in Peru, thanks to the purchase of Divemotor, a company that represents Mercedes-Benz in that country. Seven years later, Kaufmann entered the mining business, importing WesternStar, a Freightliner truck line specially oriented to large mining. In 2002, Kaufmann celebrated 50 years of life and celebrated it by significantly restructuring the administration, from family business to corporate organization. Miguel y Cristobal left their executive positions to control the group from the board of directors. In 2003, with the inauguration of the Mercedes Center, Kaufmann marked a milestone in marketing, focusing on its exclusive segment of customers with an especially dedicated center for customers of Mercedes-Benz cars. The modern facilities have a permanent showroom, personalized attention and workshop service. In 2008, Kaufmann formed a commercial alliance with Tremac, a Chilean company dedicated to the manufacture and importation of wheels and equipment. This way, Kaufmann provides its customers with a comprehensive solution to their needs, in all areas. Two years later, Kaufmann acquired Autostar, a company representing Mercedes-Benz, Dodge, Chrysler, and Jeep in Costa Rica and Nicaragua, thereby marking the definitive internationalization of the Kaufmann Group. With the inauguration of Mercedes–Haus, the company turned its attention to its auto customers, repositioning the Mercedes-Benz brand as a way of life. With this new facility, the Kaufmann network comprises a total of 36 branches throughout the country, consolidating its leadership. In 2011, with the representation of the Daimler's FUSO brand, Kaufmann entered the market of buses and light/medium trucks with greater force while Autostar began activities in Panama. The positive development and continuous growth had

The Automotive Industry in Chile

The automotive industry worldwide was fast approaching drastic changes which the traditional car manufacturers had to deal with. The 2012 launch of sales of Tesla's Model S, superior all-electric luxury car, was a strong signal of imminent disruption of an industry that has been relying on the same technology, the combustion engine, for over five decades. Changes in consumer behavior also started to affect the business model of selling cars. For the new generation in the major cities around the world car ownership becomes less and less important. Whereas the newest iPhone became the newest status symbol, the trend went to using the type of car you need when you need it, using car sharing concepts like BMW's DriveNow. Chile however, like many countries in South America, still was somewhat protected from the newest game changing developments in the international markets. New vehicle sales rose 1.4% in 2012, above sales in 2011, despite the negative forecasts while Chevrolet and Hyundai continue to be the market leaders, however with an eroding position. For 2013 a favorable performance in key factors for car sales was expected to be an estimated 357,000units being sold. This growth should bring the number of people per car to five, still leaving margin for further growth in the automobile market. Looking into the future toward 2020, the auto fleet should reach 4.8 million units in Chile. However, it remains to be seen what effects the paradigm changing developments in the international markets might have in Chile's economy and vehicle sales. So although there was definitely room to further grow Grupo Kaufman in Chile and other countries of the region it was also becoming clear to Lionel that the industry in which his family was invested was facing major challenges and change in the years ahead.

Idea Factory iF

Chile and especially Santiago in the recent years have been promoted as "Chilecon Valley", making significant efforts to attract foreign entrepreneurs to set up their

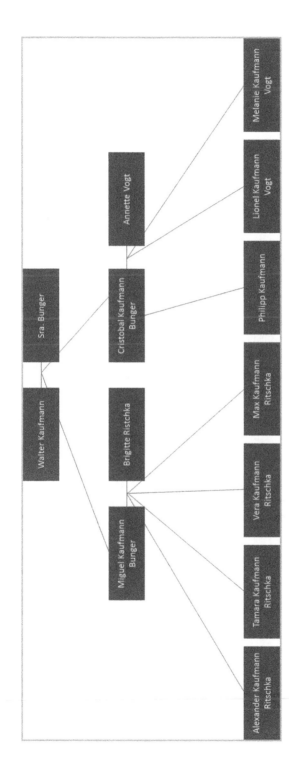

FIGURE 3.4 Genogram of the Kaufman family

new businesses in Chile with programs like Start-Up Chile, giving funding and visas to promising entrepreneurs from abroad. Aiming at sharpening Chile's profile as an international entrepreneurship hub, some envisioned Chile to become to Latin America what Singapore has managed to be for the Asian market.

In June 2012 fellow entrepreneur Alejandra Mustakis invited Lionel to develop iF, the Idea Factory. Based on discussions with innovators Manuel Urzúa, and Julián Ugarte who later joined the iF founding team, and inspired by his experience at Singularity University, Lionel analyzed the needs of entrepreneurs in Chile. Lionel and his colleagues soon realized that despite the efforts of the government and private sector initiatives like Telefonica's Wayra Santiago, there still was a great need to foster the start-up and innovation ecosystem.

They recognized "the need for entrepreneurs to have a single place to shape their ideas, seek funding, conduct tests and experiments, share knowledge, receive advice and finally develop a culture of entrepreneurship and innovation that generates value, connection, and inclusion".

Corresponding to this need they developed iFs unique model of entrepreneurship and innovation with the aim of bringing together entrepreneurs, investors, start-ups, test laboratories, universities, incubators, and innovation promoters in an integrated and collaborative environment in a single place in Chile. It was a promising idea and also corresponded very much to Lionel's vision of creating more impact in Chile and the world by selling cars.[7]

The Decision

As he was approaching his destination Lionel was debating his choices: Quitting the safe, comfortable and already designed career as future leader of the family group and dedicating himself to a very risky entrepreneurial endeavor he is passionate about or sticking to the plan and resigning on his "call for purpose"?

On the one hand there were many good reasons to continue on the prepared path and work toward the CEO position of the family group. His family would be very happy to have him lead the future development of the group, and the position came with a lot of prestige and benefits as well. On the other hand he really wanted to follow his passion and make iF his priority, a project that was not compatible with his job at Grupo Kaufmann.

The decision was complex for Lionel because on the one hand he had to choose between a very comfortable position within the family group's leadership and complete uncertainty as a start-up founder. On the other hand leaving the family business would almost certainly put the family relationships under stress and destroy his father's dream of having his son continue the family legacy as future CEO. So while he was getting closer to the headquarters of Grupo Kaufman he was considering his options. Should he quit and focus on iF or rather stay with Grupo Kaufman? Or maybe should he try to engage both challenges simultaneously?

Case 3.3 Cigar Family Charitable Foundation: The Birthplace of So Many Dreams. From Emotions to Strategy

Iluminada Severino Bueno, Belmarys Rodriguez Polanco, and Cecilia Pérez Estrella

> *"What was truly beautiful was the moment, the people and the big hearts last night coming together for a fabulous time and even more importantly raising over 800,000.00 Dollars for Charity and helping those less fortunate. My hat's off to our 4th annual event Cars and Cigars and the wonderful people of greater Detroit"*

With these words, published on June 9, 2017 through his Instagram account, Carlos Fuente Jr. (Carlito) celebrated and showed appreciation for the support received at the most recent fundraising event of the Celani Family Foundation and Cigar Family Charitable Foundation (CFCF) institution that—under his leadership—is the axis of Corporate Social Responsibility of Tabacalera A. Fuente, a company with a presence of more than one hundred years in the global premium cigar market.

After a history of successes and failures, achievements and setbacks, emotional and rational decisions, both for the company and the CFCF, this success in the work of procuring funds for the Foundation not only marked a milestone in its history, but also brought with it the challenge of what would be the next step to go beyond what was achieved in that event.

Industry Background

Tabacalera A. Fuente and Company is located in Santiago, DR. The local economy is based on several aspects, including agriculture—mostly tobacco, coffee, rice, cacao, and banana production. As far as the industry sector is concerned, the food and beverage industry is the most prominent; they are followed by manufacturing, especially furniture. Most of the cigar manufacturers in the region are located in the province of Santiago.

Dominican Republic exported six billion cigar units this year, which strengthened its leadership in this sector among the countries of Latin America, Central America and the Caribbean, generating revenue of over 700 million dollars. The revenue resulting from tobacco exports already represent one percent of the nation's Gross Domestic Product (GDP).

Regarding direct and indirect jobs, the director of INTABACO highlighted that there are more than 300,000 people involved in both the agricultural work and the collection of the aromatic leaf in the different regions where the product is grown.[8]

The Dominican Republic exports more than 90% of the tobacco it produces, both raw and manufactured in cigars of worldwide prestige. The province of Santiago is a leader in the national production of tobacco.[9]

The Free Trade Zones are one of the most important industrial compounds in Santiago and the Cibao region; 46.98% of the total amount of companies established in the country are located in the North Region, from which 29.31% are present in Santiago; and 63.38% of the total amount of the northern region companies are located in the Santiago Province. The commercial sector in this city is very dynamic (Cibao Productivo, 2006).

Tabacalera Fuente & Compañia Background

Tabacalera A. Fuente & Compañía is a firm dedicated to the production of cigars of recognized quality. It operates under the industrial free trade zone regime, exporting all the production of its twelve brands of premium cigars, its production of coffee under the Café Fuente brand and the cigar clubs in the Dominican Republic and Las Vegas, Nevada, USA. The firm is defined as a family business, after going through two processes of generational change, including the presidency and vice-presidency, with the siblings Carlito and Cynthia, respectively. Presently, the fourth generation of the Fuente family is already active in the top management of the company.

Founded in Tampa, Florida, United States in 1912, the company had a quite modest beginning. Arturo Fuente migrated from Cuba to the United States, where he settled at the age of 22. Two years later he started the operations of his company. By then, cigars were entirely handmade by the founder, using only Cuban tobacco. Ten years later, the company had about 500 employees.

Challenges Along the Way

This growth stopped suddenly because of a factory fire in 1924, which warranted a slow recovery that would take decades. By necessity, the founder was forced to work hard and postpone his entrepreneurial spirit until he felt he had the minimum conditions to restart his business. In fact, by 1940, Arturo Fuente was making cigars in the back of his house, along with his wife and two children (Oscar and Carlos), who, when they were of school age, were assigned the task of rolling 50 cigars a day as part of their homework.

As adults, the eldest of the brothers engaged in other productive activities, and only the youngest, Carlos, dedicated himself to the cigar business. With no sales experience, he took several risks by acquiring new customer accounts outside of Florida and selling on credit, which was entirely new in the cigar market. This was a critical step in creating brand recognition for A. Fuente and expanding the availability of its products in the market.

By 1956, at age 68, Arturo Fuente was eligible to retire, and his son Carlos was considered his natural successor in the cigar business. However, when asked to replace his father, as a condition Carlos asked that his brother—who was not active in the company after successfully engaging in the peanut business—sold him his part of the shares. This sale, for a dollar, would make Carlos the sole owner of the firm. Given these conditions, he concentrated all his efforts in growing the company.

Decision Amidst Contextual Crisis in Cuba and Nicaragua

Years later, in 1962, having heard rumors of the possibility of the United States imposing an embargo on Cuba, Carlos made a strategic decision: He quickly bought as many batches of Cuban tobacco as possible, thereby ensuring the permanence of the company in the market, with sufficient raw material for the next three years.

By 1965, many of his competitors had to cease operations because of the impossibility of importing their raw material from Cuba. Carlos made another strategic decision for his business: he began to produce cigars with tobacco from other countries while their reserves of Cuban tobacco were being depleted. As a result of this decision, in 1966 the company introduced its Flor de Orlando product, and by the early 1970s, Carlos experimented with producing high quality tobacco in countries like Puerto Rico, Mexico, Honduras, and Nicaragua. After a failed attempt to establish operations in the Dominican Republic, due to government bureaucracy, Carlos decided to start manufacturing operations in a factory in Nicaragua which, three years later, had about 300 employees and a daily production of 18,000 cigars.

In the midst of this new accomplishment, Arturo Fuente—who in spite of being retired never completely distanced himself from the company—passed away in February of 1973 at the age of 85. This inspired the creation of the cigar Flor Fina 8–5–8 using his own special blend as a tribute to its founder.

In 1978, the company suffered another setback due to the riots created by the rebellion of the Sandinista Liberation Front, whose passage through Nicaragua destroyed the factory. The following year, an accidental fire resulted in the loss of the factory located in Honduras. Consequently, during this time the company could barely survive producing cigars at its Florida facility in the United States. The future of the company was uncertain, with the potential for bankruptcy if extreme measures were not taken.

A New Hope in a New Place

In the beginning of 1980, Carlos and his eldest son, current president of the company (Carlos Fuente, known as Carlito) discussed business possibilities with the Oliva family and by September of that year, they decided to settle in the Dominican Republic and open their factory in the city of Santiago de Los Caballeros, taking advantage of the possibilities offered by the free trade zone regime. With production concentrated in the Dominican Republic, the facilities in Florida started to be destined only for distribution purposes. A year later, the company introduced to the market the Hemingway series, cigarettes with Figurado shapes, unique in the market, a result of the artistry in the production that had been lost many decades before. This earned the company the recognition of specialized magazines, which put the brand on the global map again.

In 1986, the Fuente family started an alliance with the Newman family, giving rise to FANCO (Fuente and Newman Company, now called Fuente-Newman) as a strategy to increase sales in the United States.

In the year 1992, Carlito assumed the challenges of producing cigar layer on dominican soil, starting "Project X from planet 9". This was something unheard of at the time. The advertising campaign resulted in the introduction to the market of Fuente Opus X, a worldwide recognized cigar, and whose name placed the company in a three year legal battle against Mondavi Opus One, of the Mondavi-Rothschild company.

Such success suffered a major setback when Hurricane George struck the Dominican Republic in 1998, destroying 17 of the 19 tobacco barns and leaving the entire community surrounding the plantation in a critical situation.

Carlito felt an avalanche of emotions due to the uncertain future of the children in the affected communities, so he started to think about how they, as a family and enterprise, could help.

Cigar Family Charitable Foundation

In 2001, the Fuente and Newman families, led by Carlito Fuente, created the Cigar Family Charitable Foundation (CFCF). This foundation was inspired by the humanitarian needs of the children of the community surrounding the tobacco plantation located in Bonao, and by their desire to give back to the country that allowed them to produce their best cigars. This foundation has as its main social initiative the Cigar Family Community Project. The main objective is to support the integral development of the population, with an emphasis on children and youth, in the rural and urban communities of the central region of the country. The project offers education, health, food, and transportation services to more than 500 children from some 20 nearby communities. For the implementation of this project, the CFCF maintains a strategic alliance with the Dominican Institute of Integral Development, Inc. (IDDI). Since it offers education and health services, the Project has the support of both the Ministry of Education and the Ministry of Public Health.

In 2005, during one of his usual visits to the Community Project, Carlito realized with great regret that what the Project offered to the children was not enough. That day in which nature was shining bright turned into a gray day, when while asking some girls who were seniors in the school project about their plans for the next school year, they replied that they could not continue their education since the closest high school was out of reach because they did not have the economic means to cover transportation costs.

That conversation was shocking and revealing: shocking because these were the two most outstanding students in the whole school who now would see their talent wasted because of the lack of financial resources of their families. Revealing, after inquiring a little more, Carlito discovered that this was the same situation for almost all the students who shared the classrooms, with a few exceptions.

Given this situation, the satisfaction that Carlito had felt for having favored the children of the Caribe and El Verde communities and other nearby areas, turned to sadness, sorrow, and uncertainty. He started to question himself about the value of the Project and its contribution to the children whom he had invited to dream of a better future with the possibility of having a profession and being successful. Remembering that moment, Carlito says that for several days, one thought stuck in his mind: "What did we do by giving these children the opportunity to dream and now take their dreams out of their hands? What did we accomplish if now they will not be able to continue with what they started here?"

The Decision

Internal Emotions Driving the Family

Faced with such a sense of responsibility for the future of these children, and the little time available before this situation altered the lives of these students, Carlito decided to implement a measure that to many within his circle was thought to be drastic. The idea was to get the necessary funds from a private bank in Florida to include the high school level in the school. With a personal loan of hundreds of thousands of dollars, Carlito arranged for the Foundation to fulfill the dream of these children to complete their high school education.

Carlito's desire to fulfill his own dreams and those of the children and youth of the Bonao community of being educated and have a different future from their parents and grandparents, lead him—as president of CFCF—to make strategic alliances with other companies. As they have often expressed "to give back to society a part of what they have given to the business".

Emotions Translated Into Intention

The alliances between companies "allows them to generate value in the different projects that are carrying out and constitute mechanisms of collaboration and a primary form of reaching short and long-term objectives" (Gulati & Singh, 1998, cited by: Rojas, Rincón, & Mesa, 2014). In this sense, the families Fuente/ Newman decided to partner for the development of the project "The Birthplace of Dreams". In addition, they formed alliances with companies such as Delta Airlines, Hublot, and Federal Cigar, to raise funds for the CFCF's education, health, water, and food projects.

This fundraising was done through different formats such as direct donations to the foundation, where for a specific amount provided annually, necessities are covered. Some of the necessities covered by these donations are: children's school uniform and shoes, the full year salary of a school teacher, immunization coverage of children in a classroom, among others.

Other ways in which funds were received for the continuity of the CFCF project was through the events held by the Fuente/Newman families among cigar aficionados. For Daniel Weber (2004),

> all events share one defining attribute, the participant or attendee gains some private benefit, be it a sense of personal achievement, an opportunity to show their generosity or simply having fun. The fact that the participants are supporting the charity may come secondary to the private benefit they gain from attending the event. Fundraising events therefore provide a means for charities to broaden their donor bases beyond those whose only motivation to support the charity is their fundamental belief in the particular charity's cause.

In 2006, the God of Fire Charity Dinner for Cigar Family Charitable Foundation, held at the Bel-Air Hotel in Los Angeles, California, USA, raised funds of more than US$200,000. This activity was attended by 250 passionate cigar lovers from different parts of the world, some of them Hollywood luminaries. In this event, in addition to enjoying fine food, exquisite wines and special cigars, participants attended the first "God of Fire" Golf Tournament.

The Foundation was further strengthened in 2010 by becoming a signatory of the United Nations Global Compact, which has recognized the Cigar Family Project as a model of community management. This gave great visibility to the Project, attracting a large number of donors.

Later in 2011, the Fuente/Newman families celebrated the third annual Toast Across America, attended by 5,000 representatives from 50 US states and 120 cigar retailers in an effort to raise funds in excess of US$300,000. Of the funds raised for the CFCF, Fuente and Newman decided to allocate US$50,000 for the victims of Hurricane Katrina in New Orleans.

In 2012, the company celebrated a century of its foundation, which Carlos described as a century of dedication and family tradition focused on high quality to make a memorable cigar. Throughout its history, the company has operated under the premise of not rushing things, but making them as they should be.

In spite of having a business that is over a century old, the family is still entrepreneurially active in business and exploring the values of the founder. "A value is a conception, explicit or implicit, of the desirable which influences the selection from available modes, means and ends of action" (Kluckhohn, 1951, cited in Rokeach, 1973, p. 10). Koiranen (2002) asked the question: how do the members of this family-owned business perceive themselves and rank their business values? For Carlito, the passion, dedication, perseverance, integrity, unwavering love for heritage of family and commitment to fulfill one's understanding is their mission in life as the values inherited from his grandfather and his parents and that have been transmitted and institutionalized to the next generation, already active in the company. "The importance

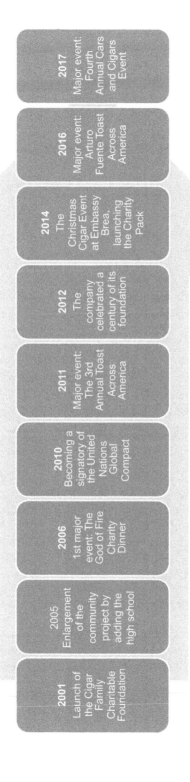

FIGURE 3.5 Timeline about the Cigar Family Charitable Foundation

of institutional values in the firm are identified with the family, either in formal company publications or in the informal traditions of the organization" (Neubauer & Lank, 1998). Some quotes of family members reveal their values.

> "We will never rush the hands of time."
>
> *Arturo Fuente, Founder*

> "We don't hurry things; we just do things the way they are supposed to be done."
>
> *Carlos Fuente Sr., second generation*

> "Our family has always taken great pride in the quest for true originality in everything we do. That's why no one can ever honestly imitate our passion for perfection."
>
> *Cynthia Fuente, third generation*

> "My family has gone through a lot, and that's what I think is the strength that holds our family together."
>
> *Carlos Fuente Jr., third generation*

> "My heart fills with pride when I learn of all my grandfather's accomplishments. But what humbles me the most is when I learn who he was as a person. My grandfather made the world a better place. Never have I met someone more humble, stronger, more true to his values, and more true to his two greatest loves: his family and his cigars."
>
> *Lidiana Fuente, fourth generation*

Although those values are implicit, they have been transferred through generations. Family business values should be defined and shared so that they create a common ground for a durable value system that benefits both realms, business and family goals (Korainen, 2002).

It is common wisdom that fundamental beliefs and values should be reflected in planning and particularly in the vision statement. Core values should also be associated with strategic control.

The Parallel Planning Process

The parallel planning process framework is driven by values and vision to support developing strategy, investment, and governance actions that exploit business opportunities and address the family's concerns. The first planning step is for the family to meet and clarify its values and then its future vision for the business—and the family's contribution to that future.

A family's investment of its human and financial capital clearly demonstrates the owners' belief that their ownership creates a competitive advantage for the business. (Carlock & Ward, 2010). In the case of the Fuente family, it was clear that their values were in consonance with the foundation project.

Continuing with the fundraising strategic activities, in 2014, the Christmas Cigar Event at Embassy Brea took place in a year in which the company introduced the Rare Aged Limited OpusX and Añejo cigars, each customer had to purchase the Charity Pack Source or the value of this in any Fuente cigar before buying the exclusive Rare Aged Limited OpusX and the Añejo.

In 2016, the companies again joined products for the Arturo Fuente Toast Across America 2016. In that occasion, Fuente and Newman offered special selections from their most luxurious cigar blends. Arturo Fuente has included their coveted OpusX blend in the new shape while J.C. Newman departs from their usual Diamond Crown Julius Caesar cigar; this time including the brand's newly introduced Diamond Crown Black Diamond cigar. Within this special edition two-pack box the clients found a pair of extremely special cigars, but what's more important is the cause behind the cigars: the funds for the CFCF.

At the beginning of June 2017, the CFCF became an important part of the Fourth Annual Cars and Cigars Event, raising more than US $ 800,000. This is the event with the greatest volume of funds raised, bringing with it the challenge of, what can we do to overcome this peak moment in our fundraising initiatives after this huge success?

What to Do?

Starting from the paper written by Hirigoyen and Labaki (2012): a) identify, in the case, the situation in which the emotion of regret significantly affected the decision-making of Carlito as President of the Foundation, and b) what emotions do you feel were influential in the decisions making?

On the other hand, how do these values influence, in practice, the business? How are these values a resource and what advantages/disadvantages can they provide?

The parallel planning process is an instrument that allows firms to integrate and balance the managerial and family issues. Could it be possible for Carlito's foundation worries and his decision-making to use this process?

Taking into account that CFCF will not stop making dreams come true and the last event having been such a remarkable success, what strategic decisions need to be made in order to increase fundraising? What types of activities would encourage donations? Are there some other strategies that could be implemented in order to extend CFCF fundraising? The philosophy modeled by the Fuente-Newman families with the development of the CFCF project marks a milestone in the history of the company, projecting the future of the firm in terms of sustainability, brand image and worth, ability to attract talent, and increased credibility.

References

Carlock, R., & Ward, J. (2010). *When family businesses are best*. New York. Springer, USA.
Cibao Productivo. (2006). Sergio Forcadell, Amigo del Hogar, Santo Domingo, R.D.

Gulati, R., & Singh, H. (1998). The Architecture of Cooperation: Managing Coordination Costs and Appropriation Concerns in Strategic Alliances. *Administrative Science Quarterly*, *43*(4), 781–814.

Hirigoyen, G., & Labaki, R. (2012). The role of regret in the owner-manager decision-making in the family business: A conceptual approach. *Journal of Family Business Strategy*, *3*(2), 118–126

Kluckhohn, C. (1951). Values and Value-Orientations in the Theory of Action: An Exploration in Definition and Classification. In: Parsons, T. and Shils, E., Eds., *Toward a General Theory of Action, Harvard University Press*, Cambridge, 388–433. http://dx.doi.org/10.4159/harvard.9780674863507.c8

Koiranen, M. (2002). Over 100 years of age but still entrepreneurially active in business: Exploring the values and family characteristics of old Finnish family firms. *Family Business Review*, *15*(3), 175–187.

Neubauer, F., & Lank, A. (1998). *The family business, Its governance for sustainability*. Houndmills and London: Macmillan Press.

Rojas L. M. D., Rincón L. C., & Mesa L. S. (2014). Alianzas estratégicas: alternativas generadoras de valor. *Universidad & Empresa*, *16*(27), 289–310.

Rokeach, M. (1973). *The nature of human values*. New York: The Free Press.

Weber, D. (2004). Understanding charity fundraising events. *International Journal of Nonprofit and Voluntary Sector Marketing*, *9*(2), 122–134.

Case 3.4 The Column: A Start-Up Looking for a Future

David E. Wong Cam

It was early 1990 and Alejandro had just finished his undergraduate degree in a recognized institution in Peru. He had a very successful time in college and he was moving to a new stage in his life. Today was a very important meeting . . . the future of The Column was being decided. The Column was a cement distribution company that he had created with his cousin Alberto, and a good friend, Cesar. They had started the business last year, and had expected that they would be better off after a year. However, the revenues were not where they wanted it to be, and something needed to be done. They were now all professionals and needed a salary. However, the company did not produce enough for the three owners, and Peru was in the middle of an economic crisis. They had already invested a lot of time and money, and needed to decide about what to do next.

The trio had three options:

1. They could continue doing the same as what they were doing now. If they chose this option, they would need to re-evaluate their goals. They could not expect to make a lot of money from the business, at least in the short run. However, they would remain employed in a job market that was very hard. They just needed to "ride this wave" and wait until the economy improved. The government was changing and experts were predicting that within 5 to 8 years the economy would revamp.
2. They could fold the company. Although this was a difficult option, their parents might be able to help them get a job with their contacts. However, none of them wanted to be perceived as a "little brat" who came back to their parents when things went wrong.
3. They could think outside the box. Innovating would be a risk for them. The formal sector was falling, and the demand for their product was dependent on economic cycles. However, the informal economy was booming, and the demand in this area remained at a good level. This approach focused on economies of scale. Thus, by having more clients, they could generate the same income as with a few rich clients. The success from this approach was working on volume to generate higher sales numbers.

Alejandro had been talking to his dad, who was a board member of a prestigious cement company, and he had mentioned that if he wanted he could talk to the owners to get him his dream job. However, he would need to let him know within one week whether this was an option that he wanted to pursue. The clock was ticking and he was getting ready to meet with the other owners to decide what to do. Today was the day.

The Beginings

Alejandro's dad was his hero. Don Pedro had started working when he was seventeen years old. He had started as a messenger in one of the companies that later became Capital Cement, one of the main cement firms in Peru. Don Pedro had worked very hard to be able to pay his way through college. He had finished an accounting degree and had become a certified public accountant. Alejandro was very proud of what his father had achieved. Don Pedro was now a Board Member of the Capital Cement, and everyone respected his opinion.

At an early age, Alejandro wanted to follow his father steps. Thus, when it came time to decide where to apply for his first internship in college, Alejandro decided to consider a position in Capital Cement. He was hired in the summer of 1986, and had a wonderful experience learning more about the cement industry. Through his experiences he had the opportunity to learn how professional offices worked, the problems that organizations could have with distributors, the concerns of the traders and carriers, and the reality of the cement industry in general.

In January 1988, when Alejandro was about to start the last year of his undergraduate career, he invited two of his college friends (Cesar and Alberto) to visit him over the weekend. Cesar arrived first. He was an extrovert and warm guy. Alberto arrived later. When he said hi to Alejandro, he noticed him restless and worried. He asked: "I don't want to kill the buzz, but do you know what you want to do once you finish school? We only have one year to go . . .". Cesar stood up and said: "We need to create our own company . . .".

Alejandro liked the idea. He thought: "We could do something in the cement industry. I had an internship in Capital Cement, one of the leading cement manufacturers on Peru. My dad is the Chairman of the Board and he can serve as a sounding board". Alberto responded, saying: "people will say we are successful because we are spoiled kids". However, the seed was planted in their minds.

Soon after they decide to create a small company so they can serve as Capital Cement dealers. This is how the The Column was born. Before 1989, Capital Cement's major distributors were San Ignacio, Icaza, and Alegría, with 46%, 22% and 12% of sales, respectively (Exhibit 3.1). Their goal was to become one of the most profitable distributors of cement in Lima, the capital of Peru.

The beginnings of this family business were set. Different from other family businesses that start with one founder, The Column was founded by two cousins (Alberto and Alejandro) and their friend. They received support from their fathers, who were directors at Cement Capital, and a recognized architect in the central region of Peru.

Percentage of cement sales per distributor before 1989	
Distributor	**%**
San Ignacio	46%
Icaza	22%
Joy	12%
Particulars	7%
Others	13%
Total	100%

EXHIBIT 3.1 Percentage of cement sales per distributor

The Peruvian Context

Peru is one of the countries in South America. The country is characterized by its natural resources. Peru is considered a place rich in flora, fauna, culture, cuisine, and natural resources—especially minerals, like copper and silver. Peru has a long ancestral culture, and Cusco—including the Inca Citadel, Machu Picchu—, is the emblematic city that attracts millions of tourists from all over the world.

Between 1943 and1976, the situation in Peru was marked by a demographic expansion, exacerbated by a process of internal migration to Lima. This prompted both the industrial and services expansion. The migration also caused the development of slum neighborhoods, which in 1981 represented the 25.5% of the population of Lima (Exhibit 3.2). This was affected by the military dictatorship that was prevalent in the Peruvian document during 1968–1979 decade.

In 1983, the production and the consumption of cement was close to two million metric tons a year, which accounted only for around 70% of the production. There were only five cement factories. Of these, Capital Cement was the main company that catered to the Lima market, which would become the future supplier of The Column. National cement production had, in general, an evolution growing during this period, although, in some years, it was insufficient to meet domestic consumption (see Exhibit 3.3).

In the 1980s there was economic crisis in Peru. In the cement industry, this enabled the government to control prices through ownership in cement companies (Exhibit 3.4). At the same time, the national demand for products and construction diminished as a result of the worsening economy. During this time, manufacturing saw a decline in production of 19% while construction decreased 16.1%.

However, demand grew from the informal economy that was developing in the slums. The demand was boosted by home improvement projects in the city slums, where the number of hardware stores and warehouses was increasing. During this time, the total value of informal settlements in Lima amounted to US$8319.8

Years	Metropolitan Lima	Population of the slums	Slum as % of metropolitan Lima
1956	1,397,000	119,886	8.6%
1961	1,845,910	316,829	17.2%
1970	2,972,787	761,755	25.5%
1981	4,608,010	1,171,800	25.5%

EXHIBIT 3.2 Metropolitan Lima 1956–1981: Evolution in slum population

Year	Metric ton production	Internal consumption metric ton
1983	1,965,672	1,962,110
1984	1,757,337	1,929,321
1985	2,206,639	2,219,302
1986	2,584,256	2,612,892
1988	2,514,306	2,498,264
1989	2,104,622	2,146,345

EXHIBIT 3.3 Cement production and market. Peru 1983–1989

Factory	Private capital	Government participation
Arequipa Cement	0%	100%
South Cement	0%	100%
Chiclayo Cement	51%	49%
Andean Cement	51%	49%
Cement capital.	51%	49%

EXHIBIT 3.4 Government and private capital participation in cement companies

Year	Real GDP (var. %)	Exports (mill. US $)	Import. ($mill.)	NET External Indebtedness (mill. US $)	Economic result (% GDP)	ICC (Yearly var.)
1985	2.1	3021,4	1822,6	997	−3.5	158,3
1986	12.1	2572,7	2649,3	916	−5.8	62.9
1987	7.7	2713,4	3215,1	1252	−8.8	114,5
1988	−9.4	2719,9	2865,1	1369	−5.5	1722,3
1989	−13.4	3503,3	2286,5	1603	−9.5	2775,0

EXHIBIT 3.5 Macroeconomic variables. Peru 1985–1989

billion, and 5% of the estimated cost of each house represented the costs of cement. Thus, the yearly growth of the slums represented US$17 million a year.

By 1985, a new government was in power, and they had implemented an increased public spending policy. Although this infusion of the economy seemed to work initially, the economy did not change. This resulted in a freezing of prices and exchange rate, ending with the country plunged into hyperinflation and another economic crisis (see Exhibit 3.5).

The Family Business

The Founders and Their Desires

The three partners who created The Column (Alejandro, Cesar, and Alberto) had initially invested US$12,000. Alejandro, the eldest of the three, enjoyed reading and writing. Thus, one of his goals was to travel and live in Paris for a while. He wanted to experience the European life. To him, The Column was a way to achieve his goals. He also wanted to create a company that could help people work for the development of people. He had always said: "the achievements of the company reflect positively on society; thus we need to be a company that can help". Cesar had always been the sales guy. He had started developing these skills as a child through the creation of a lemonade stand outside of his home in Pimentel, a small town to the North of Lima. He had also been very entrepreneurial, starting his first business at 14 and later focusing on marketing. Cesar had worked in a tourism agency, becoming the salesperson of the month. He loved traveling, and had studied abroad in London to perfect his English. Alberto, on the other hand had inherited from his dad the love of numbers, and was very good at managing complex processes. He wanted to follow in the steps of his dad and become a successful professional.

They had met in college, and had worked together developing their undergraduate thesis. Although the three had worked on the project (i.e., the creation of The Column), it was Alejandro's baby. The company reflected Alejandro's identity, given that he had completed most of the work. During this development process, they faced the challenge of understanding "The Column's" competitive advantage. What was their source of differentiation? After much discussion they decided to focus on customer satisfaction and efficient financial management. They also wanted to make sure that their firm could provide for the financial needs of them and their families. For example, Alejandro was planning on getting married soon, and the three of them wanted to complete their MBAs abroad.

The Challenges of the Founders

Although the macroeconomic context was unfavorable for all companies, for The Column this represented an opportunity. Given that Capital Cement had decided to expand their network of distributors after noting the drop in sales precipitated by the economic crisis of 1988, they had been able to enter the distribution network with seven other companies. By February 1989 they were official distributors for Capital Cement and had developed the following objectives:

1. Become the leading distributor of Capital Cement in the span of 2 years.
2. Focus on enhancing profitability through efficient financial management and a high market share.

At the end of 1989, Alberto believed that the Peruvian market was in a severe crisis. They had already been in operation for 6 months, and they were not hitting the numbers that they were hoping for (See Appendix 1). To achieve their goals, they would need to sell cement at a lower price and only hire staff if they absolutely needed them. Alejandro also suggested that they needed to begin working with the informal companies in the slums. He said: "if we focus exclusively on doing business with those in formal business structures, the economic crisis will push us to fail. However, if we also consider informal businesses, this can really help us". Cesar complemented his ideas by saying "the people who live in slums need to make sure that they have their supplies just in time, since it is impossible to accumulate large amounts of cement and other materials in their homes under construction. Thus, this can be a good opportunity for us".

To be able to expand this way, they would need to develop a financial component to their business. "This population came to Lima to thrive and does not have much capital to pay all of the services at once, and does not have access to a bank loan. Thus, if we want to work with them, we need to offer them financing options", Alberto had mentioned. Alejandro replied saying "I know the cement market, I am not aware of cement distributors who offer the option to pay in installments. These companies even hesitate selling to people in the slums because they think they will not pay". Cesar, who had sales experience responded by asking: "And, what if we became part of this informal economy?"

Cesar was aware of the different cooperatives that had been developed in this part of the city. Cooperatives were organizations that replaced financial institutions in this part of Lima. They were developed by groups of people who saved money every month, and created an informal credit system that would allow members to borrow money to pay for their expenses. It was their experience that people who lived in this region of the city were often ignored by large corporations because they believed that they did not have money, thus they did not reach out to this market.

The trio thought that they needed to come up with an innovative and cost-effective solution to serving this particularly difficult market. However, did they want to risk everything in the middle of an economic crisis? They did not know what to do.

The Decision

The group of friends was faced with an important decision. They had three options:

1. They could innovate and develop a new informal market for the cement company. This would require them to move the majority of their efforts to the informal sector. It would also require changes within the company that would include: computerizing the cement shipment processes, develop a way to provide credit to the informal market, and reduce transaction costs. However, this would enable them to accelerate growth during the next three years while being an active part of the business and then relax this growth.
2. They could also continue working on the formal market and deepen contacts with the government and private companies that demand cement. If they did this, they would need to computerize cement shipping processes, and reduce

transaction costs to accelerate the growth of the company for the next three years. After this, they could relax the growth plan and establish a program of redemption of shares (equivalent to creating a procedure to assess actions).
3. Graduate from college and close the company.

It was time for them to plan their futures. That was the reason they were here today. So, Alejandro shut off the TV and the three started a discussion.

Appendix 1

Balance Sheet and Income Statement

Balance Sheet Adjusted by inflation Until December 31, 1989 (expressed in american dolars)	
Assets	
Cash	65,854
Accounts receivable	101,154
Other accounts receivable	29,527
Expenses paid in advance	
Total current assets	196,535
Investments in securities	2,942
Fixed assets	9,425
Cumulative depreciation	(53)
Total long-term assets	12,314
Total assets	208,848
Liabilities & Shareholders' Equity	
Taxes payable	12,875
Salaries payable	106
Accounts payable	129,432
Other accounts payable	46,574
Total current liabilities	188,987
Provision of social benefits	191
Total long-term liabilities	191
Capital stock	4
Retained earnings	
Net income	19,665
Total Shareholders' Equity	19,670
Total liabilities & Shareholders' Equity	208,848

FIGURE 3.A1

Income statement Adjusted by inflation From February 14 to December 31, 1989 (expressed in american dolars)	
Revenues	6,604,258
COGS	(6,523,509)
Gross Profit	80,749
Administrative expenses	(80,957)
Sells expenses	(70,094)
Operation profit	(70,302)
Financial expenses	(6,200)
Financial incomes	30,077
Other incomes	78,153
Extraordinary expenses	(1,311)
Profit before taxes	30,418
Labor participation	(106)
Taxes	(10,646)
Net Profit	19,665

FIGURE 3.A1 (*Continued*)

Notes

1. This firm was previously studied by the author as part of the Babson College's STEP (Successful Transgenerational Entrepreneurship Practices) Project for Family Enterprising in 2009.
2. The pre-university educational system in Puerto Rico, as in the United States of America, includes twelve years of study after kindergarten (K) or playschool.
3. A Limited Liability Company (LLC) in Puerto Rico is a business form of legal organization that is included in the General Law of Corporations (Law Number 164, December 16, 2009, as amended). In Puerto Rico, this type of business legal entity is a hybrid that combines the advantages of limited responsibility of the owners provided by the corporate structure and the tax advantages provided by the civil societies.
4. The building permit requires that it be identified as "Convenience Store".
5. In September 2008, it was incorporated under *El Mesón de Felipe*, Inc.
6. Background readings: www.migrationpolicy.org/article/chile-growing-destination-country-search-coherent-approach-migration
https://en.wikipedia.org/wiki/Immigration_to_Chile
https://en.wikipedia.org/wiki/German_Chileans
7. Background reading: www.theguardian.com/small-business-network/2016/dec/22/chile-accelerator-startup-grants
www.economist.com/node/21564589
8. www.diariolibre.com/economia/republica-dominicana-exporto-6-mil-millones-unidades-cigarros-GK7950495
9. www.eldinero.com.do/39950/el-sector-agropecuario-fortalece-la-economia-dominicana/

4

FAMILY DYNAMICS

4.1 The Dynamics of Family Business: Virtuous and Vicious Cycles

Torsten M. Pieper

Family businesses are the most prevalent type of organization in the world. They account for the lion's share of employment, employment growth, and economic production globally (IFERA, 2003; La Porta, Lopez-de-Silanes, & Shleifer, 1999). In the United States alone, depending on the definition of family business used, family businesses contribute more than half of the gross domestic product, 60% of total employment, 78% of new jobs created, and 65% of all wages paid (Astrachan & Shanker, 2003). These numbers are similar in the Latin American countries where family businesses can represent upwards of 75% of all firms (Poza, 2010).

A family business is any business where one or several families have effective control over the strategy of the business and where the business contributes significantly to the wealth and identity of the family (Astrachan & Shanker, 2003). Family businesses come in various sizes and configurations: They range from relatively small operations over medium-sized enterprises up to multi-billion dollar global corporations. As a matter of fact, some of the largest businesses in the world are controlled by families, such as Walmart (Walton family), Volkswagen (Porsche/Piëch families), Arcelor Mittal (Mittal family), or América Móvil (Slim family), to mention but a few. Even in the United States, the birthplace of public markets, about one-third of Fortune 500 firms are controlled by families (Anderson & Reeb, 2003).

What makes family business different from other forms of organization is the reciprocal influence that a family (or several families) has on the business, and the business (or several businesses) has on the family. A family can influence the business in a variety of ways (see, e.g., Astrachan, Klein, & Smyrnios, 2002; Klein, Astrachan, & Smyrnios, 2005). For instance, by holding ownership stakes or leadership positions in the firm (e.g., in the top management team or the board of directors), family members can exert influence on the business and the ownership of a firm. On a more subtle level, a family can influence the business also through its experience in terms of the number of generations that are involved in the business and through its culture, namely in terms of the overlap between family and business culture (i.e., is the family's culture reflected in the business culture and vice versa), and the extent to which the family wants the business to continue its operations as a family business (versus an anonymously held entity).

The business can also affect the family in a variety of ways. Most importantly, the business usually provides financial returns, jobs, and opportunities for venturing (buyer-supplier relationships) to the owning family. These financial returns can also benefit the extended family when they are passed along to nonowning family members (e.g., children or cousins). In addition, the business provides the family with a host of nonfinancial returns, such as reputation and identification, which is especially important when the business bears the same name as the owning family (think of companies like Porsche, SC Johnson, or Rothschild) (Zellweger, Kellermanns, Eddleston, & Memili, 2012).

The mutual influence between family and business can have many positive effects, both for the family and the business. However, the mutual influence between family and business can also have negative effects. Indeed, some researchers argue that families in business who do *not* experience conflict are, in fact, rare "anomalies" or "outliers", as conflict is omnipresent and, essentially, inevitable in family business (e.g., Grossmann & Schlippe, 2015).

The argument is based on the fact that family businesses—unlike their nonfamily counterparts—accommodate two subsystems: the family and the business, each with its distinct goals and values (Hollander, 1983; Lansberg, 1983; Tagiuri & Davis, 1996). [For a recent literature review on goals in family business, the reader is referred to Williams, Pieper, Kellermanns, and Astrachan (2018).] Families generally operate on the basis of equality and pursue multiple goals, such as stable family relationships, work-family balance, and adequate income, among others (Danes, Zuiker, Kean, & Arbuthnot, 1999; Olson et al., 2003), whereas (nonfamily) businesses typically function by the principle of meritocracy and pursue profit or shareholder value maximization as their ultimate goal. Because of the apparent incompatibility of family and business goals and values, the two systems are often in conflict, the argument goes. However, we also know of many family businesses where family and business goals are in harmony and one supports the other, creating a symbiotic relationship with many positive outcomes for all parties involved.

A "vicious cycle" is often created when friction in the family spills over to the business, or vice versa. For instance, the business with its needs for time and financial resources may put pressure on the family system, which is often intensified when significant portions of family wealth are tied up in the business, thereby increasing the pressure in case the business would not perform well or perhaps even fail. Likewise, examples abound where conflicts among family members spill over to the business and cause significant problems. As a matter of fact, the popular press is full of feuds involving prominent business owning families, such as the Ambani brothers in India, the Gucci family in Italy, or members of the Bettencourt family (owners of L'Oréal) in France. Another example pertains to situations where unqualified family members are appointed to leadership positions in the firm (Kidwell, Kellermanns, & Eddleston, 2012), which causes not only discord in the family, but also sends negative signals to the nonfamily employees and other stakeholders of the firm.

When family and business systems are aligned and mutually support each other, they create a "virtuous cycle" that often brings out the best in family businesses. For example, a harmonious family that wants the business to continue as a family business can provide the business with "patient capital" (Sirmon & Hitt, 2003) below market rates, "sweat equity" (Zellweger, 2007), and trusting relationships (Eddleston & Morgan, 2014; Steier, 2001), all of which may give the business an inimitable strategic advantage over its competitors (Ruiz Jiménez, Vallejo Martos, & Martínez Jiménez, 2015). Perhaps as a result of these characteristics, some studies have identified family businesses as performing better financially (Anderson & Reeb, 2003; Wagner, Block, Miller, Schwens, & Xi, 2015), retaining employees more effectively (Stavrou, Kassinis, & Filotheou, 2007), being more socially responsible (Dyer & Whetten, 2006), and engaging in more environmentally responsive behaviors (Berrone, Cruz, Gomez-Mejia, & Larraza-Kintana, 2010) relative to their nonfamily counterparts.

While conflict in family business cannot be avoided, there are means to manage it and reduce potential detrimental effects (Pieper, Astrachan, & Manners, 2013). Conflict can even prove healthy, when managed well (Kellermanns & Eddleston, 2004). Chief among the mechanisms that seem to be effective is a cohesive family that engages in frequent communication, develops unifying emotional attachments to the business and to each other, creates clear and widely shared expectations, builds a sense of purpose and mission, and creates formal mechanisms for recognizing and resolving conflict (EY, 2016).

From a scientific perspective, the bivalent attributes of family businesses (Eddleston & Kellermanns, 2007; Tagiuri & Davis, 1996) provide for a unique research context in which to investigate novel phenomena that go beyond what is typically studied in the mainstream literature. The better we understand the intricacies of family businesses, the better we can assist families in business in avoiding the pitfalls of negative dynamics and creating "virtuous cycles" instead. Given the economic and social importance of family businesses, it is a goal worth pursuing.

References

Anderson, R. C., & Reeb, D. M. (2003). Founding-family ownership and firm performance: Evidence from the S&P 500. *Journal of Finance, 58*(3), 1301–1327.

Astrachan, J. H., Klein, S. B., & Smyrnios, K. X. (2002). The F-PEC scale of family influence: A proposal for solving the family business definition problem. *Family Business Review, 15*(1), 45–58.

Astrachan, J. H., & Shanker, M. C. (2003). Family businesses' contribution to the US economy: A closer look. *Family Business Review, 16*(3), 211–219.

Berrone, P., Cruz, C., Gomez-Mejia, L. R., & Larraza-Kintana, M. (2010). Socioemotional wealth and corporate responses to institutional pressures: Do family-controlled firms pollute less? *Administrative Science Quarterly, 55*, 82–113.

Danes, S. M., Zuiker, V. S., Kean, R., & Arbuthnot, J. (1999). Predictors of family business tensions and goal achievement. *Family Business Review, 12*(3), 241–252.

Dyer, W. G., Jr., & Whetten, D. A. (2006). Family firms and social responsibility: Preliminary evidence from the S&P 500. *Entrepreneurship Theory & Practice, 30*, 785–802.

Eddleston, K. A., & Kellermanns, F. W. (2007). Destructive and productive family relationships: A stewardship theory perspective. *Journal of Business Venturing, 22*, 545–565.

Eddleston, K. A., & Morgan, R. M. (2014). Trust, commitment and relationships in family business: Challenging conventional wisdom. *Journal of Family Business Strategy, 5*(3), 213–216.

EY. (2016). *Can embracing conflict spur positive change? How the world's largest family businesses resolve disagreement.* Retrieved from www.ey.com/Publication/vwLUAssets/ EY_-_Can_embracing_conflict_spur_positive_change/$FILE/ey-family-business-embracing-conflict.pdf

Grossmann, S., & Schlippe, A. V. (2015). Family businesses: Fertile environments for conflict. *Journal of Family Business Management, 5*(2), 294–314.

Hollander, B. S. (1983). *Family-owned business as a system: A case study of the interaction of family, task, and marketplace components.* Doctoral dissertation, University of Pittsburgh, Pittsburg, PA.

IFERA. (2003). Family firms dominate. *Family Business Review, 16*(4), 235–239.

Kellermanns, F. W., & Eddleston, K. A. (2004). Feuding families: When conflict does a family firm good. *Entrepreneurship Theory and Practice, 28*(3), 209–228.

Kidwell, R. E., Kellermanns, F. W., & Eddleston, K. A. (2012). Harmony, justice, confusion, and conflict in family firms: Implications for ethical climate and the "Fredo effect". *Journal of Business Ethics, 106*(4), 503–517.

Klein, S. B., Astrachan, J. H., & Smyrnios, K. X. (2005). The F-PEC scale of family influence: Construction, validation, and further implication for theory. *Entrepreneurship Theory and Practice, 29*(3), 321–339.

Lansberg, I. S. (1983). Managing human resources in family firms: The problem of institutional overlap. *Organizational dynamics, 12*(1), 39–46.

La Porta, R., Lopez-de-Silanes, F., & Shleifer, A. (1999). Corporate ownership around the world. *Journal of Finance, 54*, 471–517.

Olson, P. D., Zuiker, V. S., Danes, S. M., Stafford, K., Heck, R. K. Z., & Duncan, K. A. (2003). Impact of family and business on family business sustainability. *Journal of Business Venturing, 18*(5), 639–666.

Pieper, T. M., Astrachan, J. H., & Manners, G. E. (2013). Conflict in family business: Common metaphors and suggestions for intervention. *Family Relations, 62*(3), 490–500.

Poza, E. (2010). *Family business* (3rd ed.). Mason, OH: South Western Cengage Learning.

Ruiz Jiménez, M. C., Vallejo Martos, M. C., & Martínez Jiménez, R. (2015). Organisational harmony as a value in family businesses and its influence on performance. *Journal of Business Ethics*, *126*(2), 259–272.

Sirmon, D. G., & Hitt, M. A. (2003). Managing resources: Linking unique resources, management, and wealth creation in family firms. *Entrepreneurship Theory and Practice*, *27*(4), 339–358.

Stavrou, E., Kassinis, G., & Filotheou, A. (2007). Downsizing and stakeholder orientation among the Fortune 500: Does family ownership matter? *Journal of Business Ethics*, *72*(2), 149–162.

Steier, L. (2001). Family firms, plural forms of governance, and the evolving role of trust. *Family Business Review*, *14*(4), 353–368.

Tagiuri, R., & Davis, J. (1996). Bivalent attributes of the family firm. *Family Business Review*, *9*(2), 199–208.

Wagner, D., Block, J. H., Miller, D., Schwens, C., & Xi, G. (2015). A meta-analysis of the financial performance of family firms: Another attempt. *Journal of Family Business Strategy*, *6*(1), 3–13.

Williams, R. I., Pieper, T. M., Kellermanns, F. W., & Astrachan, J. H. (2018). Family firm goals and their effects on strategy, family and organization behavior: A review and research agenda. *International Journal of Management Reviews*, *20*, S63–S82.

Zellweger, T. M. (2007). Time horizon, costs of equity capital, and generic investment strategies of firms. *Family Business Review*, *20*(1), 1–15.

Zellweger, T. M., Kellermanns, F. W., Eddleston, K. A., & Memili, E. (2012). Building a family firm image: How family firms capitalize on their family ties. *Journal of Family Business Strategy*, *3*(4), 239–250.

Case 4.1 The Complexity of a Sibling Partnership

Alvaro Vilaseca

That winter afternoon in 2006, María Elisa O'Reilly de Azcuenaga was determined to play her part in a matter that caused a deep anxiety: what should she do with Jaime's loan? She was conscious that time went by and with it, the last years of her existence, unveiling the idea that the family which she dedicated her entire life, was divided forever.

This year had been a tough year. She had lost her husband, her children were fighting with each other, and it seemed that all she had worked for in her family was falling apart. She could not believe that after six years of working together her two sons could not even talk to each other. Their business had collapsed, and now they were fighting like cats and dogs. On one side Damian thought that Jaime was "a parasite" trying to take advantage of the family. On the other side, Jaime thought that his family was being unfair to him. Although he had incurred a debt with his father, the debt was not all his responsibility, and his father had forgiven the debt in 1994. So why were they trying to get back at him? Was it Damian and his anger or was it his other siblings?

Maria Elisa was meeting with the lawyer today. He was preparing the Domingo's Estate and wanted to know what she wanted to do with the loan so that he can finalize the estate and set up a meeting with all family members. She had several options:

1. Follow Domingo's wish and forgive Jaime's loan, and separate the estate into equal parts.
2. Charge Jaime for the loan, and separate the estate into equal parts.
3. Divide the estate into equal parts, and deduct the amount of the loan from Jaime's part.

However, how could she be fair with all her children? What was she going to do?

The Azcuenaga Family

Entrepreneurship was prevalent in the Azcuenaga family. Starting with Juan Bautista Azcuenaga (1888–1918), Jaime Azcuenaga O'Reilly's great grandfather, all male figures in the family had been very entrepreneurial. Even though Juan Bautista had died very young, he had gained considerable prestige as a lawyer, journalist, judge, and professor in Guatemala. He had created his private practice and, using his knowledge and contacts as leverage, he had helped change the education system in Guatemala. He had been one of the main leaders in the education reform that had banished the predominance of the private Catholic education for the privileged elite and transformed education to become the responsibility of the State, and a right for the citizen.

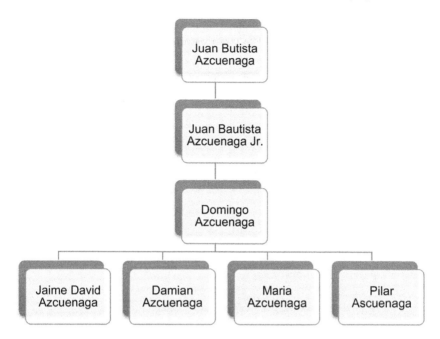

FIGURE 4.1 Genogram

Jaime's grandfather, Juan Bautista Azcuenaga Jr. (1910–1985), followed in the steps of his father and founded "Banco Obrero de Guatemala". This bank was responsible for safeguarding money from the working class. Junior had created a management system comprised of responsible and respectable individuals in the city in a management approach that was not primarily concerned on profits, but also wanted to protect the hard-working class. Those involved in the bank were deeply religious and believed that part of their responsibilities was to promote Christian values, and to help protect those who were less educated and fortunate by helping with the management of their money.

His father, Domingo Azcuenaga Sotogrande had also been a serial entrepreneur and was recognized by the community. Domingo, as Public Accountant, was one of the most respected accountants of the region. Early in his life he had met Maria Elisa O'Reilly, who he married and with whom he had four children: Jaime, Damian, Maria, and Pilar.

Jaime was a Veterinary Medicine Doctor, and had met his wife Maria Jesus in College. They had married soon after finishing college and had three daughters.

The Beginning . . .

After successfully working for different companies Jaime was ready to take the leap and start his own company. This became a reality in 1990, when Jaime joined forces with one of his best friends, Francisco Ugarte, to create Ugarte

S.R.L. The company was dedicated to the production and trading of mineral salts for the agricultural sector. This was a very unique venture that had great potential for growth and impact.

The creation of the venture required working capital of US$300,000 to buy the inventory and to acquire all of the technology to start operations. Given that they did not have the money, Jaime and Francisco decided to request a loan from Domingo that would help them get Ugarte S.R.L. on the right path. Domingo agreed to loan the amount to the two entrepreneurs. However, he had to bring the money out from the US Treasury investments, and requested that Jaime and Francisco pay the 9% annual rate that he was receiving from the investment. For them, this was a great deal given that other bankers that they had consulted were requesting between 10 and 12 percent for the same loan.

Confident in the success of the business, they accepted and signed a promissory note agreeing to pay an annual rate of 9%, with biannual interest payments and without an expiration date.

Jaime, who by then was 36, clearly remembers the conflicting emotions while he signed the document. Although he valued the support of his father the formality of the agreement made him very nervous. It was the first time he took such a formal approach to a loan from a family member.

The Early Years and the Unexpected

The company started production in the middle of 1990, and launched its main product into the market with great success. By the end of 1991, they were billing US$1,700,000. This success kept replicating for the next two tears, and by the end of 1993 it seemed like the following year would be the best year yet. However, on the morning of March 20th, 1994 the unexpected occured. That morning Jaime received a call from Patricia, Francisco's wife, telling him that Francisco had committed suicide and had been found dead in a hotel room. Jaime was in shock; he could not believe that his best friend and partner had committed suicide leaving his family and him when things were going so well. How could he not notice anything? What was he going to do?

The day after the regrettable incident, Jaime went to the company and, while reviewing the books, he realized that Francisco had not been properly taking care of the books. The company was heavily in debt as a result of Francisco's actions. He had taken money out of the business to pay some of his personal debts, and to start other new ventures. He had never consulted Jaime. Thus, instead of being the profitable and in good standing, Ugarte S.R.L. was in major debt and heavily leveraged. With this news, Jaime had no other choice but to start the process of filing for bankruptcy. Everyone was asking for their money, and Jaime did not know how to handle this situation. Jaime had never felt the need to monitor Francisco. They had a relationship of complete trust. He just asked: "how are the figures doing?" And would always receive the same response: "Do not worry . . . . We are in the black".

In less than three days Jaime's life had completely changed: He was now broke, in debt, and suffering from the loss of his best friend. He was physically and psychologically hurt. Everything he had worked for was now gone. How was he going to get out of this hole? It was at this time that his father provided the emotional support that he needed. He came to his son and said: "Jaime, the most important thing here is that you are healthy. You can stand up again and get out of this situation. You can rebuild your professional career. Don't worry about the debt, don't pay any more interest, we will figure this out later. For now focus on your family, and how to get out of this situation."

Brother Support

It was at this time that Damian, Jaime's youngest brother, came to the rescue. Two years earlier, Damian had started a small business dedicated to the rental of canopies, tents, and accessories for parties and events with an investment of US$25,000. When he had started he had asked his brother and his partner Francisco, if he could use a small part of their facilities at the factory for the storage of his rental equipment (i.e., pipes, canvas, tables, chairs, etc.). Due to their close relationship and after observing Damian's business progress, the partners had expressed interest in investing in his business. Thus, six months after Damian started, he sold 50% of his company for US$25,000 to Francisco and his brother Jaime. He had recovered his initial investment, keeping the 50% of the company. The ownership composition of the company was now 50% for Damian Azcuenaga, 25% for Jaime Azcuenaga and 25% for Francisco Ugarte. Since then, the company used the facilities of the fertilizer company as a storage and operations base. Meanwhile, the ownership of the company of fertilizers remained the same: 50% for Jaime Azcuenaga and 50% for Francisco Ugarte.

After seeing his brother in such a bad condition, Damian had said to Jaime: "We are going to move forward. Even though the company filed for bankruptcy and things seem uncertain, we still have the machinery to manufacture products, and that is what matters". Damian was the only sibling that seemed interested in helping Jaime come out of this difficult situation. He was optimistic and constantly motivating his brother to move forward. Damian's strategy was to first reactivate the fertilizer business through a partnership under a new denomination, but with the same customer database. Second, he wanted to reorganize the ownership of the two companies so that both of their work was equally compensated through ownership in the firms. Before Damian executed the plan, he presented this offer to Jaime. Jaime accepted his brother's offer and agreed to:

1. Reactivate the fertilizer company under a different name and with equal ownership for each brother (i.e., 50% ownership).

2. Continue to work on the Canopies and Tent Company with equal ownership for each sibling (i.e., 50%).

Although this was a risky move due to the economic crisis in the country, Jaime was sure that working with his brother he could once again make the company successful. With this goal in mind, in the middle of 1994, Damian and Jaime started their joint ventures. During this time, Maria Elisa and Domingo were the proudest parents. They were very humbled to see how their sons translated a difficult situation into an opportunity to work together and be successful. For them it was a "dream come true".

Partnership Between Brothers

The first few years, the partnership worked very well. The two styles of management seemed to be very complementary. On one hand, Damian was a risk taker. He had very useful ideas that when implemented helped the companies move forward. He was the innovator and always saw the new opportunities for growth. On the other hand, Jaime was more conservative, and now focused greatly on the financial aspects of the firm. After his experience with Francisco, he wanted to make sure that he would not go through the same situation again.

By early 2002, the differences in styles began to have a toll on the brother's relationship. Even though Jaime never stopped any of the ideas that Damian proposed, Damian thought that his brother was not making business life easy for him. He also thought that Jaime was not working as hard as he was. Thus, he started to believe that to be fair, he should earn a higher salary than his brother. Jaime, on the hand, though that Damian was getting riskier with each proposal that he came up with. What if something went wrong, how would they get out of that hole? After what had occurred with Francisco he was very hesitant of taking too much risk. Initially, Domingo and Maria Luisa stepped in to help the brothers manage their conflict. They would listen to each side, and try to come up with ways to reconcile and manage both sides of the conflict.

By December 2002, Damian was feeling like the current arrangement was not very fair for him given all of the time that he was dedicating to the business. So, he approached Jaime to say:

> "Jaime, I am very pleased with this partnership. However, I would like for us to re-evaluate our compensation structure as I consider that my contribution to the company is greater than yours, and I think is not fair for both of us receive the same remuneration".

Although Jaime was surprised, he accepted the proposal from his brother to receive a higher salary. Jaime said that as long as his currently salary is not affected, he is okay with this change. However, differences continued. In particular,

Damian's administration style became careless because he was so focused on the new opportunities for the business. Jaime got mad because Damian was not providing any expense reports besides the banking records, and he wanted to make sure that the books were clear and up to date.

By the beginning of 2004, the conflict between them increased. So Damian talked to a friend who recommended the services of an advisor who specializes in the management of family companies. They contacted the advisor, and he accepted mediating the conflict. After talking with both brothers, and listening to their concerns, he proposed three initial processes to clarify the roles and responsibilities of each brother, and to better understand the current state of the business. The three processes that the advisor suggested are:

1. **Clarify the accounting figures.** In order to know how much is earned by each business unit and understand the contribution of each brother they would first need to understand their accounting. This would include how much was invested, how much were the sales, and the profits generated in each firm. This information would provide a better understanding of each company.
2. **Assign clear responsibilities within each company**. The advisor suggested that the brothers clearly outline what each of them was responsible for within each firm. This could help in the accountability of actions.
3. **Clarify remuneration criteria.** The advisor suggested that the remuneration criteria should be based on the responsibilities and activities that each brother had in each of the firms.

The advisor understood that his plan would help correct the difference in remunerations. He argued that: If one of the partners worked less, they should gain less. If they work more, they should earn more! The "discomfort" will be corrected with the contribution and performance of each employee in each business unit. If this does not mitigate the conflict, it means that disparities are at a higher level. "If there is no trust or there is lack of the necessary corporate esteem, there are fewer things that can be done to resolve the conflict".

The Breakup

Even though both brothers seemed willing to sort out their differences and accept the help of an external consultant, none of the suggestions were implemented. By October 2004, the conflict had become worse and the relationship between the brothers was now plagued with all types of conflicts that not even their parents could help them solve. It was then that Damian came to Jaime and said: "I want to end this, I don't want to be your partner anymore".

Jaime was deeply astonished by his brother's reaction. And, at this time, remembered that due to the embargoes that he had when the business started, both of the companies were legally under Damian's name. He continues working and trying to negotiate with his brother how to separate the business. However, Jaime is so overwhelmed by the family conflict that he suffers a heart attack, and, to recover, takes a medical leave to seek medical treatment in United States. Jaime's wife is very concerned and decides confront her in-laws and Damian by saying: "This family is going to kill Jaime! Is it that you want him dead? Why are you all pressuring him and treating him so unfairly?"

Given the situation, Jaime and Damian decided to ask the advisor for help in terminating the partnership. As a result, the advisor proposed to cancel the partnership by splitting the companies. He suggested that given each brother's expertise Jaime should take the fertilizer company, while Damian should take the canopies and tents business. Damian refused the offer and decided to send his "pending invoices" to Jaime charging him for his services from the time he had helped coming out of the bad situation that Francisco had left him in. This complicated even more the dissolution of the partnership, and put a huge dent in the brothers' relationship. Damian became so disgruntled that he went on a rant in front of the employees, saying that his brother Jaime was:

- "Completely useless"
- "He only comes to the company to drink some coffee"
- "He only wants to benefit from the partnership, but does not want to make a contribution"
- "He is useless. He is a parasite!"

Another Rock in the Road . . .

To make matters worse, during this difficult time Domingo passed away unexpectedly. This made the relationship between siblings even worse. In addition to the problems that emerged from the separation of the business, Damian and the other siblings find the note that Jaime had signed in 1990 when he developed his company with Francisco. Although his father had verbally forgiven the debt, they had never destroyed the note, and the siblings were demanding that Jaime pay his debt to the family, or for that to be taken into account in the division of Mr. Domingo's state.

Maria Elisa, their mother, feels that she needs to do something. She just lost her husband and she is about to also lose her family in this conflict. But what should be her course of action?

Jaime's position in this matter is clear: If you are going to charge me for the note, I should only be responsible for US$140,000. Although the note was for US$280,000, there were two parties that signed giving them 50–50 responsibilities. Thus, he should be responsible for half and Francisco Ugarte's family should be responsible for the other half. However, even if I wanted to, right now I do not have the money to pay this debt.

Damian's position was that Jaime had always played the role of a martyr when this topic was discussed. How could he be trusted? Did the family really buy the fact that "he didn't know anything about the situation of the business at that time? How could he? What type of manager was he?" He actively lobbied with the rest of his siblings not to finance his madness, and to protect their mother from Jaime. He argued that "Jaime's wife and her family had a lot of money and they could use that money to pay his debt".

The Decision

Maria Elisa's apartment is located close to the layers office. He is coming in one hour and she has to communicate her decision to him. What should she do? What is fair in this situation? Should she:

1. Follow Domingo's wish and forgive Jaime's loan, and separate the estate into equal parts.
2. Charge Jaime for the loan, and separate the estate into equal parts. Jaime could sell his part and pay the debt.
3. Divide the estate into equal parts, and deduct the amount of the loan from Jaime's part.
4. Or is there another option for her?

She knows that Jaime had a good economic status. He was married to a woman from a wealthy family. They had a good house, two cars, and were able to enjoy holidays in Riviera Maya. However, her two daughters didn't have a good economic position and this extra money would bring them some needed benefits. She did not want to be unfair with Jaime or any of her children. Right now she was feeling empty. The idea that her children were strongly distanced hurt much more now that she was a widow. She questioned what she had done wrong in her life in order to have her sons fighting over economic differences, were these the values that she had instilled in her children? In the bottom of her heart she was at peace, knowing thatDomingo tried to help each of their children depending on their needs. Now she was asking herself, are there any rules that can help me treat them in a more equitable way? What can I do now to help them understand that we are a family that can work through this?

Case 4.2 Textech of Nicaragua

Eduardo Artavia and Enrique Ogliastri

José Saldaña, co-owner and general manager of Textech of Nicaragua, was faced with a difficult situation. After selling important assets of the company he had cofounded with his brother Alvaro, and moving his operations and store to a less than ideal location in the suburbs of Managua, he had just been informed by the local government that he would have to move again, less than two weeks before opening.

He did not have the resources—or at least the cash flow—to invest in preparing a "second new location", but the government had been very clear: either he gave up his operation as an Internet services provider and his business in data transmission or he had to relocate, since the foreign embassies around the new location he had just finished furnishing and preparing had asked that no antennas be installed near their residences, probably for fear of some form of espionage. He could not believe this was happening after the enormous effort they had just made to downsize and rebalance the company.

It is true that over the years they had overextended based on their natural optimism and entrepreneurial spirit, but after the sacrifices they had just made—even asking his son to find a job outside the company—this just seemed unfair. To complicate matters Alvaro, his brother and co-owner, kept thinking in entrepreneurial terms and was already looking for new ways to expand the business again. José both admired and resented the fact that Alvaro never focused on the problems and limitations, but was rather always looking for new angles to grow. At least, now that he had managed to pay off the multiple debts with local banks and had successfully renegotiated their commercial debt, he had freed himself from that additional pressure, but he was at the limit of his resources and needed to decide what to do.

History of the Company

In 1986 José Saldaña was working in a fast growing IT corporation in Texas when he received a call from his brother Alvaro, who asked him to resign from his job and come join him in Miami. Alvaro was launching a new company— SM TexTech, Inc.[1]—which would supply brand and care labels for the textile assembly industry operating in drawback operations throughout the Caribbean Basin.[2] The idea, Alvaro insisted, was to "be their own bosses" and, as quickly as possible, diversify their offer of technologically based services to this fast-growing textile industry.

Although labels were not exactly high tech, Alvaro, an accomplished software developer and programmer, had developed new software capable of designing and printing labels at fast speed and with great flexibility. José was an electronics engineer from the University of Texas, and could provide the support he needed for the success of the firm.

José asked for half the shares of the new company, to which Alvaro agreed; and immediately quit his promising job. Two weeks later he landed in Miami and started working in the new company, which formally opened operations in early 1987, operating literally from the small den of Alvaro's apartment. At this time, Alvaro was 27 and Jose was 25 years old.

The company grew and diversified quickly. Alvaro continued developing software for the textile industry, while José designed and installed servers, computer terminals, and their connecting network. Alvaro's experience and understanding of the textile drawback industry operating in Florida and servicing the Caribbean helped in the initial success of the firm. By early 1989 the company was growing at a nice rate and seemed to have a great future. By this time José and Alvaro had both married and the headquarters of SM TexTech had moved to a small warehouse. This new location provided space for an office, a workshop, and storage for their small inventory.

Moving to Nicaragua

Alvaro and José were both born and raised in Nicaragua. They lived as "political refugees" in the United States (US), which meant they held a conditional residence status, limiting their travel outside the country. They always felt—in their words—"living in a foreign land and hoping to get back to their beloved Nicaragua". However, they could not return as long as the self-declared Marxist-Leninist Sandinista Regime was in power and enforced a mandatory military draft to fight against the rightist guerrilla movement (i.e., "Contras").

The Sandinista Regimen called for a national election to democratically elect a new government in the beginning of 1990. This opened the possibility for their return. In August of 1989, before the elections, the brothers decided that José would move back to Nicaragua, abandoning his conditioned residence in the US, to open SM TexTech of Nicaragua. This new company would sell and install computer systems (i.e., hardware designed and developed by Jose; and software, designed and developed by Alvaro) in Nicaragua. At this time the country had been in a technological and trade embargo imposed by the US against the Sandinista Regime, which had left a wide gap in technological development of the country. The plan was that if the Sandinistas won the election Jose "could always try to get his US residence back; after all, his older daughter and his first son were American born".

In February of 1990, the Sandinista Regime lost the election and a democratic government led by Violeta Barrios came to power. This change resulted in a lift of the embargo, which provided an additional boost for the growth of the company. TexTech had been growing and José had developed a great reputation for his capacity to design and install tailor-designed computer systems. And now, Alvaro had the opportunity to join his brother in Nicaragua.

By the end of 1990, TexTech was a prosperous company. They focused on software and hardware development and had added accounting software to their offered products. Their headquarters were now in Nicaragua. However they had a trading company in Florida, which was run by childhood friends and served as procurement office for parts and peripherals for the Nicaraguan operation. Their focus was now on growth.

Strategy and Growth

TexTech was growing fast. The need to close the technology gap provided a fertile environment for the business. However, TexTech would go through three different stages in its strategic development. For its first three years the company grew very fast and achieved sales of nearly US$2 million per year. During this time they had specialized in offering:

- High quality servers
- Personal desktop computers designed and manufactured with their own brand name (i.e., SM TexTech)
- Structured network systems
- Accounting and control software with their own brand name
- Maintenance of systems and equipment
- Peripherals[3]

The fast growth and good yields results led Alvaro to abandon the software development side of the business. This part was time consuming and faced strong competition from "packaged software" developed in Costa Rica and Mexico. Additionally, the growth in the hardware sales provided enough income to sustain the business.

By 1996, TexTech sales came primarily from hardware. At this time, software services were only provided to clients who had accounting software and needed specific updates. However, by 1998 the company was 100% focused in hardware and related services (i.e., cable network, data communications, and maintenance). By this time, two new business lines were developing: (1) the installation of transmission antennas and radios for companies with remote operations in the country,[4] and (2) the rental of transmission capacity from their antennas.

By the late 1990s, laptop and notebook sales were surpassing PC sales. To compete in this market, Jose decided to travel to the US and look for opportunities. He negotiated to become one of the representatives of Dell and Toshiba notebook computers in Nicaragua. This helped TexTech become a market leader. Their competitive advantage centered on their ability to repair computers, to connect the notebooks into existing company networks and the support service. This became a new source of steady growth. However, new competition came from the creation of multiple stores selling appliances and computers, and providing easier credit options for families and smaller enterprises. TexTech could not compete in this credit market due to its financial commitments, but Jose and Alvaro adapted and started assembling inexpensive computers with the brand names of the new stores and quickly became an important supplier of the most successful companies with over 100 stores in the country.

By this time, TexTech had also developed Internet Services Provider (ISP) serving to provide high speed Internet to commercial clients and providing another source of income for the company. The company served private businesses primarily, and started working with the government, who at times provided up to 40% of monthly sales. Government contracts required participating in an open bidding process that frequently resulted in significant income for TexTech from designing and assembling tailor-made equipment and systems.

By 2006 sales had reached almost US$9 million a year (see Exhibit 4.1). The strategy now had evolved in terms of products, services, and commercial footprint. TexTech was very competitive importing parts, cases, and designing and assembling its own brand of desktop computers and servers. The government had become the most important client. However, these changes consumed José's time with bid preparation and contract negotiation. Additionally, the government was a "bad client" because it often paid late (up to 6 months), which created financial pressure for the company and required the brothers to fund the growing inventories and payroll for the company.

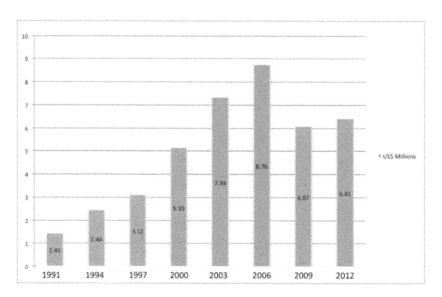

EXHIBIT 4.1 Gross Sales of TexTech

Subsidiary in Costa Rica

In 1997, the brothers convinced their sister Ramona, who lived in Costa Rica and had a degree in Information Systems, to open a subsidiary of TexTech. The subsidiary offered the same product line as the Nicaraguan operation until 2009, when competition became stronger. After running the company for 14 years, Ramona decided to close in September of 2011 when she decided to move out of the city and did not want to commute. The company had never grown beyond US$600,000 in sales a year. Ramona had always put her own family and welfare first, and did not want a larger commitment, even though the brothers believed the operation had potential. The subsidiary was a source of prestige with clients and suppliers and a safe haven in case the Sandinistas came back to power.

Growing Pains

The company's growth was primarily funded through commercial credit lines from the US and Eximbank credit, which they used aggressively. The interest rates were high, however their working credit line did not require to pay back the principal, and by 2007 the line offered $1M in credit. The line of credit helped fund their infrastructure growth and their payroll. Alvaro believed that having a large commercial footprint was an important part of their image and success.

As part of their interactions with the bank, they requested a formal audit of their operations in Florida. To their surprise, they found that the manager in Miami, Alvaro's lifetime friend, had been stealing from the company, there was a gap of US$130,000 between the audit books and their banking accounts. They fired the man, and decided not to prosecute. However, they had to completely reorganize their Florida operation, hire a new manager, and establish control systems. To make up for the missing funds, and avoid any trouble with Eximbank, they transferred funds from Managua by borrowing against their credit lines with local banks.

Physical Expansion

In 1993, TexTech acquired an 8000-square-foot store in one of the main streets in Managua. It included a smaller space of 1000 square feet to house the workshop and maintenance departments, as well as storage space for their inventories.

In 2002 the brothers opened a second store in the Northern Highway, another important commercial and industrial area of Managua, with a cost of US$250,000. The idea was that by expanding their footprint in key locations around the city, their sales of computers and peripherals would grow at least proportionally. A new store meant an investment in inventory, a store manager, three to four salespersons, one storage operator, and 24-hour security. In 2003 they opened a smaller store in a popular middle-class neighborhood, with the same logic. This space they rented, but still had to cover the operational costs.

In 2004 Alvaro insisted in acquiring a 1000-square-foot store in the recently inaugurated shopping mall, about two kilometers away from their main store, which made TexTech the only company in their industry to hold such a store, although by this time many appliance stores offered desktop, laptop, and notebook computers, as part of their products. This was an important investment in excess of US$210,000, plus similar operational costs to the other stores, with the exception of security which was provided by the mall.

By 2007 TexTech had four stores in Managua, all strategically located and the company seemed to be ready for its next strategic stage (see Exhibit 4.2). The payroll had grown to over 135 full-time employees, which the brothers did not consider overload since most of them worked for the very low wages of Nicaragua and they considered generating employment an important contribution to society. It was not unusual to find the son of a former maid of their mother's working in computer assembly, driving a truck, or even in a sales position.

Growth, particularly in sales to the government and to the corporate market implied giving commercial credit conditions with payment normally in 30 days, but in some cases up to 90 days after completion of a contract. The Nicaraguan government always paid late, sometimes by months; and the corporate market, although a little better, was usually a few weeks late, too. This created enormous cash flow stress for the company, and they ended up using local commercial banking credit to supply their cash needs. They found themselves opening credit

Real Estate Investments:	
Main Store in Central Highway to Masaya and Granada	8000 SqFt
Maintenance workshop and storage room	1000 SqFt
Total investment of US$ 645,000, market valuation in 2016 of US$ 708,000, funded with a mortgage loan, all of which had been repaid on time.	
Shopping Mall Store in Central Highway to Masaya and Granada	1000 SqFt
Total investment of US$ 210,000, market valuation in 2016 of US$ 250,000, funded by loan from their parents' retirement fund, all of it still pending	
Store in Northern Highway	1200 SqFt
Total investment of US$ 250,000, market valuation in 2016 of US$ 280,000, funded with a mortgage loan, of which 80% was still pending	
Rental	
Rental house in Altamira Neighborhood, Managua	2000 SqFt

EXHIBIT 4.2 TexTech Commercial Footprint in Managua in 2006

lines—in addition to the mortgage loans to expand their footprint—with local banks. Whether they realized it or not, they were borrowing money to fund their payments to Eximbank and also to fund their own personal needs.

So complicated had become the cash flow situation since the late 1990s, that the brothers recruited their mother, a well-known lady around Managua, to be in charge of the recovery of their receivables. The situation improved somewhat, but was never effectively solved. Doña Ana however became a fixture in the main room of the company working endlessly on the recovery of pending accounts and cost control.

Family Business

By 2004 Alvaro's family had grown to include a second wife, two daughters, and one son. The two older kids from his first marriage, then 18 and 17 years old, applied to expensive universities in the United States, after finishing high school in one of the most exclusive private high schools in Managua. They ended up graduating abroad in four years, but thanks to scholarships for academic performance, their university education ended up costing less than US$200,000 altogether. Both the son and the daughter became engineers, the son coming back to Nicaragua, while the daughter remained in the US. Exhibit 4.3 shows a family tree for the Saldaña Mujica family and for those of Alvaro and José in 2016.

Alvaro had moved into a new house in 2004, a large house in one of the most trendy neighborhoods in Nicaragua. Between land and construction he had spent close to a half million dollars. By then he drove a Toyota Land Cruiser, with a price tag of US$120,000, and he had invested in a summer home in an exclusive resort near Granada, investing another US$120,000.

José's family had also grown to include four daughters and one son. In 2004 they were 17, 16, 14, 13, and 9 years of age and the first two, who had been born in the United Sates, were planning on going back to Florida to study at one of the State's universities, which meant they would get subsidized tuition costs. As it turned out, they both spent two years in Florida and then, due in part to the financial pressure, came back and finished their careers in Nicaragua. The third child went to school in Costa Rica for a year, before returning to finish college in Nicaragua in 2014 and continuing on to a one year Master's Degree in Marketing in Spain, with a total cost of nearly US$80,000, and the fourth graduated from a Texas University, which implied an overall education cost of nearly US$200,000. The youngest daughter was still in high school, but her expectations were high.

Jose also built a house in an exclusive neighborhood of Managua at a cost of nearly US$300,000; invested in a modest house of US$40,000 in a nearby lake, and bought a piece of land on a Pacific Ocean beach on which he built a small house at a total cost of US$60,000. He had three cars for the whole

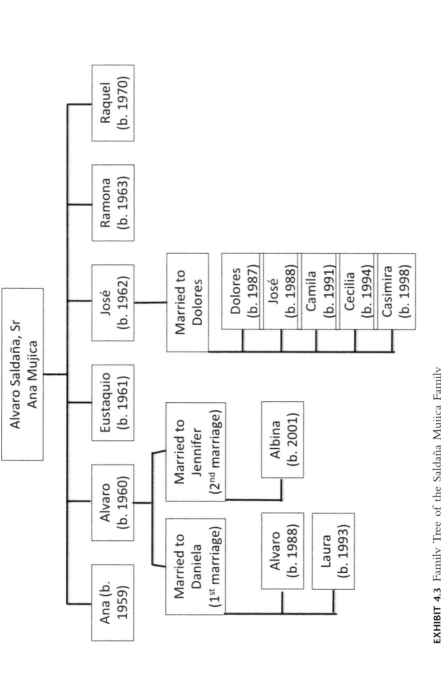

EXHIBIT 4.3 Family Tree of the Saldaña Mujica Family

family, including a Toyota FJ Cruiser that he drove. Later he invested about US$15,000 in a sand buggy, for weekend use.

In general, the remuneration policy for the brothers was flexible. They set "nominal salaries" for themselves in the order of US$10,000 per month, but when they needed money to make personal investments, they retired extraordinary dividends as needed. The only rule was that there needed to be balance between their personal compensations, which meant that when one of them declared the need for an extraordinary dividend, they both got it, regardless of their need at the time.

In general, the cash flow seemed large enough to accommodate their personal and TexTech's needs, as long as they did not repay the principal of the Eximbank loan.

Decision-Making in TexTech

All important investment and operational decisions were made by Alvaro and José. Although there was a "nominal Board of Directors" made up of their wives and their other brother, in addition to themselves, the fact is that the Board only existed on paper.

Several times in the life of the company they had appointed general managers, some of them very qualified and experienced, but the fact is that the brothers, Alvaro in particular, always made decisions bypassing the managers who then protested to José. José talked to Alvaro every time, but always left the office laughing, understanding that his brother was just too impulsive and entrepreneurial to respect the limits set by the managers.

One time they appointed a cousin who held an MBA from a prestigious school of business. He worked for three years, earning good money, but it got to the point—in his own words—when he only came to go through the motions since it was clear that the brothers would continue making all relevant decisions. He left after three years, grateful for the opportunity, but recommending them not to ever hire anyone else for that position, since it was just a waste of their money.

Over time several family members were hired in different positions, particularly in sales, but every time the relative left soon after. They seemed to use TexTech while they found something better. In one case, a distant cousin who was particularly good in sales and who learned very quickly the dynamics of the business, left the company to set up a small competitor, taking with him important clients, particularly in the countryside. The brothers learned the lesson and never gave any other relative a position of power and access, but did not challenge him in any way.

The rest of the extended family saw Alvaro and José as successful businessmen, admired them for the growth and prestige they had achieved in their industry, and considered them a source of pride.

2007, the Sandinista Regime Returns to Power

In 2007 the Sandinista Regime returned to power, winning the national presidential election and maintaining a majority in Congress. In this new government, the regime did not declare itself Marxist and, in many ways, became a pro-business government, maintaining good relationships with most of the business sector. It was a "tense calm"; one that the private sector seemed to accept as long as it did not interfere with their operations. The government let business go along their own way, unless someone in the regime decided that there was a piece of business that they wanted. This was the case with TexTech. One of their main competitors was close with the Sandinista regime.

As soon as the Sandinista regime returned to power, the government's procurement became biased toward two competitors—friends of the authorities, José argued—and the customs processes for TexTech, which had always worked fairly well, all of a sudden became problematic, taking weeks to import goods that up to then took only a few days.

Sales started dropping significantly, as the government contracts had remained an important part of the business and each month they won fewer and fewer bids in public institutions. To make matters worse, one year later the international financial crisis hit directly the international trade of Nicaragua. The economy slowed down; and what had seemed a never-ending race to close the gaps caused by the regime and the embargo in the 1980s, came to a hard stop. Sales of computers to the corporate market became a fraction of what they were up to then, and sales to the commercial and family sectors slowed down. All things together meant that by 2010 the brothers faced a smaller domestic market, with virtually no sales to the government.

The commercial bank in Florida that managed the Eximbank credit line quickly realized that import orders were down, but noticed that the line of credit remained at close to US$1,000,000 and, although the brothers never missed an interest payment, pressure to cancel a portion of the principal started to increase.

From the brothers' perspective the Eximbank line of credit was part of their overall credit, including lines of credit for US$700,000 in Managua, and what remained of the debt for the acquisition of the stores. Total debt was at US$2.2 million dollars and although in the current situation they could face the interest payments, it was impossible to think about reducing the principal on any of the debts. To complicate matters, one of the debts, specifically that of the shopping mall, was guaranteed by their parents' retirement fund.

In 2008 and 2009 José and Alvaro's older sons came to work for the company. Young Alvaro became a management assistant, overseeing marketing and sales and Young José became the manager of the workshop and storage rooms. Both received good salaries, higher than those paid to others in the company. Young Alvaro quickly realized that his sales and marketing ideas were not going to be implemented as his father in particular always responded with something like "that is a terrific idea, but not the way to do it in Nicaragua . . ."

2016, Reality Check

By 2016 sales remained at nearly US$6 million (Exhibit 4.4). Young Alvaro had resigned his position in less than two years and, following in his father's footsteps, quickly became an entrepreneur of his own with three different businesses in tourism, vending services, and marketing.

Young Jose worked well in his position for almost five years, until it became clear that the company would soon have to downsize to start repaying the Exim-bank credit. In 2014 he resigned and got a job with an international electronics firm, in sales; and quickly became a successful salesman, being recognized both with promotions and bonus payments each year.

Once the two young men were secure in their own activities, the brothers faced up to the Eximbank situation. In order to pay back part of this credit and reduce exposure to what the lower level of inventories justified, they had to generate cash locally. After exploring all kinds of options and not willing to expose further their personal and family assets, they decided to downsize.

First they checked the market value of their infrastructure and decided that they could generate US$1.3 million dollars by selling their store spaces in the market and, given the prime locations they held, this should not be hard to accomplish. Alvaro was initially opposed to such a change, but after very hard meetings between the brothers, in which they both laid part of the blame on the other for the personal investments they had made, they agreed on a plan.

They would sell all the real estate assets and repay their loans, liberating their mother's fund, and eliminating all local debt. They would refinance the local lines of credit and, between the lower interest expense and some of the cash they would generate, they would start repaying the principal of the Eximbank loan. They would also downsize, separating all the personnel from the stores in the Northern Highway and the shopping mall, as well as at least one-third of

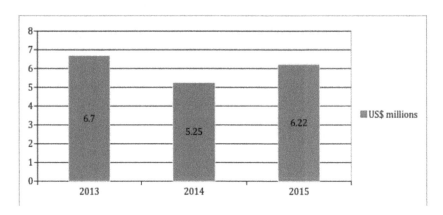

EXHIBIT 4.4 Sales of TexTech 2013–2015

the personnel in the main branch. Altogether they would end up with 60–65 employees, a little under the highest headcount in 2007.

The plan went into effect and it advanced well. The brothers were very disciplined in the execution and paid directly each credit as the money came in, avoiding any temptation to use the funds in any other way. Once they had sold all their real estate, they negotiated a three-month period to vacate the premises of the main store and found a house in the outskirts of Managua, near where they lived, that would become their new headquarters. It was not a perfect commercial location, not a high traffic road as they felt they had before, but was good enough to restart.

They rented the place, started renovations and cabling, and were enthusiastic to get their company on a path to growth once again, even if the government no longer seemed to be a feasible client. But a big surprise awaited them once they started installing the antennas for their data transmission and Internet Services Provider businesses. The neighborhood in which they had rented space included some European and Latin American embassies that, when they noted the antennas, immediately requested to the government that they be removed. TexTech could not operate without them and regardless of all their arguments, the government asked them to eliminate the antennas. They lost the money invested in the renovations and rent. Their investment capacity was gone as was most of their enthusiasm.

But once again their parents came to the rescue. The family home in which they had grown as kids was a large house located in an even better place, with better access and traffic volume and enough space to meet their needs. The only problem was that the same property also held a small house in which their older sister lived by herself. Their father offered to buy out their sister for US$100,000 and offered them the house in rent, assuming that the sister's house might rent or sell, independently, later. Their parents would move to a much smaller rental house, since they really did not need all the space they had. Of their siblings, Ramona and two others were fully supportive of the idea, while the affected sister, although willing to sell to her father if necessary, was strongly opposed to displacing their parents and herself.

Alvaro immediately warmed up to the idea, but José remained uncertain. They had to do something and rent another place, that was for sure; but did it make sense to displace his parents and sister? If this did not work, their parents would end up with a damaged house and no rent income.

José offered to look for a job elsewhere and leave the company to Alvaro to show that he was willing to sacrifice his own position, but this would not work, as his knowledge was indispensable to keep the most valuable services of the company operating profitably.

He also considered selling the company to a competitor or to a "wealthy Sandinista", but he wasn't sure how much the company might be worth and he was sure that without Alvaro and himself, the current strategy could not

Sales	100,0
Cost of sales	72,0
	———
Gross Margin	28,0
Administration expenses	13,0*
Sales expenses	6,0
	———
Net Margin	7,0
Profit Tax	1,4
	———
Profit (Loss)	5,6
Depreciation	5,5
	———
Free cash flow	11,1
*Includes depreciation	

EXHIBIT 4.5 Profit and Loss Statement (in percentages of sales)

be sustained, as it was fundamentally based on their complementary talents and experience. Besides, how long would the income from a sale last and what else could he and Alvaro do in Nicaragua? Would there be anything left after completely canceling the Eximbank loan?

He felt that there was no reason for them not to do well in the corporate, domestic, services, communications, and ISP markets from their new location, but the company would be smaller and with limited initial capacity. Alvaro and José had assigned themselves salaries of US$6000 per month, a fraction of what they were taking out of the company in salary and dividends in 2006, but he still did not know what to do.

Case 4.3 Should I Continue Working for My Family Firm?

María Piedad López-Vergara and Luz Elena Orozco-Collazos

It was 7:00 a.m. on Monday June 19, 2017. María, the Chief Commercial Officer at JKL, a family owned company construction company in Bucaramanga, Colombia, was finishing her preparation for today's board meeting, scheduled for 9:00 a.m. The succession process would be the central point of the agenda. María had spent the entire weekend thinking about her 25 years working in the family business and what she had learned.

She was now 50, and felt that she needed to assume new professional challenges. She had always thought that becoming CEO at JKL would be the next step, but now this did not seem a realistic expectation. Hernán Saldarriaga (76), her father, who had led JKL as CEO since the beginning, had postponed his retirement several times due to different family and business events.

For some years, María had considered opening her own residential housing construction and real estate company. Her contacts in the construction industry endorsed this idea, and she knew she had the necessary knowledge and skills. Although this option would offer her personal and professional development, it also would mean leaving the family firm, with complex implications for both the business and the family.

María also contemplated other alternatives. Continuing to work for JKL without succession expectations; accepting a job offer to be the marketing manager of another company—she had just received an offer and had to answer in the next 15 days—; or motivating her father to start the succession process with external facilitators who could help them in this situation. This third option would be no easy task, given his past behavior.

María was hoping that today's board meeting would address the need to start planning for succession in the management of JKL. However, if this did not happen, she needed to decide the next step. Should she stay, or should she go? If she decided to go, where should she go?

The Construction and Cement Industries in Colombia

The construction activity in Colombia is divided into two branches: residential/commercial construction, and public/private infrastructure. The economic dynamics of the construction sector includes cycles of expansion and contraction directly related (among other things) to demand for the product, interest rates in the financial market, the availability of financial resources, and policies implemented by the government. Government policies generally try to stimulate the employment generation.

These phenomena make it difficult to establish firms with sufficient capital and infrastructure to ride out cycles of decreased demand. Companies in the construction sector grow and contract according to the economic cycle. And, because of this, they lose continuity. This dynamic makes efforts to develop labor security and health ineffective, and developing the skills and capacities for blue-collar workers becomes more difficult.

In recent years, construction has been one of the most dynamic productive activities, with a growth of 7.9% between 2000 and 2015. This growth has been aligned with an increasing participation in GDP, rising from 4.4% in 2000 to 7.5% in 2015. The construction sector also makes an important contribution to the Colombian employment rate. In 2016, around 1.4 million people were employed in this sector (ANDI Colombia: Balance 2016 y Perspectivas 2017[5]).

In 2016, the favorable dynamics of the sector were explained in part by residential and commercial building construction, where the growth rate rose from 0.5% in 2015 to 8.1% in 2016, making it the fourth fastest growing sector. In comparison, the infrastructure sector grew by 6.8% in 2014, 16.47% in 2015, and 0.66% in 2016. Figures in the construction sector are associated with an increase of 6.5% in approved building construction sites, which reached more than 1.5 million m². Of this, the area approved for housing was around 1.3 million m².

The dynamic of the construction sector is aligned with the dynamic of the production of cement, the original business unit of JKL. In contrast to the construction activity, the cement industry is highly concentrated into three main producers: Holcim (Switzerland), Cemex (México) and Argos (Colombia). Minor producers, like JKL, have traditionally supplied the regional demand for their location. However, governmental policies regarding national highways and social interest housing motivated part of the 25.7% in growth of the production of cement between 2012 and 2016[6] (El_Tiempo, 2017). This, in turn, motivated the participation of five new large competitors to make it a total of 11 companies. During 2016, production of gray cement in the country was 13 million tons.

Appendix 1 presents selected financial data for the Colombian construction industry and for JKL Constructions. Although JKL represents a small percentage of the total, it should be noted that the eight biggest companies serve among 75%–80% of the Colombian market.

JKL Constructions

JKL Constructions was established in 1967 when Mr. Saldarriaga saw a business opportunity in the construction sector with interesting options for firms located in Santander, one of the 32 Colombian administrative states. This region is characterized by a culture where males are encouraged to work and women are encouraged to stay at home with the children. These cultural expectations have transferred to the construction sector, which is considered a traditionally masculine industry, leading to a predominance of males in this sector's workforce.

Since its beginnings in the 1970s, JKL has been an important producer of cement. At the end of that decade, Mr. Saldarriaga decided to diversify the company by developing a branch focused on residential and commercial construction. This decision allowed him to grow and expand the family firm.

With effort and the collaboration of his staff, Mr. Saldarriaga transformed his business idea into a large company. JKL established a strong reputation with its clients and suppliers. Its founder was recognized as an exemplary, charismatic, and benevolent leader. For him, the achievements of the business were the result of the efforts and support of his work team. Promoting social and environmental responsibility in the region was always present in his mind and influenced his decisions. He said: "We are not only here to make money, but also to support the people who work with us, contribute to their well-being, and contribute to the local community."

JKL is now the best known supplier to large construction companies. It offers high quality cement and a high level of customer service. As well as supplying cement, JKL builds houses and apartments in the region. The design department of JKL Constructions plans and develops the architectural design of its projects and takes part of the selling process.

Becoming a Family Business

Milena and Hernán met in Barbosa, a small town in Santander, in 1965. As the town was very small, it was common for people to meet at social events where music, dance, and poetry were shared with good food. Hernán had finished high school two years before, and Milena was a high school senior. They got married after she finished her high school degree.

For a long time, Mr. Saldarriaga was the only family member who worked in JKL. Although Milena was not directly involved in the business, she always emotionally supported him and offered her opinions about specific business issues and decisions. The Saldarriaga marriage was very close. Mrs. Milena took leadership in caring for the children: María, Claudia, Andrés, and Carlos. They are now aged 50, 45, 40, and 30, respectively. (See Appendix 2, the Saldarriaga family tree)

A climate of peace and love filled the Saldarriaga home. Discipline, thoroughness, professionalism, and excellence were part of the rules, particularly for María, because of Hernán's deep wish that María would be his successor. Loyalty among their members, service to other people, thankfulness, and cohesion to protect the family also characterized the Saldarriaga family. They embraced humility, honesty, respect, and gratitude as their family values. Mr. Saldarriaga always tried to uphold the importance of his family's values and their effect on the organizational culture of JKL.

María obtained her degree as an industrial engineer in 1986, and Mr. Saldarriaga invited her to become part of JKL. Don Hernán thought: "What I have built is for my family. It is for them. I am very proud that my eldest daughter has decided to work with me." María still remembers that day.

> My first day of work was exhilarating. I remember entering our JKL offices with a different frame of mind. Before, these offices were my playground, On that day, the offices became my professional environment. My role now was to make important contributions and support my father in anything he needed.

As assistant to Mr. Saldarriaga, the first position María held at JKL, she learned about the operations of the business and the industry. Mr. Saldarriaga taught her the key elements of the business and how to negotiate with clients and suppliers. He insisted that María had to be both strong and conciliatory, because most JKL clients and suppliers were male. Five years later, María moved to the Human Resource Department. This move allowed her to learn and to apply her managerial skills. After five years, in 1996, she moved to the Finance Department. However, some months later in the same year, the firm's growth led to her appointment as Chief Commercial Officer (CCO). As CCO, María positioned JKL as a brand in JKL's hometown of Bucaramanga and in the entire region of Santander. With new contracts for JKL, she drove the firm's economic growth and negotiating power in the region.

In 2001 two of her siblings, Claudia and Carlos, also joined JKL. While Carlos was hired as Chief Architect to lead construction projects, Claudia, with previous professional experience in a different industry, came in as Purchasing Manager, and was also in charge of the administrative direction.

The youngest sibling, Andrés, joined the business in 2012 as the Chief Operations Officer. As soon as he completed his degree in Business Management, he started work as a marketing assistant for a company in the food industry. After three years, he decided to ask his father for a place in JKL.

Although Mr. Saldarriaga invited his daughters and sons to work with him, his relationship with his children was influenced by the masculine culture of the region and his leadership style. Mr. Saldarriaga tended to overprotect his daughters, especially María. In contrast, the relationship with his sons was more open. Mr. Saldarriaga intervened in several of Andrés' business decisions, but although Andrés felt that his discretionary power was limited, in most situations he could make his own decisions. Despite this disparity, the relationship between Andrés and María was not affected; Andrés had always shown his admiration of her and recognized her professionalism.

In general, the siblings felt that their father's leadership style was limiting their contributions and their space to make decisions. Although Claudia, Andrés, and María agreed that they should have a more active role as chief officers and owners, they followed Don Hernán's ideas and proposals instead of proposing their own projects. This situation generated some disagreement between Hernán and his children.

Some years ago, for instance, there was an opportunity to buy a piece of land for an apartment building. Given that this would require taking out a significant loan, the siblings did not agree with this proposal because Hernán's health could be affected. In particular, María and Claudia are risk averse and prefer to leverage with own equity while keeping a low debt level. They thought that the financial commitment required would generate a lot of stress for their father. However, Mr. Saldarriaga decided to buy the land and extend his credit with the bank. He was a risk taker. For him, borrowing more money from the banks was a good strategy to ensure the company's future, grow its business, and survive the associated economic cycles. Taking on debt also increased the capacity of JKL to develop commercial relationships. These debts were backed by the assets of both JKL and Saldarriaga family.

On another occasion, when a supplier increased prices by 25%, Claudia and Andrés suggested looking for another supplier. Given the company's long-term relationship with this supplier, Mr. Saldarriaga rejected the suggestion without considering their opinion. In moments of high tension, it was common for Hernán to say: "There is no one who does things like I do; that is why I cannot hand JKL over."

A Failed Succession Process

In April of 2014, Mr. Saldarriaga, with the support of his family, decided to hire a consultant specialized in advising family firms. His objective was to restructure JKL's corporate governance to help the family make better decisions. The complexity of the industry and national economy were increasing, and JKL needed fresh ideas to guarantee its long-term continuity.

María and her siblings were excited by this initiative; once again they had expectations of a promising future for themselves and JKL. The siblings thought that their father would start to create opportunities for them to participate and make decisions in JKL. However, the consultant's action plan did not fully achieve these objectives. The family members were very willing to attend the family council's meetings, and these helped solve the communication troubles that had emerged in the family over recent years. However, Mr. Saldarriaga was not prepared to accept either a board of directors with outside members or an executive committee to make operating decisions. The consultancy firm had recommended starting the succession process, and Mr. Saldarriaga wanted to do so. However, when it came to defining the process and the steps to be taken, he had doubts and stopped the initiative. The last recommendation was to organize the companies led by Mr. Saldarriaga into a holding structure; this suggestion was not followed either.

Step by step, JKL had improved its functional structure and decision-making processes, making them more professional by establishing managerial committees. By 2016, Mr. Saldarriaga was having a monthly meeting with the accountant and the fiscal reviewer. When any additional information was required, María, Claudia, and Andrés were invited to the meeting. This was what Mr. Saldarriaga called his board.

Additionally, the siblings met their own work teams in small departmental committees in which the activities and performance of the unit were analyzed. In the end, the owners' annual meeting was symbolic; although the shareholders were present, there was no distribution of revenues. Don Hernán, as majority owner, made the decisions, while the other shareholders listened to him, neither discussing nor objecting. Although María and her siblings (apart from the youngest one) held shares, they did not feel like owners. "We are only paper owners; clearly my father is the owner of JKL."

Given this series of events, María wondered if her father would ever decide to retire and give her the opportunity to assume leadership of JKL. "He has been training me for that position since my first day in JKL, at least it was what I understood. Otherwise, I would have made other decisions or would be in another place".

Different Ways, Only One Decision

After 25 years of hard work in the family firm, María feels ready to lead it. She knows the firm; she has been involved not only in its day-to-day operations but also in shaping and implementing its strategies. She has good relationships with clients, suppliers, and employees. However, her father thinks that María needs more time before becoming CEO. For him, the construction sector is too masculine. It moves to the male beat, and it is hard for women to assume high positions and succeed in it. These thoughts have discouraged Mr. Saldarriaga from starting the succession process.

María has been thinking about her choices and their implications. She sees several options. First, she could continue working for the family business under the same conditions and without succession expectations. Second, she could start her own business in housing construction projects, becoming a competitor of JKL. This option also includes selling those housing projects. For this option, she would need to make important investments; she would need money and a good work team. Third, she could accept the job offer she just received to be the marketing manager in another company. Or, fourth, she could try to persuade her father to start a succession process with external facilitators. This would be no easy task.

Giving up her job in the family firm would have a negative impact on the family's unity and harmony. Her father would take offense at this decision. For him, "María is the future CEO". On the other hand, María feels that staying in the firm will only have negative consequences for her personal and professional development. However, moving to a different company or creating her own company could also be risky. But how can she convince her father to start the succession process?

María is facing a big dilemma: should she stay or should she go? She only has 15 days to respond to the job offer. However, if she decided to start her own business, she could stay in her current position for one more year. This option has fewer negative consequences for JKL but might affect the family, mainly her relationship with her father. Given that JKL anticipates important growth, the firm would need a new marketing manager. However, María knows the business very well and has a good relationship with clients and suppliers; no one could replace her at this time. Her siblings are not prepared for her leaving, and they do not have enough experience to assume Maria's responsibilities. Additionally, Claudia and Andrés have expressed their intention to support and follow María in her new entrepreneurial venture. They feel that their father is not able to give them more space in the family business. They have decided not to wait until their 50s to see any future that JKL might offer them.

María has been thinking for one and a half hours about the different options she has. Now, it is time to attend the board meeting. Mr. Saldarriaga will be there as well as her siblings. María wants to give her decision to her father at this meeting, but she is not sure about which option to choose and the best way to communicate her decision.

Appendix 1

Financial Figures for the Construction Industry and JKL Constructions

	2012	2013	2014	2015	2016
The Colombian Construction Industry					
Sales	3,604,810	3,621,621	3,145,063	2,664,224	2,732,721
Total	9,188,371	9,427,154	8,914,398	6,970,753	7,561,971
Earnings	414,470	280,929	350,237	336,659	436,324
Equity	5,955,149	6,503,097	5,748,260	4,316,278	4,787,278
Sales growth	0.17	0.09	0.08	0.12	-0.02
JKL Constructions					
Sales	9,817	11,102	10,732	9,625	9,784
Total	5,555	5,754	11,140	10,469	9,527
Earnings	583	755	668	792	592
Equity	3,251	3,739	8,425	7,192	4,110
Sales growth		0.13	-0.03	-0.10	0.02
JKL/Industry	0.27%	0.31%	0.34%	0.36%	0.36%

Source: EMIS Benchmark main Indexes: Construction

Appendix 2

Saldarriaga Family's Genogram

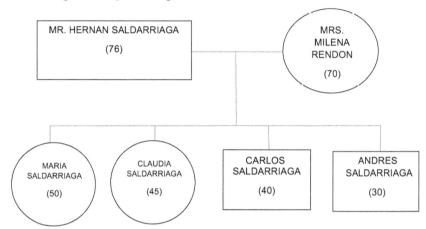

FIGURE 4.A1

Notes

1. SM stands for Saldaña Mujica, their paternal and maternal last names, and all companies in the group would always carry these two initials in front as part of their commercial brand names.
2. Drawback operations consisted of sending cut parts of textile products to be sewn and assembled at lower cost of labor venues, saving on labor costs and making the products more profitable for the brand owners.
3. Peripherals are printers, mice and mouse-pads, commercial software (Microsoft products mainly), power surge comptrollers, batteries, and power back-up systems, computer monitors, etc. In short, all the peripheral equipment and software needed to complete the systems designed and installed by TexTech.
4. Examples of this business were banks that connected their branches to the main office through direct communications or sugarcane mills connected to their Managua offices through the antennas.
5. Andi. Colombia: Balance 2016 y Perspectivas 2017. Retrieved from www.andi.com. co/Documents/Documentos%202016/ANDI-Balance%202016-Perspectivas2017.pdf
6. Granados, O. Colombia vive un auge de la industria del cemento. May of 2017. Retrieved from www.eltiempo.com/economia/sectores/auge-del-cemento-en-colombia-93426

5

ORGANIZATION PERFORMANCE

5.1 Organizational Performance in Family Firms

Gaia Marchisio

Family firms challenge the #1 rule we teach in business schools. In fact, the maximization of shareholder value is not necessarily the only or even the primary goal (Chrisman, Chua, & Litz, 2003, p. 468). This is the first (yet not the only) attribute that differentiates family from nonfamily firms. In addition to that, literature shows that family firms pursue unique, family-related aspirations and goals, many of which are nonfinancial objectives (Miller & Le Breton-Miller, 2006). Family owners, much more than other shareholders, display a strong preference for a broad spectrum of noneconomic utilities, collectively labeled as "accumulation of social capital" (Arregle, Hitt, Sirmon, & Very, 2007), "socioemotional wealth" Gómez-Mejía, Haynes, Núñez-Nickel, Jacobson, and Moyano-Fuentes (2007) or "affective endowments" (Berrone, Cruz, Gomez-Mejia, & Larraza-Kintana, 2010). Families have considerable discretion to pursue these goals and enact particular strategies that are targeted toward their fulfillment (Galve-Górriz & Salas-Fumas, 1996). Notably, the pursuit of these family-related goals, such as the perpetuation of the family's legacy, is neither random nor unknown to the family members involved with the business, and is likely systematic. This seems to indicate that the family firm's goals and aspirations lead it to adopt strategies that are not designed to focus solely on wealth maximization or other financial outcomes (Chrisman & Holt, 2016). Indeed, empirical findings suggest that the family-related aspirations and goals lead to unique strategic choices, which ultimately impact firm financial performance and family outcomes. Unfortunately, these empirical studies have largely relied on indirect tests to draw these conclusions, rather than directly assessing the extent to which goals and aspirations of the family shape and influence the firm (Kotlar, Signori, De Massis, & Vismara, 2017)

By recognizing this shortcoming in the literature, several scholars have argued that these approaches lead to significant disconnects between theory and practice, where the existing research appears to confuse cause and effect, suggesting that outcomes can be misattributed to the family's pursuit of family-related aspirations and goals. This happens even when there is additional evidence that there may have been differing motivations behind the behavior. Based on this, Schulze and Kellermanns (2015) suggest to address a few areas when applying the construct to family firms, to the advantage of a greater correspondence between the theoretical construct and its empirical correlate. One of the major risks is, in fact, to default to the pursuit of family-centered objectives, which might contribute to determine a lack in the clarification of the core theoretical assumption.

In a way this chapter is designed to take a step toward filling this gap. Specifically, the authors expose the readers to three cases where they show the extent to which family values and aspirations shape the strategic orientation of the firm, and its outcomes, whether related to the family, the firm, or both.

Case 5–1 The case of Sucos Lima faces that the family was deciding whether they should keep business under family control, or alternatively, to sell the control of Sucos Lima, thereby cashing out for the second time. The family had experienced this when the founding generation had sold the control of the company and it had taken them 25 years to buy the company back. They had been able to buy Sucos Lima because it was an underperforming company and they had invested a lot of time and effort to promote a successful turnaround. While executives from big companies such as Souza Cruz, Nabisco, and Kraft Foods tried to make the juice business relevant to their portfolio, it was only under the administration of the Lima family that the business prospered.

In the Case 5–2 Viñedos Del Pacífico, the family is faced with a decision that will mark the future of the business, when the eldest and third-generation son returns from France with a master's degree in wine management. The family's long-term vision and values help to make the best decision in the case.

Case 5–3 Grupo Transoceanica, is about five different Ecuadorian families, who co-own a group of more than 10 logistics related companies. They need to decide whether or not to accept a very interesting offer from a multinational. An agreement first needs to be reached within the founding family, before including the others.

All these cases beautifully display both the complexity of factors that play out in decision-making in family firms, and the degree of interdependence among not only these family and nonfamily dimensions, but also of context and moderators.

One of the biggest challenges posed by family firms is managing a critical paradox: while for theory building purposes, it is important to isolate different phenomena; in practice it is crucial to maintain a systemic approach that is able to account for both family and nonfamily attributes.

References

Arregle, J. L., Hitt, M. A., Sirmon, D. G., & Very, P. (2007). The development of organizational social capital: Attributes of family firms. *Journal of Management Studies*, *44*(1), 73–95.

Berrone, P., Cruz, C., Gomez-Mejia, L. R., & Larraza-Kintana, M. (2010). Socioemotional wealth and corporate responses to institutional pressures: Do family-controlled firms pollute less? *Administrative Science Quarterly*, *55*(1), 82–113.

Chrisman, J. J., Chua, J. H., & Litz, R. (2003). A unified systems perspective of family firm performance: An extension and integration. *Journal of Business Venturing*, *18*(4), 467–472.

Chrisman, J. J., & Holt, D. T. (2016). Beyond socioemotional wealth: Taking another step toward a theory of the family firm. *Management Research: Journal of the Iberoamerican Academy of Management*, *14*(3), 279–287.

Galve-Górriz, C., & Salas-Fumas, V. (1996). Ownership structure and firm performance: Some empirical evidence from Spain. *Managerial and Decision Economics*, *17*, 575–586.

Gómez-Mejía, L. R., Haynes, K. T., Núñez-Nickel, M., Jacobson, K. J., & Moyano-Fuentes, J. (2007). Socioemotional wealth and business risks in family-controlled firms: Evidence from Spanish olive oil mills. *Administrative Science Quarterly*, *52*(1), 106–137.

Kotlar, J., Signori, A., De Massis, A., & Vismara, S. (2017). Financial wealth, socioemotional wealth and IPO underpricing in family firms: A two-stage gamble model. *Academy of Management Journal*, amj-2016.

Miller, D., & Breton-Miller, L. (2006). Family governance and firm performance: Agency, stewardship, and capabilities. *Family business review*, *19*(1), 73–87.

Schulze, B., & Kellermanns, F. W. (2015). Reifying socioemotional wealth. *Entrepreneurship Theory & Practice*, *39*, 447–459.

Case 5.1 Returning to the Founding Family after 25 Years: The Case of Sucos Lima[1]

Fabio Matuoka Mizumoto[2]

Marcos was looking at the clock in his office on a sunny morning in[Recife, one of the largest cities in the Northeast of Brazil.

Another Board of Directors meeting would take place in twenty minutes, and the future of Sucos Lima was at stake. While flipping through his notebook, Marcos realized how busy the last couple of months had been. He had met with shareholders, advisory strategists, lawyers, and family members to determine the future of the company. He had spent many hours analyzing the 'pros' and

EXHIBIT 5.1 Northeast of Brazil

Note: Recife is the capital city of Pernambuco (PE) Federal State

'cons' for each alternative for Sucos Lima. The family was deciding whether they should keep the business under family control, or alternatively, to sell the control of Sucos Lima, cashing out for the second time.

Taking the first option would require the family to change their current strategy and invest a significant amount of money to internationalize their market and diversify their investment portfolio outside of the juice industry. Marcos was not sure how the family would react to this idea. This would be a big commitment, and require several family members to join the business, to be able to achieve these goals.

On the other hand, they could sell the business again. They had experienced this when the founder generation had sold the control of the company and it had taken them 25 years to buy the company back. They had been able to buy Sucos Lima because it was an underperforming company, and they had invested a lot of time and effort to promote a successful turnaround. While executives from Souza Cruz, Nabisco, and Kraft Foods tried to make the juice business relevant to their portfolio, it was only under the administration of the Lima family that the business prospered.

For many members of the Lima family, Sucos Lima was an important component of their legacy. However, some of them also recognized that once the juice business model was adjusted, investors would have advantages over the family's capacity to finance the expansion. Additionally, some family members preferred to cash out to finance their private plans.

As the president of the Board, Marcos was the member of the second generation that was responsible for helping the family make a decision. He had pushed back the decision-making meeting several times to give others the time for an open discussion, and to help the family reach a consensus. However, the investors' deadline required them to make a decision for the beginning of July 2015, which was a couple of weeks away. Board members had struggled to decide whether or not to accept the offers from investors to completely sell the company. A partial selling was not an option since both sides were reluctant, family shareholders and investors were not comfortable with sharing control. It was time for this long-awaited meeting. Marcos would have to convince the Board to make a decision today. They were running out of time.

The Lima Family and Businesses Background

Daniel, Marcos's father, was a born entrepreneur. He had started his ventures in the ethanol and sugar industry by acquiring an existing company in 1940. A couple of years later, he associated with his father-in-law and brother-in-law to prepare the expansion of all operations. However, in 1953 the family came across an interesting opportunity and founded Sucos Lima, a company designed for the production of tropical juices. During the 1980s the family also entered the ice cream business, and started to diversify their company to include sandal production, where they became the second largest producer in Brazil. Although this was a completely different businesses, the Lima family had leveraged its own capacity to provide corporate financing and organizational expertise among other competencies. Meanwhile, competitors would struggle to finance their operations due to the underdeveloped Brazilian capital market, and faced challenges hiring qualified executives from the labor market.

After the initial success in the 1940s, the other founders had left the business. Daniel was the one leading the group. As a self-made entrepreneur, he believed that a businessman should take risks based on their intuition and what they learned from previous experiences. However, he found value in formal education too. Thus, he had encouraged his children to have formal education and required them to work with the family starting at an early age so they could learn how to manage a business. In 1985, when he passed away, his sons and daughter were involved and already led the business.

Marcos, the oldest son, had inherited his entrepreneurial abilities from his dad. He had started working with his father a couple of years after the foundation of Sucos Lima. Part of his initial job was to find ways to get the juice distributed locally and, later, to all the state of Pernambuco. As the commercial director, Marcos became well known for his negotiation skills and his ability to develop and maintain a relevant business network. These abilities were very important in a context where institutions failed to enforce contracts. For instance, in the case of a client's default, rather than going through the court system, it was more effective to negotiate the debt or even to find common friends to help with the bills. Indeed, with the help of his friends, Marcos drove investments in the juice market and also in other businesses. He also started new ventures that facilitated the entrance of Ana, his sister.

Ana entered the group in the early 1980s to develop the ice cream business. Although she had tried to replicate Marcos's success leading Sucos Lima, she failed to manage the production and logistics of ice cream, even with help from market experts. This situation had almost turned into a family crisis, when Marcos wanted to take over the ice cream business and Ana resisted.

It was in this context that Paulo, the youngest sibling, returned to the group to attend his father's wish. Paulo had been involved in the business after he obtained his degree in business. However, he had also failed to manage some minor operations. At that time, he decided to work in the financial market despite his father's plans. His career in the banking industry began in Recife and, a few years later, he moved to São Paulo to be prepared for the top management of the bank where he worked. But he had to change his plans: "I could not resist when Dad called me to ask for help to Marcos and Ana". By that time, Paulo suspected that his father had planned changes in the near future but he could not anticipate what he was planning.

Sucos Lima Background and the First Selling Decision

The family founded Sucos Lima as a regional company in 1953. After initially focusing on pineapple juice exclusively, the company succeeded in introducing cashew, passion fruit, grape, and orange juices into their production line. This portfolio expansion was linked to the company's geographical expansion to the southern area of Brazil, where it was possible to find diversity of fruit supply and to increase their number of consumers.

After 31 years working to establish Sucos Lima, Daniel decided to sell the company in 1984 to Souza Cruz. Souza Cruz was a large company that was originally focused on the tobacco industry, and had recently entered the food and beverage industries. Even though the selling was financially interesting, the move created ripples in the family's relations. At this time Marcos had been totally against the selling of the juice business. He had led Sucos Lima, and was particularly proud to have promoted the geographical expansion, to have driven all product innovations and, more importantly, to have established a great brand reputation. Ana was also reluctant to sell the control of Sucos Lima since the change would drive Marcos' interests and attention to the ice cream business. Both Marcos and Ana were figuring out how to conduct business without Sucos Lima when Daniel passed away in 1985.

Family and Business Governance in the 1980s and 1990s

Sucos Lima left the family portfolio in 1984. As the founder, Daniel had been very involved in the selling decision. He passed away shortly after the sale was finalized (i.e., in 1985). Thus, the remaining businesses were left to the three siblings—Marcos, Ana, and Paulo. To avoid major conflicts between them, the siblings created some agreements and clarified the chain of command that they would use. This left Marcos as responsible for the ethanol and sugar businesses. Ana took over the sandals operations after shutting down the ice cream business. And, Paulo took responsibility for the group's finances. They also agreed not to interfere with each other's scope of decisions to prevent fighting based on preferences or opinions. Finally, to avoid conflicts, they also agreed to have their mother mediate any issues between the siblings to avoid negative conflict.

In the beginning of the 1990s Marcos, Ana, and Paulo decided to change the initial agreement. Ana decided to step down from her management role to dedicate more effort to her family and to her mother. She was especially worried about how to keep the family united, which was her mother's wish after their dad passed away. The third generation was still very young but Ana felt that it was already time to nurture the entrepreneurial spirit in all of them.

Marcos and Paulo stayed focused on the business. Marcos took over all operations; he was leading the ethanol, sugar, sandal, and real estate businesses. Paulo was responsible for all the group's finance; he was especially worried about the economic and political scenarios since driving businesses under those circumstances was challenging.

Doing Business in Brazil in the 1990s and 2000s

After experiencing many years of skyrocketing inflation rates (e.g., 2,477% in 1993), Brazil started controlling their inflation in 1994. Before the success of Plano Real,[3] the government had tried six different plans, including changing the national currency, to stabilize the economy. Brazil had enforced a new Constitution in 1988 in the context of a new democracy developed after the military that was in place since the 1970s.

In the 1990s the sugar and ethanol business markets were uncertain. The international commerce of sugar was exposed to political decisions based on quotas, tariffs and technical barriers that eroded margins. Similarly, the national market of ethanol had changed given that automakers had focused on the production of gasoline-fuelled cars instead of ethanol-fuelled models.

However, in the 2000s the market changed completely. The sugar market faced a turnaround to become an open driven market. At the same time, the automobile industry launched the flex-fuel models that allowed the consumer to decide to use gasoline or ethanol at the gas station instead of having to decide at the car dealer. This created an opportunity to adjust the relative price between gasoline and ethanol more frequently. Moreover, in the mid-2000s the United States of America established the adoption of ethanol as progressively mandatory, which opened the export market for sugarcane ethanol from Brazil.

Sucos Lima Returns to the Founding Family

After operating Sucos Lima for a while Souza Cruz had sold the business to Nabisco. Nabisco later sold it to Kraft Foods who now controlled the business. Even though all the companies had invested and made changes to Sucos Lima, they had been unable to make it a relevant part of their business. Thus, after selling the ethanol and sugar operations in 2007, the family worked on reconfiguring their portfolio with a focus on investments toward infrastructure. In this process they reconsidered investing in Sucos Lima.

Sucos Lima returned to the founding family in 2009, 25 years after being sold. The company had changed. Previous controllers had invested to distinguish the quality of Sucos Lima products, and had replaced the glass bottle with carton box, plastic bottles, and cans. However, once under family control, Sucos Lima started to grow again and obtained a high-value segment of the market. It launched ready-to-drink coconut water in 2011, and a functional (i.e., related to health promotion or disease prevention) beverage line in 2013. Sucos Lima was now the leader in the concentrated juice segment with 27%

of market share in 2013, reaching about BRL500 million revenue per year (about US$220 million).

Why would the founding family be interested to return to the business after 25 years? "Sucos Lima means a lot to the family"—said Marcos, one of the company shareholders. Besides the emotional attachment to Sucos Lima, the family knew how to make the business prosperous. In fact, the Lima family had assembled a set of new competencies and business networks from their work in multiple industries since 1984 that helped them when rebuying the business. Given its previous history it seemed as though the founding family was the only one able to assemble the appropriate conditions to promote a performance turnaround at Sucos Lima.

Family and Business Governance in the 2000s and 2010s

Ana kept all efforts to develop the family governance since the 1990s. By late 2000s the third generation was now ready to work for the group, or to ask for seed money to open their own businesses. Ana was particularly proud to keep her father's entrepreneurial spirit in the younger generations of the family. She liked to open a family meeting by saying: "I'm the CEO of this group and I'm referring to CEO as chief emotional officer!" Ana became an important voice among other family businesses and she started planning how to provide help and advice to other families besides her own family.

By mid-2010s the family had established a Family Board composed by two members of each of the three family branches, and Ana's mother as honorary president of the Board (see Exhibit 5.2). At the beginning, most activities were driven to prepare the heirs and to promote social meetings with all family members. Finally, they decided to create a family constitution, which took about two years of ongoing clarification and negotiation. The family governance results varied. According to one of the heirs from the third generation: "On a role-play process, I had tried the shoes of a manager and the shoes of a shareholder . . .

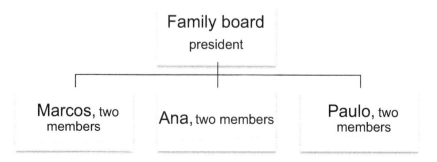

EXHIBIT 5.2 Family Board

I realized how tough it could be to have these duties, I need more preparation to help with the diversification strategies of the group!" Another heir from the third generation said: "I've been preparing since I was a kid inspired by my grandpa, but now it is time for me to take care of business! I'm looking forward to making our juice business prosperous in the international market".

Marcos had controlled the business since the 1990s using the same model as his father, centralized decision-making. He felt he could rely on Ana and Paulo's confidence to make decisions quickly, changing initial plans and intentions without previous notice. In the past he had mentioned that "business is about being quick. If I have to listen to everyone's opinion, I need time and I will lose money!" Ana and Paulo tried to establish a Board of Directors in the 2000s but Marcos resisted.

It was only in the mid-2010s that the Board of Directors was established. After Marcos was hospitalized for almost one month to treat heart disease, the need for a board became evident. Marcos also decided to structure the executive director's position, opening room for nonfamily managers. After acquiring Sucos Lima in 2009, Marcos stepped down as CEO to concentrate all efforts as president of the Board. Paulo became the new CEO, working with a nonfamily COO and CFO (see Exhibit 5.3). The five seats of the Board of Directors were allocated as follows: Marcos was the president of the Board; Ana represented the interests of her family branch and also was the eyes of her mother; Paulo represented the interests of his family branch; Director Four was external but not independent—he used to be former executive director of sugar and ethanol business of a Lima controlled operation; and Director Five was an independent member with long experience in multinational food and beverage businesses.

EXHIBIT 5.3 Board of Directors and Executive Directors

Brazilian Juice Market Size and Growth

According to ASBRASUCO, the Brazilian Juice Association, Nectar, and Juice market size grew 15% on a CAGR (compounded annual growth rate) from 2009 to 2014 (see Exhibit 5.4). The beverage industry describes nectar as a drink that contains some percentage of fruit juice with other ingredients, preservatives, and/ or sugar. Juice refers to 100% fresh fruit juice that can be processed to extract water from it. Grape, peach, mango, passion fruit, guava, cashew, and orange are the main flavors in this market (see Exhibit 5.5).

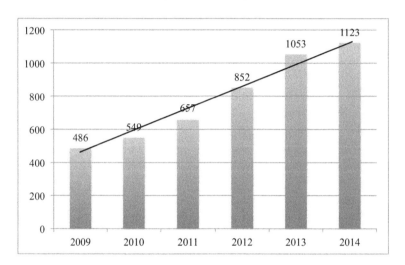

EXHIBIT 5.4 Nectar and Juice Brazilian Market Size and Growth (million liters)
Source: ABRASUCO—Brazilian Juice Association

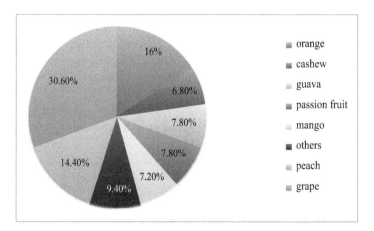

EXHIBIT 5.5 Nectar and Juice Brazilian Market Size and Growth (million liters)
Source: ABRASUCO—Brazilian Juice Association, 2015

In 2014, the Brazilian market for Nectar and Juice reached a size of 1,123 billion liters compared to the soft carbonated drinks companies, which sold 20,491 liters. In comparison, while one Brazilian consumer drinks 5.6 liters per year of Nectar and Juice, the consumption of soft carbonated achieves 101.9 liters per capita. Thus, considering the healthy trend in food and beverage consumption, there is a huge potential for growth for Nectar and Juice companies.

However, it is important to note that Nectar and Juice markets are very sensitive on income levels. In 2010, ASBRASUCO conducted research that concluded that 53% of the consumption power was due to class "C" level of income level—about BRL1,338 or US$790 per month.

Investors in the Waiting Room

Consolidating Sucos Lima as the top leader of the concentrated juice segment, competing with giants such as Coca-Cola was, to a great extent, unexpected by the market. Since 2009, the underperforming company had a turnaround based on changes in the top management team that supported innovative initiatives led by the founding family. Obviously, many investors have shown up seeking opportunities with this privately held company. The family and shareholders can be divided into two groups.

Those against the investors' offerings argue that Sucos Lima could develop on two possible paths under the Limas' capacity to finance the expansion:

1. They can explore the international market. "Sucos Lima could benefit from exporting tropical atmosphere in juice boxes! Let's benefit from our own financial capacity to reach a worldwide scale"—claimed a market expert. The COO, on the other hand, argued that additional costs of the supply processes, and all efforts to fulfill compliance policies for many countries would erode margins. Marcos was aware that going abroad would be in line with part of the Lima family's private plans to have international access to education and living style. But he could not explain at what stage these private plans were to support this alternative.
2. They can also diversify the product portfolio. "We could benefit from the good reputation of our brand to introduce food products to complement the juice portfolio"—defended a business consultant. Finance people were completely against this alternative when considering CAPEX and OPEX to be paid by "uncertain demand and unclear synergies that consultants like to tell us about but ask us to make it happen afterward".

On the other hand, those supporting the selling of the business criticized the plans to go abroad since "people talk about exports but so far we have nothing". In addition, they mistrusted the diversification strategy because they did not have the money and expertise of investors to control the enforcement of this alternative. They promoted a sell again strategy.

3. Sell it again. "It's time to change again like we did in 2007, when we have sold our sugarcane-based industries and the sandals business to reconfigure our portfolio toward infrastructure. Let's cash-out on the peak of Nectar and Juice market, I'm afraid the market will not be able to sustain the average growth of 15%, like in previous years"—said the CFO. Paulo, the CEO, was reluctant to consider this option. According to him: "We did what no other executive team was able to do. It's more than a financial turnaround! We are leading the concentrated juice segment with enough room for growth. We have quick wins that can help us to explore the valuable ready-to-drink segment". Marcos knew that some family members were already counting on the money from selling Sucos Lima's shares to finance their own particular endeavors.

It Was Time

The clock marked 9:00 a.m. and members were ready to begin the Board of Directors meeting. Marcos' notebook was opened on the page "why should I sell the juice business?" It read:

1. 2015 is a great time to cash-out and invest in infrastructure.
2. Our experience to sell and reconfigure portfolio (just the way we did with sugar and ethanol).
3. We can leverage our knowledge to get a good deal.
4. The money from the selling would help Ana's private plans.
5. The advice from our CFO and COO.

When flipping the page, he reviewed his notes on "why should I keep the juice business?"

1. It was my first great endeavor and I finally bought back in 2009.
2. We are making money on a market with reasonable potential for growth.
3. Paulo believes that we can continue to get quick wins on this business through diversification and internationalization.
4. The interests of heirs from the third generation.
5. The expertise in our board (i.e., one of our directors from the Board is an expert in food and beverage industries).

Without a clear decision in mind, Marcos, holding his notebook, is about to say the initial words for this session that has only one topic: to decide the future of Sucos Lima.

Case 5.2 Viñedos del Pacífico: Harvest Time for the Valls Family*

Claudio G. Müller and Ana C. González L.

The end of the harvest—gathering the grapes—was scheduled during the last week of March, 2014. This was the first harvest where the Valls Family, specifically Juan Valls-López—a third-generation family member—would see the results of a long road traveled: first, persuading his father, Pedro Valls-Beltrán, and then, convincing the Family Council and the Board of Directors to transition the business from conventional handcrafted wines to organic and biodynamic wine and/or expand to other agricultural endeavors, like cattle or dairy. The family faced a key strategic dilemma regarding focus and growth, specifically how to reorient the business strategy and execute the plan with a high level of efficiency.

Nine years before, as Juan Valls-López packed his briefcase to attend the 2005 quarterly meeting of the Board of Directors, he already knew what his father, Pedro Valls-Beltrán thought were the three diverging paths to growth. One option was to increase production of their conventional wines, which had established the vineyard's reputation for quality and had given the company sufficient scale to move from handcrafted wine to large-scale production. Alternatively, Viñedos del Pacífico could focus less on wine and more on the dairy business, taking advantage of its strengths in farming and leveraging its primary asset—the land and a stable dairy business. A third possibility and more radical decision could be to produce organic and biodynamic wine in Chile. Given the pros and cons of each of these strategies and the resources needed to move forward, the Valls Family and Viñedos del Pacífico could only choose one option. What should it be?

Wine Industry Background

Producing and drinking wine has been a millenary practice and its beginnings date from ancient Egypt (3,000 B.C.). However, it was not until the year 200 B.C., when Romans worshiped their God named Baco—symbol of festivity associated to wine consumption—that they demonstrated their extensive technological knowledge for the time, with regard to grape-growing and wine making.

Over the centuries and especially in the last 50 years, the wine industry has become one of the more competitive sectors worldwide, with a permanent incorporation of new countries, and the development of advanced processes of manufacturing and formats, with USA and Europe as the main consumer regions and China joining recently (Exhibit 5.6).

Consumption has risen above 42 liters per year per person in countries like France, Portugal, and Switzerland and more than 30 liters in countries like Austria, Italy, and Greece, whereas in USA and Canada the average consumption is 10 liters per person per year (Exhibit 5.7).

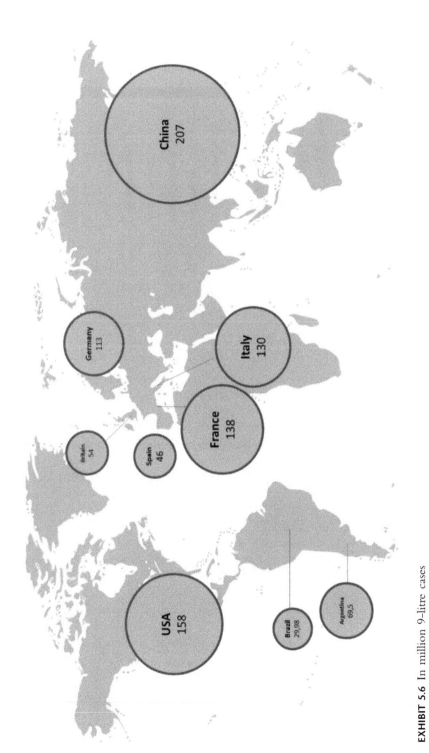

EXHIBIT 5.6 In million 9-litre cases

Source: Vinexpo (2016), https://www.theiwsr.com/iwsr_vinexpo_report.html

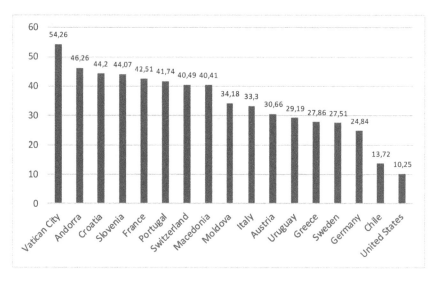

EXHIBIT 5.7 Annual wine consumption per capita
Liters per capita
Source: The Wine Institute (2015)

The wine sector continues to be highly dynamic in Chile, in terms of production, exports, and generation of employment, as well as in the development of high quality products. Taking advantage of the particular weather conditions and soil that are characteristic of the valleys located at the central and southern zones of Chile, and the selection of proper strains, this industry has recently specialized increasingly in high quality wines, which are the base of the export viniculture.

According to the figures of 2017 of the International Organization of Vine and Wine, Chile is placed seventh in the wine producers' world ranking, and fourth among the main wine exporters.

The Wine in Chile

Chile's wine industry dated back to the 1500s, when the first Spanish settlers in the region brought vines from Europe. These settlers established early vineyards with cuttings from France and other parts of Europe, brought to Chile before the European phylloxera epidemic in the late 1800s. It was not until the 1990s, after the country had stabilized politically and undergone a period of economic reforms that the wine industry began to grow, modernize, and compete on a global stage. From 1992 to 2017 total production grew from a half million cases to 54 million cases,[4] definitively establishing the strong export focus of the Chilean wine industry.

During this time of global expansion, Chile developed a clear reputation with consumers in the United States and Europe for consistent, low-priced wines, particularly Cabernet Sauvignon and Sauvignon Blanc. The price per case for exported wines highlighted this trend. While in the 1990s and 2000s volume grew enormously, the price per case stayed quite low. In 2013 the average price per exported case was $20.76, which would imply a price per bottle in the United States of roughly $5 to $6 in retail stores.

Since the 1990s, Chile had developed a global reputation for commercial value wines that were predictable and drinkable. In the United States, this reputation came partly from the limited exposure of US consumers (Beltán et al., 2006), who generally encountered the wines from a few large producers. Critics of Chilean wine classified the wine industry as being too industrial and fixated on volume.[5] However, a small group of independent winemakers, including Viñedos del Pacífico, had sought to change that image by producing small-lot wines that were sophisticated, complex, and able to stand up to great wines from all over the world. But despite a growing community of high-end winemakers, it was an uphill battle to convince influencers in key markets abroad to buy in to high-end Chilean wines. In 2016, a large number of high-end Chilean wines, from a number of wineries, are fighting to overcome US consumer perceptions that wines from Chile are affordable and drinkable, but unsophisticated.

The Chilean industry's primary target markets are the USA, China, and the UK. The main consumer-level trends in those markets are: a change in consumer habits; television food channels and food-related blogs are increasing in popularity; and a new market segment has appeared, the Millennials. These consumers were born between 1980 and 2000 and represent 92 million consumers in the USA.[6] Forty percent of the wine they drink is imported. They learn about products and communicate with others online. These new consumers are currently driving the new trends in wine consumption. Producers have responded to these trends by selling more wine online and using the internet to educate consumers. Thus, US consumers, broadly speaking, have greater access to a broader range of wines and distribution channels than ever before.

Viñedos del Pacífico Background

Ernesto Valls-Garrido, a Spanish immigrant, arrived at Chile in 1937 after escaping from the Spanish Civil War, and at the age of 15 years old he settled in the southern zone of Chile. He rapidly got employment as a farm worker in agricultural tasks related to the vineyard. Due to his strong character and intelligence, he assumed more responsibilities, becoming Chief of Production. At the age of 22 he moved to Casablanca Valley, located in the central part of Chile, a well-named production sector of white wine and pinot noir of high quality. Conjointly with a Croatian partner, they started producing wine in small-scale, founding Viñedos del Pacífico on just 25 acres.

The first years were hard. The selected region met the ideal climatic conditions to produce quality wine, but did not have a supply chain network with the expectations of Ernesto Valls-Garrido and developed a sales strategy focused on volume production and market share.

The following were successful years. The company became known in the local market for its wines and grew at average sales rates of 15% per year. However, due to the management differences, Ernesto bought his Croatian partner out in 1958. The next years, the company put effort in a strategy to increase its market share, given that very few companies in Chile could offer a quality wine produced for the local market.

By the end of 1970, the first succession occured when Ernesto Valls-Garrido stepped down and his eldest son of, Pedro Valls-Beltrán, took over the company. Through his tenure, French white wine varieties like Sauvignon Blanc and Chardonnay were incorporated into the winery's offerings. Pedro Valls-Beltrán also included a new technology to the business, integrating innovative techniques and nutrient inputs treatments to the vines, new frost control systems and advanced quality control systems for harvesting and the winery, such as process techniques, inverse osmosis and micro-oxygenation.

With the introduction of these technological advances, Viñedos del Pacífico ranked as one of the most relevant vineyards in the high quality production of white wine in Chile, competing directly with the white grapes wines from the New World produced in South Africa and Australia. In addition, profits and volume of exports for Viñedos del Pacífico had rapidly increased; its wines were traded in more than 21 countries all over the world, mainly in the demanding market of the United Kingdom.

In 2003, Juan Valls-López, grandson of the patriarch (Exhibit 5.8), enrolled at the Institut des Sciences de la Vigne et du Vin at the University of Bordeaux, to undertake a specialization program, a Master of Business Science in Vineyard & Winery Management. Upon Juan's arrival in France, Pedro Valls-Garrido passed away, and in his sadness for the loss of his beloved grandfather, Juan had second thoughts about spending the following two years abroad. Juan's motivations included eventually running the family business and exploring opportunities to introduce more improvements to the process that Viñedos del Pacífico could identify.

Juan had big shoes to fill, though. Pedro had been a very successful businessman in the local wine industry and had created a prestige of quality around the vineyard, leaving an innovation legacy and growth. He chose to stay and finish graduate school.

Juan Valls-López Returns

In 2005, Juan Valls-López returned to Chile, after finishing his studies in Bordeaux. He went back loaded with new projects for him and Viñedos del Pacífico. As an Agricultural Engineer, Juan had the intuition and tenacity to start incorporating key concepts into the family business that would have a twist to his activity.

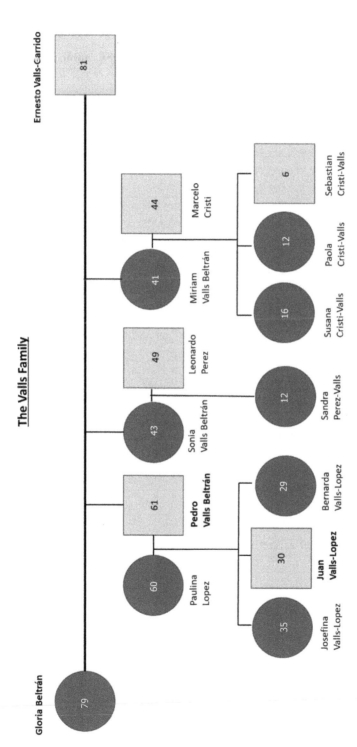

EXHIBIT 5.8 Genogram Valls Family (year 2014)

When he arrrived, Juan was appointed as a new winery production manager for Viñedos del Pacífico, a position that would allow him to move forward with the first draft of a sustainability project for the Vineyard. He wanted to implement what the Brundtland's Report[7] promotes for sustainability: "the capacity to satisfy the needs of the current human generation without supposing the cancelation that future generations also can satisfy individual needs". In particular, thiscroa concept implied the incorporation of environmental practices to the wine, changes to the systems of production, water recycling and a new winery with LEED world-class standards (see Exhibit 5.9).

Unlike the usual tasks of the Chilean wine industry, Juan Valls-López envisioned a need to incorporate organic crops and biodynamic practices into the business. In other words, working toward the sustainable development of the company.

It turned out to be a tremendous challenge, though, to change more than 60 years of history in the harvesting and wine producing processes founded by his grandfather. His project was to transform the vineyard, seeking to take care of the environmental conditions, respecting the ecology and giving priority to soil management as a central part of the system. This implied fertilizing with organic compost and natural materials to protect the environment, making the brushwood clearance manually—never using herbicides—, while the illnesses would be handled through biological control and prevention, without relying on chemical elements. Water was particularly essential, as its use had to be pure.

His father was skeptical at the beginning and used to make comments like:

> Son, this management policy of 'mystical approach' does not have scientific seriousness, stop insisting on that, or it'll drive us to the bankruptcy and market loss. All successful vineyards conduct industrialized processes, which means, techniques such as ours, applying herbicides and soil fertilization, with the purpose of having plagues under control and improving the performance during the harvest.[8]

The Board of Directors Meeting in 2005

The day had arrived and Pedro Valls-Beltrán needed to introduce the three alternatives to the Board:

> The market is sluggish, we need to make changes. The numbers are not good and the price by case is falling. Our first option would be to increase production of our wine using our conventional process. We have the know-how but we will need raw high-quality material, a new plant and acquiring additional land. Option number two is to take advantage of our strengths and expertise in farming and dairy products and develop our dairy products. A third path would be more radical, which means to begin producing organic and biodynamic wine, proposed by Juan some time ago.

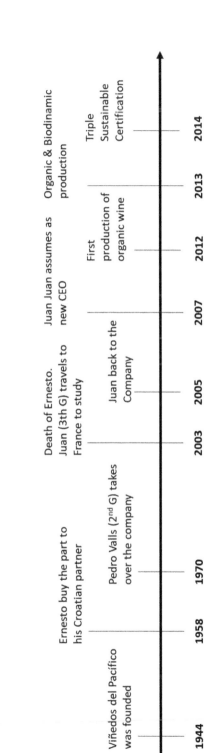

EXHIBIT 5.9 Timeline for the business

Timeline content:

1944 — Viñedos del Pacífico was founded

1958 — Ernesto buy the part to his Croatian partner

1970 — Pedro Valls (2nd G) takes over the company

2003 — Death of Ernesto. Juan (3th G) travels to France to study

2005 — Juan back to the Company

2007 — Juan Juan assumes as new CEO

2012 — First production of organic wine

2013 — Organic & Biodinamic production

2014 — Triple Sustainable Certification

Strategy in market share

Strategy in quality

Strategy based in sustainability

Over the months, tension between father and son increased to a point where they did not speak during office hours. Thus, Juan decided to leave his family home.

One year after assuming his position in the family business and after a series of tensions and confrontations on how to run the business, the different points of view between father and son ended up with Juan quitting his position as winery production manager and leaving his family business to start his own business, leaving the sustainability project inconclusive.

The Valls Family's Dilemmas

A year before the patriarch died, Pedro decided to create a Family Council. He had seen many families finish the business because of family disputes and difficult family relationships. The Family Council was formed by his sisters and their husbands, Juan's wife and his eldest daughter (Exhibit 5.10). Although neither of them worked at the company, the sisters had a percentage of shares (15% each) inherited from their grandfather. Juan's brothers-in-law had a very cohesive family perspective and made a contribution from a business point of view.

Juan's sisters, Josefina and Bernarda were shocked by his brother's decision to leave, and decided to bring the case to the Family Council. Josefina Valls-López, expressed the following premise in the extraordinary session:

> We are very sad for Juan's voluntary leave off. The project he presented makes a lot of sense to us like a family and honors the legacy of our grandfather and founder of the business. We cannot understand that all his talent is now in another firm. I think Juan didn't have the space and time necessary to implement the project and see its benefits, not just for Viñedos del Pacífico, but also for the family, the employees and our community.[9]

Pedro Valls-Beltrán intervened and commented that, in order to carry out the project, the level of investment required would need external funding, as the company didn't have enough resources. Besides, he was skeptical about its possible results, in spite of the fact that organic wine production was consistent with a global trend across the world

Family Council Valls Family

Pedro Valls Beltrán	Sonia Valls Beltrán	Miriam Valls Beltrán	Josefina Valls Lopez	Paulina Lopez	Leonardo Perez	Marcelo Cristi

EXHIBIT 5.10 Family Council

The Family Council voted, and Josefina was left in charge of presenting a new project in the next two months. If the pros/cons of the project in the long run balanced its environmental and social impact, Juan would be asked to return to the company again, but this time as CEO, having to report directly to a Board of Directors composed by family shareholders and one external advisor (Exhibit 5.10). This Board of Directors was formed at the request of the banks, as a control measure to oversee the business financial health and transparency in its management. The property remained entirely owned by the Valls family.

Pedro Valls-Beltrán accepted this proposal and requested to put on record the following statement.

> Our family has led the wine innovation market in Chile for the last 60 years. This is the time to give space to new generations, I'm open to support Juan if the long-term project is rewarding for the family unit.[10]

With the path clear to move forward with Juan's project, Josefina took charge.

Juan's Return and Cost Benefit Analysis

At the beginning of 2007, Juan Valls-López returned as the new CEO of Viñedos del Pacífico. He made peace with his father and had a new opportunity to implement the project. Nevertheless, his return was not exempted from difficulties; his father was a Board member and was watching each step strategically.

The project should begin to bear fruit in some five years. The first productive cycles were expected to reduce the harvest by 35%, but that would only happen until the vineyard adapted to the changes.

The way to convince the Family Council and the Board of Directors would be calculating the performance—financial and social—of the vineyard in terms of production with a change of the system, from the traditional way to a model with organic and biodynamic crops. Based on this, the company started to add costs and net benefits for both the company and other stakeholders including employees, customers, and society in general. The impact on some of these groups could be small or even nonexistent, but would probably be significant on others. Juan Valls-López should consider each group to monitor whether there was impact or not, if it was positive or negative and its magnitude. When possible, he would try to quantify the impact.

Productive System and Price Changes

The impacts on the productive system would be the most relevant, as they would lower the production levels. Juan bet that the reduction of volume could be compensated through the final product price. The consumption of organic wine in the US has increased at an average annual growth rate of 15% during the last 5 years and the price of a bottle of an organic wine is over $20.00 vs. $9.00 for traditional wine in the US.

Employees and Contractors

Juan's proposal considered the social equity concept, that is, a fair treatment to the company's workers and contractors, ensuring care plans in terms of occupational health and process certification through OHSAS 18001 (Occupational Health and Safety Assessment Series). This new system increases costs in the first years by 20% but would reduce the risks of accidents, fines, and other.

Customers

Every certification process such as the organic and biodynamic process, would be conducted by international companies, with the aim to show customers absolute transparency in their practices. The certifications have a cost and time of implementation, but present to the consumers information about healthy and safe production of wine.

Suppliers

Juan Valls-López addressed that all input suppliers would have a fair treatment in their payments and conditions, ensuring a higher competence in the offer. A Supply Chain Management system would be designed.

Competitors

The companies of the sector in Chile would have access to a code of good practice, with the objective to disseminate and promote that more firms can be able to conduct organic and biodynamic processes.

Community

Juan observed that most workers came from the local community; others from places close by Valle de Casablanca. Therefore, Juan had a special concern for working hand by hand with the local community, with programs for promotion of local wool handcrafts, a project known as Entre Cerros.

In addition to this social equity concept, a look at the required investments for the three options in 2007–2009 in USD and gross margin by option was forecasted (see Exhibit 5.13).

With the evaluation of the social and long-term impact of the organic wine alternative, plus the projections of the other two options, the Valls Family could look at the economic and sustainable future of the world from a different perspective.

Board of Directors
Viñedos del Pacifico

| Pedro Valls Beltrán | Sonia Valls Beltrán | Leonardo Perez | Juan Valls Lopez | Arturo Gonzalez (External) |

EXHIBIT 5.11 Board of Directors

Country	2007	2008	2009	2010	2011	2012	2013
UK	43.090	59.298	76.654	96.902	132.261	175.052	144.630
Brazil	19.947	28.627	37.005	66.495	54.461	49.822	69.821
USA	19.749	14.313	14.313	22.717	14.313	13.700	34.911
China	–	12.269	12.269	12.269	12.269	14.109	29.923
Russia	3.770	13.700	13.700	22.388	13.700	15.745	33.414
Germany	2.370	9.201	9.201	9.201	9.201.	11.246	22.443
Austria	2.154	2.454	2.454	2.454	2.454	4.069	5.985
Sweden	3.232	3.681	3.681	3.681	3.681	4.294	8.977
Switzerland	1.759	6.748	6.748	6.748	6.748	8.997	16.458
Others	83.468	54.186	88.299	91.291	139.917	151.817	132.162
	179.540	204.476	264.323	334.144	389.004	448.851	498.723

EXHIBIT 5.12 Exports by country, Viñedos del Pacífico

Increase the production	2007	2008	2009
Invest in land	2,500	1,500	0,000
Invest new plant & winery	1,500	1,500	1,500
Other cost	0,500	0,500	0,500
	4,500	3,500	2,000

Launch dairy products	2007	2008	2009
Invest new diary plant	6,500	1,500	1,000
Packing plant	0,750	0,500	0
R+D	0,150	0,150	0,100
	7,400	2,150	1,100

EXHIBIT 5.13
Source: Viñedos del Pacífico

Organic wine	2007	2008	2009
EMS System	1,500	1,000	0,500
OHSAS 18000	0,500	0,500	0,500
Social responsibility program	0,500	0,500	0,500
Biodinamic program	0,250	0,250	0,250
	2,750	2,250	1,750

EXHIBIT 5.13 (*Continued*)

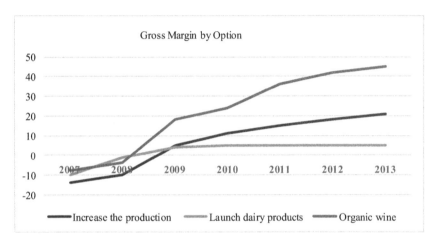

EXHIBIT 5.14
Source: Viñedos del Pacífico

References

Beltrán, N. H., Duarte-Mermoud, M. A., Bustos, M. A., Salah, S. A., Loyola, E. A., Peña-Neira, A. I., & Jalocha, J. W. (2006). Feature extraction and classification of Chilean wines. *Journal of Food Engineering, 75*(1), 1–10.
Brundtland, G., & Khalid, M. (1987). *UN brundtland commission report.* Our Common Future.

Case 5.3 Grupo Transoceanica: The Meinlschmidt Family's Strategic Choices

Johannes Ritz and Marc-Michael Bergfeld

Context

In 2017, the Meinlschmidt Family, together with four other families that formed and own Grupo Transoceanica were facing a complex decision. Grupo Transoceanica is Ecuador's main logistics company, providing services in the main commercial hubs, seaports, and airports. Founded in 1953, it currently represents companies like Hapag Lloyd, Lufthansa, and LAN Cargo. Facing a decline of profitability in the main business unit due to international market consolidation the executive team had to take decisive action or accept declining profit margins. One option was to start conversations with a multinational which had made them an attractive offer. The other option was to invest in strengthening business lines to compensate for the declining performance main business.

This case can be used to discuss the sale of a family business as well as shareholding by multiple families.

The Grupo Transoceanica Story

Wilfried Meinlschmidt and his son Volker were standing by the huge windows of their modern office, overlooking the river Guayas across the street from their company headquarters in Guayaquil, Ecuador. As they were looking at the ships passing by on the major stream leading to Ecuador's biggest port they were considering their company's future.

They recently had received a very interesting offer from a multinational company to start conversations to buy the logistics company that Wilfried has led since 1981. As they were preparing to meet with the representatives from the other four families that were shareholders in their companies they agreed that they needed to come to agree on a course of action. There were many factors to consider and this was not a decision to be taken lightly. The offer came at a time when industry consolidation pressured Transoceanica's profit margins and the political situation in Ecuador, with a populist left wing government and rising corruption, preoccupied them.

Ecuador

Ecuador is a country on the west coast of South America. Its diverse landscape includes the Amazon jungle, the Andean highlands and the Galapagos Islands with a diverse wildlife. Quito, its capital city, is located in the foothills of the

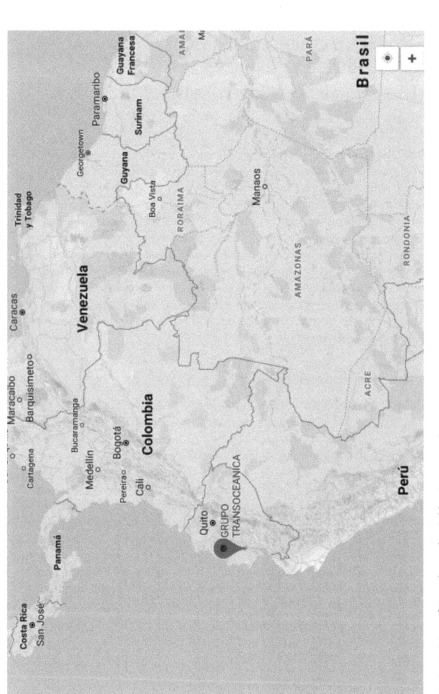

FIGURE 5.1 Map of Ecuador and neighboring countries

Andes at an altitude of 2,850 m. The city is known for its Spanish colonial heritage, with palaces from the 16th and 17th centuries and religious sites such as the magnificent church Compañía de Jesús. Guayaquil, the largest city in the country and its main sea port, was the headquarters of Grupo Transoceanica. Ecuador borders with Colombia and Peru. With about 16 million inhabitants it also represents one of the smaller markets of the Andean community economic zone. With GDP per capita of US$6,074 in 2013, its economy is behind Peru (US$6,583) and Colombia (US$8,030) but has significantly improved in recent years due to rising oil prices. Ecuador's economy relies on exporting primary goods, especially oil, banana, shrimp, canned fish and flowers. Manufacturing is focused on the local market. Ecuador adopted the dollar as its national currency in 2000, following a major banking crisis and economic recession in 1999. Such context provided stability; however it also makes Ecuador's exports more expensive relative to neighboring countries with national currencies. After decades of political instability and turmoil, a stable government since 2006 has helped the country to grow at favorable rates and reduced poverty significantly.

Company Profile

Wilfried Meinlschmidt came to Ecuador in 1976 from Bremen, Germany. In 1981 he took over the leadership of Transoceánica in Guayaquil, which was founded in 1953 as an independent and fully Ecuadorian company. Initially it represented Norddeutscher Lloyd and Hamburg-Amerika Linie as its General Agent in Ecuador. In 1958, Lufthansa chose Transoceánica as general commercial agent for Ecuador. One year later, NYK Line chose. Transoceánica as its general agent. In 1973, CSAV entrusted Transoceánica with its general representation in Ecuador. One year later, SEA CONTAINERS LTD., chose Transoceánica as its agent in Ecuador. In 1981, Chilean airline LADECO named Transoceánica as its general commercial agent in Ecuador. In 1993, the passenger and cargo divisions of Lufthansa choose Transoceánica as its general agent throughout Ecuador. After that in 1996, LAN CHILE returned to Ecuador after 20 years, taking the routes of LADECO and selecting Transoceánica as its general agent in Ecuador. In 2001, CSAV chose TRANSAVISA (a company belonging to the Transoceánica Group) as commercial agent in Ecuador, maintaining Transoceánica as general agent in the country. In 2004, Grupo Transoceánica, with its companies Transoceánica Cia. Ltda., Transavisa S.A., Tercon Cia. Ltda. and Navecuador S.A. obtained the ISO 9001: 2000 certification for quality management system, covering all the processes of the four companies in all offices nationwide. In 2006, NYK Line selected TRANSNIPPON (a Transoceanica Group company) as a commercial agent in Ecuador, maintaining Transoceanica as a general agent. Over the years Transoceánica developed into a group of several related companies in the logistics industry, gaining a powerful position in the Ecuadorian logistics market, operating offices in four major cities in Ecuador.

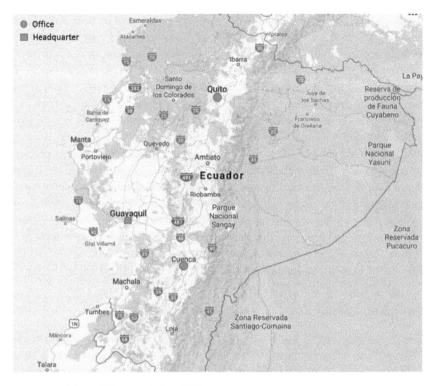

FIGURE 5.2 Map of Transoceánicas Offices

Wilfried Meinlschmidt and his partners relied on a German approach to run an Ecuadorian company. German organization and precision made Grupo Transoceánica a very profitable endeavor.

Group Structure

Grupo Transoceánica comprises more than 10 related companies within the logistics sector in addition to the main firm Transóceancia C. Ltda, such as Tercon—Terminales de Contenedors Cía. Ltda., a company that operates container terminals; Transpoint S.A. a company running a fleet of trucks to transport containers within Ecuador to their final destinations; and Transnippon S.A. represents shipping lines. Other companies of the group comprise Nacecuador S.A., Hansamaritime S.A., Transsky S.A.,. Figure 5.3 shows the leadership structure of the main group of companies. As can be seen the companies are controlled mainly by Wilfried Meinlschmidt together with his son Volker and representatives of the Riemann and Rivera families.

Figure 5.4 shows the revenue and profits for the group of companies in recent years. The group achieved a steady revenue growth in the years following 2010. However, profits started to decline despite growing sales.

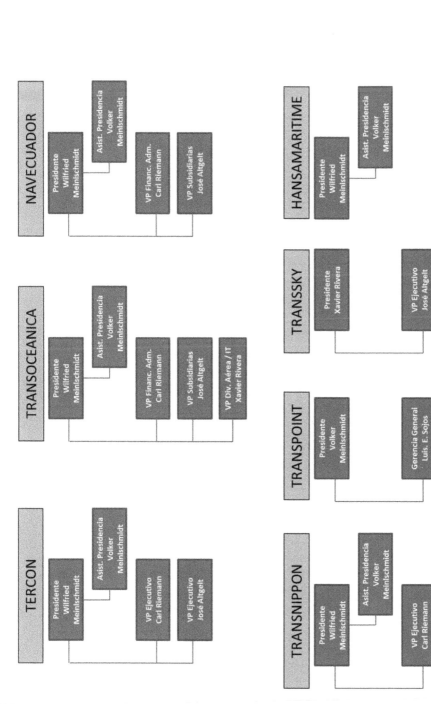

FIGURE 5.3 Leadership structure of main group companies

Transoceanica Group	2010		2011		2012		2013	
Companies	Revenue	Profit	Revenue	Profit	Revenue	Profit	Revenue	Profit
TRANSOCEANICA C. LTDA	$ 20.795.858,00	$ 3.810.336,00	$ 25.684.800,00	$ 9.047.095,00	$ 30.062.971,00	$ 8.981.337,00	$ 30.338.109,00	$ 8.887.373,00
NAVECUADOR S.A.	$ 1.484.008,00	$ 130.978,00	$ 2.405.587,50	$ 272.424,00	$ 3.327.167,00	$ 413.870,00	$ 6.350.193,00	$ 183.584,00
TERCON TERMINALES DE CONTENEDORES C LTDA	$ 2.754.172,00	$ 436.836,00	$ 2.952.508,00	$ 764.312,00	$ 4.005.782,00	$ 939.251,00	$ 4.024.902,00	$ 739.036,00
TRANSPOINT S.A.	$ 5.038.896,00	$ 326.730,00	$ 5.956.171,00	$ 368.850,50	$ 6.718.334,00	$ 410.971,00	$ 7.673.709,00	$ 121.876,00
Total	$ 30.072.934,00	$ 4.704.880,00	$ 36.999.066,50	$ 10.452.681,50	$ 44.114.254,00	$ 10.745.429,00	$ 48.386.913,00	$ 9.931.869,00

FIGURE 5.4 Transoceanica Group financial statement (estimates)

Shareholder Structure and Governance

The shareholder structure of Grupo Transoceanica is unusual as the main companies are owned by five family groups. The majority of these families have German heritage. Currently, as Figure 5.5 shows, the Hoppe, Riemann, Meinlschmidt, Altgelt, and Rivera families hold 15.3%, 22.5%, 29.7%, 22.5% and 10% respectively of the six main companies through investment companies: ANKARI S.A., FARIMAR S.A., NIMARO S.A., PEAL S.A. and RIDEYCA S.A.

With regards to the governance the owning families have established boards of directors for each firm. The board members are the leaders of the five owning families. The families' designated successors can join the board meetings without voting rights. The voting rights are granted according to percentage of ownership. There is a written agreement that every family must have only one successor for the leadership role within the companies' board.

Logistics Industry Trends[11]

The positive development of the group during recent years had been fueled by the general economic development in Ecuador. However local competitors like Hamburg Süd Ecuador and Maersk Ecuador as well as global industry trends started to affect the group's position and profit margins.

A recent study from PWC shows that there are a lot of M&A transactions in the logistics sector. Dietmar Prümm, PwC Partner and Head of Transportation & Logistics in Germany expressed:

> The reasons are as varied as the industry: growth in new markets, better regional coverage, but also participation in growth areas such as online trading and the automation of logistics processes are key drivers for logistics companies to drive the consolidation of the still highly fragmented industry.

This trend is worldwide. In 2013, 82 deals were allocated to the logistics and transport sectors.

However, the shipping industry remained the most active individual unit within the transport and logistics sector: in 2013, 53 deals were closed with a volume of 50 million dollars or more, with a total of 56 deals in the following year. However, this was different from the booming logistics business of the past. Dietmar Prümm said

> The industry continues to face immense consolidation pressure. Freight rates continue to be low, and the world trade has still not started well after the financial crisis. In this environment, large corporations are able to hold their own and make better use of their capacities. This is exacerbating the pressure on mergers and acquisitions (for example, Hapag Lloyd/CSAV), but also on cooperation, as the example of the Maersk and MSC shipping companies, which founded Allianz 2M in autumn 2014.

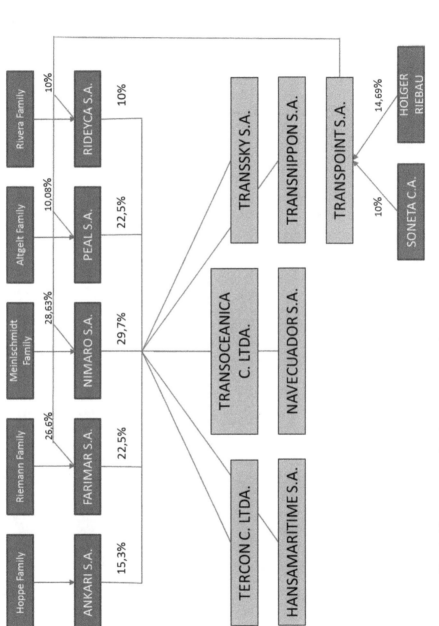

FIGURE 5.5 Shareholder structure of main group companies

Given the high demand for high-yielding targets, the prices of companies in the industry are currently at a historic high with a doubling of sales (median). For 2015, the PwC experts expect a slight revival of mergers and acquisitions in the transport and logistics sector. Dietmar Prümm attributes such revival to the following reasons:

> Increasing e-commerce in the B2B and B2C business and the reduction of trade restrictions mean that more and more companies are gaining access to international markets. At the same time, consumer spending in the growth markets, particularly in Asia and Latin America, is growing. Against this background, many logistics service providers have to develop technologically and geographically in order to be able to build reliable supply chains around the world. Added to this is the fact that many large companies and private equity houses have large cash reserves that they have to invest on a profitable basis. For them, M & A activities in a low-interest environment continue to offer comparatively attractive returns.

The Key Decision for Grupo Transoceanica

As the meeting with the other shareholding families approached, Wilfried and Volker considered the current situation, the PWC highlights and the possible choices. Their companies had been profitable and successful for a long time within a very instable political context thanks to a German approach and visionary leadership of Wilfried and his partners. Wilfried had spent more than half of his life growing the business and Volker had spent many years preparing for succession and future responsibilities. They also acknowledged the responsibility of employment for several hundred employees in the different firms. Yet, they were also facing a deteriorating economic outlook in Ecuador due to low oil prices and strong pressure on their margins due to industry consolidation on a global scale. The offer to buy their company became really attractive.

To be able to make a decision with the other shareholders, father and son had to agree on possible options. Should the company be sold for the owners to retire or start a new business, maybe back in Germany? Or should they commit to continue their firm in the risky Ecuadorian market? Further commitment would mean investing heavily into other businesses in the group to counterbalance the declining profit margins. For such an option to work all shareholders would need to agree to rely on recapitalizing the company with family funds. They were uncertain about how the meeting would go and what the other shareholders may propose.

Notes

1. This case study was elaborated based on a true history added by disguises to serve only for didactic purposes and does not propose to evaluate the managerial effectiveness or to serve as a primary source of data. The protagonist and the decision scenarios are fictional.

2. Fabio Matuoka Mizumoto is professor at FGV—Fundação Getúlio Vargas and partner at Markestrat.
3. Plano Real was a huge economic program established on February 27, 1994 to control inflation and to stabilize the economy. A new currency, the "Real", was launched by that time and still is current nowadays.
*. The authors wrote this case solely to provide material for class discussion. The authors do not intend to illustrate either effective or ineffective handling of a managerial situation. The authors may have disguised certain names and other identifying information to protect confidentiality.
4. www.winesofchile.org/es/estudios-reportes/168
5. Beltrán, N. H., Duarte-Mermoud, M. A., Bustos, M. A., Salah, S. A., Loyola, E. A., Peña-Neira, A. I., & Jalocha, J. W. (2006). Feature extraction and classification of Chilean wines. *Journal of Food Engineering, 75*(1), 1–10.
6. Goldman Sachs Global Investment Research 2017.
7. Brundtland, G., & Khalid, M. (1987). UN Brundtland Commission Report. Our Common Future.
8. Interview with the founder.
9. Ibid.
10. Ibid.
The incorporation of the first organic and biodynamic farming practices by the company Viñedos del Pacífico in Chile, had resulted in high expectations for the wine industry, calling the attention of international organizations such as The Bio-dynamic Association and prestigious journals like Winemaker. A transformation that had experienced high costs, not just from the financial point of view, but also from the family side: the Valls clan had lived very difficult times for this decision-making.
11. Source: www.pwc.de/de/pressemitteilungen/2015/m-und-a-in-der-transport-und-logistikbranche-2014-schifffahrtsektor-unter-druck-logistik-nimmt-an-fahrt-auf.html

6

INNOVATION AND INTERNATIONALIZATION

6.1 Innovation and Internationalization of Family Businesses in Latin America

Paloma Fernández Pérez

Innovation and internationalization are two strategies that historically start more often as a reaction to severe crisis and economic difficulties, than as a positive plan to open new business opportunities in times of economic expansion and growth. This is exactly the problem that affects most family firms that need to make decisions about innovating and going abroad. Most of them have to make the decision without having the time to think, react, or analyze if it is appropriate to change the business model, or go outside the family. The four cases analyzed in this section are good examples of this common situation: family firms try to analyze these decisions when there are serious problems inside the family, in the sales or the indebtedness of the family firm, or in the external economy.

Second, it is common to find in family firms abundant cases of entrepreneurial founders who start businesses that have an innovative aspect, from a technological point of view, or from a market or organizational perspective. It is also extremely common to find that the family firm's second or third generation does not share the same innovative vision of the business. Second or third generations have different visions about the family business, and are the ones that usually must face the problem of what to do, how, where, and who, to maintain the founder's business. Again, the problem is particularly serious if these decisions must be taken in times of heavy debts, losses, government changing regulations that negatively affect the future of the business, and changing economic cycles.

It was in the 1970s, in the midst of a world industrial crisis, and the coming of the new generation of baby boomers to family firm ownership and management, that old founders who created businesses in the Western world before World War II started to retire and think that they needed some advice to survive. Family business scholars emerged as a new field of scientific research devoted to help those founders in need. The greatest academic innovation found in those times when there was no internet, and heavy financial controls at the national level, was to suggest to these family firms in need to implement innovations in the business model of management, in their organization, in their professional education and international training of younger generations; and in large firms also introducing professional outsiders more acquainted with world finances and world competitors.

These outsiders, and the better educated and internationally trained family members, have helped family firms in the last three decades to follow new strategies of organization, diversification, international operations of mergers and acquisitions, international alliances, and financial operations. Also, new professional training and international experience has helped younger generations of family businesses in developed and emerging economies of the world to adapt to changing institutional regulations. In Latin America and Asia, for instance, there has been a proliferation of business groups controlled by families, organized by professional executives of the same family or outsiders, as business groups are often an efficient organizational form in contexts of high risk of economic or political turbulence.

Small and medium family firms, in developed and developing economies of the world, have been extremely slow, or reluctant, to adopt the strategies that large family firms have learned to implement in the last decades. They do not plan innovation or internationalization in the good times of economic expansion, in general. They are reluctant to think, therefore, in the long-term efficient use of qualified outsiders in the top management, or in devoting time and space for knowledge transfer from abroad. Internet and the low cost of long-distance transportation should be tools that must be used to train young generations to organize diversified businesses to reduce risks of the central historical core business, or to search for potential partners outside (from whom to obtain not only potential capital, but innovative ideas) to diversify the old business.

Latin American countries have historically faced much political and economic turbulence. Two books have presented the chronology of these turbulences, and the transformations family businesses have faced in the region (Balmori, Voss, & Wortman, 1990; Fernández Pérez & Lluch, 2015, 2016). Between the mid-eighteenth century and the early nineteenth century an elite of family firms was composed mainly of immigrants from Spain and Portugal, working in foreign trade, and increasingly becoming large landowners and controlling the political rules of the game. Between the 1830s and 1880s a second generation of family businesses emerged, in close connection with opportunities coming from the innovations in trade and industry that meant a wave of foreign investment from Europe and the United States, immigration from Europe, Middle East and Asia, and new technologies. This extraordinary increase in opportunities meant the emergence of enduring innovative family businesses linked to mining, agriculture, cattle, consumer, and light industries (textiles, shoes, food, beverages, maintenance, and repair of equipment), expansion of mercantile firms, and alliances between the entrepreneurial families in each country. Large family firms of this period engaged in international export of mineral products and agricultural raw materials much in demand in world markets. The end of world demand of scarcely elaborated raw materials, at the end of the nineteeth century and until the end of World War II, meant the beginning of the decline of a whole generation of family businesses in Latin America. Diversification, and intraregional trade were the painful solutions survivors and emerging family businesses found, between the end of the nineteenth century and the 1950s. This strategy was reinforced during the Import Substitution Industrialization (ISI) period in Latin America, until the 1990s. State firms and big national champions and very big family businesses innovated and internationalized with state support in this ISI period, but smaller and medium-sized family businesses remained in their former strategy of diversification and intraregional trade. In these two rather inward looking strategies they accumulated an expertise that would be the basis of their competitiveness after the 1990s, with the new wave of globalization and new foreign investment that benefitted most of the region (with exceptions linked to anticapitalist regimes and countries like Venezuela or Cuba or some Andean countries).

The lessons from the historical experience of innovation and internationalization experimented by three or four generations of family businesses in Latin America are that times of crisis are times to initiate innovative diversification, and rapid knowledge transfer. Diversification means that often the business initiated by the founder may have to change, or disappear, in order for new generations to be able to endure in business. Diversification also means that often founders and older generations have to keep an open mind and a relatively stable percentage of their expenditures linked to someone in the firm (outsider, or family member) focused on finding innovative diversification. The four cases in this section demonstrate often there is no time to do complete changes, or willingness to sell, so a rather cheap strategy is to diversify in related or nonrelated businesses in which young generations have a motivation and a feeling that it might be good for them and for their family. Diversification means, therefore, also, tolerance to new ideas, tolerance to risk, tolerance to a certain amount of losses implied in having a junior or an outsider trying to help. Knowledge transfer means, following the variety of historical cases we know from past family businesses, and from the lessons of expert consultants, that there are no simple straightforward directions for success. Knowledge can and should be obtained combining a variety of sources of information that can be used to analyze internationalization and innovation plans: employees first of all; consumers second; competitors and suppliers third. Innovation studies confirm that these are major sources of ideas to orient business practice, and family firms often disregard or plainly ignore them. However, most founders of family firms started their visionary businesses exactly by seeing, listening, and learning from other firms as employees, consumers, competitors, or suppliers. The four cases in this section have no reference to them; the family firms worry only about what the family would do or think, what the competitors will do against them, or how the State may damage the future sales of the business. Family firms in Latin America are used to individualistic behavior, and maybe this is one of the lessons their own history shows they can do to help family firms: to believe that their clients, their employees, their competitors, are part of the business. Innovation, or internationalization, in many cases, has come from a close connection with them.

References

Balmori, D., Voss, S. F., & Wortman, M. (1990). *Las alianzas de familia y la formación del país en América Latina*. Mexico D.F.: Fondo de cultura Economica, S.A. de C.V.

Fernández Pérez, P., & Lluch, A. (Eds.). (2015). *Familias empresarias y empresas familiares en América Latina y España. Una visión de largo plazo*. Bilbao: Fundación BBVA (available online in pdf the book, the appendix, and a microsite with interactive database). In English, (2016). *Evolution of family businesses: Continuity and change in Latin America and Spain*. Cheltenham, UK: Edward Elgar Publishing.

Case 6.1 Harvest Products LLC (S.A. de C.V.)[1]
Marcos A. Vega Solano

The Opening

What do we do now?, wondered Mr. Madecadel Barriere and his daughter Claudia, one cold January afternoon in 2014. As founder of the Harvest Products company, Madecadel was in the middle of an internal war that concerned the course of his company. Should they sell assets? Should they continue to operate at a minimum profit level? Should they cut down their product portfolio? The current internal financial crisis meant a high level of debts and illiquidity, since the company start outsourcing the distribution operation, with terrible results. It had been nearly three decades of experience and hard work and now this had to come along. A downturn in the El Salvador economy, which might point toward an eventual exit from the market, and the innovation in the technical process have been the key to sustaining the operations. Maybe innovation in the business model was now necessary.

The Context: El Salvador

The World Economic Forum declares, in the Global Competitiveness Report of 2014, that El Salvador had in 2013 a GDP around US$24.5 billion, with a population of 6.3 million people. The GDP per capita is about US$3,875, under the Latin America and the Caribbean average. This report points to the most important problems in the business environment as: crime and theft, access to financing, inefficient government bureaucracy, policy instability, inflation and corruption.

In the middle of the 80's political crisis in Central America and the civil war in El Salvador, there was a lack of price control by the Salvadoran Supply Regulation Institute, creating opportunities in the business environment.

In the early 2000s the CAFTA RD was signed and governmental economic policies were put in place to provide support to companies producing ethnic foods that qualified as small and medium scale companies. These policies sought to train and position the personnel working for these companies so they would comply with requirements, affording the benefit of brand promotion through all media channels indicating that these were small-scale companies that were reaching their objectives.

The financial world economic crisis in 2008 affected El Salvador, reducing the purchase power of the middle class. This situation put the country in a recession scenario, decreasing the GDP in the next years.

The Harvest Products Company

The Harvest Products Company (THPC hereafter) is a family-run company established in 1989 with an equity of US$11,000, beginning in the Barriere family's living room as a natural person company. The sales were meant mainly for the local market as well as international markets, especially in the USA. Appendix 6.1 shows the company's financial information from 2002 to 2013. The company jumped off by packing and distributing staple products, such as rice, beans, and sugar. Given the instability of the local production of these items, other products were added, covering the demand for spices, powdered drinks (traditional and fruit flavored), as well as poultry feed; thus contributing by supplying healthy items with excellent flavor, high quality and efficient service.

At present, 30 people work for the company; they are distributed in commercial, production, and administrative areas. It is their mission to contribute positively to their customers' health by supplying first-rate natural food products and with the clear vision of being the main regional supplier of natural flavors in a responsible manner (management of THPC 2014).

The Company's Evolutionary Chronology

From 1994 to 2000, investments in working capital had to be made, as it was common practice to provide credit to any customer who purchased product until the working capital availability started to diminish. It was at this time that the company searched for new ways to collect so the money would flow faster. Factoring was then implemented to have immediate resources and still cover the market's needs; moreover, some companies occasionally offered their customers discounts for prompt payment. THPC also used this method during the first five years of its existence.

The company had an initial installed plant capacity of 300 hundred weights per month of production and labor was limited to family members. Between 1989 and 1999, the number of workers grew, starting from two to three people until 10 permanent workers were hired.

In 1998, with more hands being available due to the presence of the new hires, product diversification was driven by the seasonality of the bean harvest. The company was limited to working seasonally under the effect of price variability which affected their costs and sales, so there were moments when product would become scarce and prices would skyrocket and there were others when the opposite would be true; an abundant supply but low prices, while trading in the marketplace would be stable. Therefore, the company diversified, searching for an alternative for the scarce bean harvest during this crop's low season, the introduction of new products that were able to maintain a steady demand over time.

The solution was the creation of powdered products with a mission to attend to the housewives' market in presentations marked for middle-income families with classification and packaging to make them attractive to the consumer's wallet.

This project made reaching the final buyer with a distinguished and clear image possible, which made the buying decision easier. Super markets provided the paths for the new product lines. Moreover, in this same year (1998) an export window was opened. Sales to their client, La Tapachulteca, started when they opened a branch store in Los Angeles, USA, thus promoting enough sales to fill one container per month filled with nostalgic products meant for export.

Close to the year 2000, the owners decided to turn the company from its natural person status to a share company with five shareholders: the parents and three siblings. In the same year the free trade treaty with the US was formalized, which meant a commercial openness with a positive impact on sustainable sales growth in the next 7 years, with a market having developed which had been latent until that moment. With this new opportunity having presented itself, Guatemala began to penetrate El Salvador's retail sales sector, which led to an accelerated competition among the players, mainly with a national supermarket known for its fondness for Salvadoran society with the result that La Tapachulteca shut down its local business, although it kept its export activity extant. It was at this moment that Claudia Barriere, daughter of Mr. Barriere stood out within the company, taking charge of the day-to-day management, accounting, marketing and organizing it all to solidify the fundamental pillars of THPC.

She took advantage of the opportunity afforded by the Salvadoran chamber of commerce of an export window to develop as an export company and also to improve local sales by providing better conditions for sales and distribution by doubling local and international sales.

On the other hand, in the period 2002–2003 a discount club gave the company a chance to sell barley and horchata in its venues, which led to a constant growth from that time on, a third of their monthly sales in just two of their salesrooms.

Due to this increase in sales THPC decided to invest in technology by purchasing technolink, a specialized software which estimates sales orders and their provenance with immediate and accurate information on their buyers. For example:

- There is no formal platform of the national supermarket clients; sales vary according to the client's needs.
- Weekly sales are constant.

THPC took advantage of governmental economic policies to provide support to small and medium companies producing ethnic foods. Taking advantage of the support provided by the government in the technical area the company's position was consolidated in the estimated time, reaching a sales record of $1,000,000 in the 2007–2008 period, which allowed for the transfer of the production facility to a wholly owned production facility in Santa Tecla that would accommodate 50 permanent workers.

At the end of 2007 and the start of 2008, the world economic crisis took place. This provoked an increase in the company's costs promoting a gradual breach in the payment of financial obligations. Before the financial crisis detonated, a decision was reached to subcontract the company's product distribution to a 400-worker Salvadoran company that sought to increase its item portfolio. This would allow the company to lower its distribution costs and to have a greater reach to those markets where demand was now greater.

After 11 months of working with this new scheme, the relationship with the distributor came to an end as it was ascertained that sales had fallen alarmingly due to the fact the distributor was delivering products to its clients without receiving due payment. These clients would later declare payment default. There were no sales for two months due to the commercial relationship having been terminated, which left Harvest Products with a large debt, which was counterweighted by the sales of that same year because it overbalanced expected profits. As a result of this, working capital was reduced to a bare minimum and it was necessary to return to the direct product distribution scheme as it had originally been conceived and executed. In the end, the handling of semi-industrial products was turned over to the discount club, which was still Harvest Products' client. In 2009, $600,000 in product sales was reached at the same time that marketing and management processes were put in place to recoup previous sales levels, which was difficult given the difficult conditions then extant. The middle-income population opted for lower level products, limiting the recovery of the market once controlled by the company.

More than a year was invested seeking a balance between costs and sales. On that same year, the agriculture ministry, through its fruit department, set itself the task of developing a contest on innovative ideas dealing with fruit- based refreshing drinks. The winner would get technical advice from Texas A&M University. THPC entered the competition with a product called "fresco de tamarind" (tamarind juice), and took first prize. Thanks in part to the help provided by the staff of the food science lab of UCA, the Central American University, "José Simeon Cañas" of El Salvador and by a professor from Texas A&M, THPC fulfilled the requirements needed to obtain a dehydrating machine manufactured in India with specifications especially adapted to the company's needs. This became a competitive advantage due to the features that added value to the company's products, among which the following stand out:

- 100% natural products
- Products free of preservatives
- High nutritional value products
- High quality products
- Original organoleptic qualities without the need for chemical additives.

Mr. Barriere had analyzed his start in the business and its pillars, which were the foundation for differentiating him within the market. What was his position in the market? Did he have his clients' loyalty?

The Specific Challenges

Target Market

For being a 100% natural product, the target market aimed for was that with the greatest purchasing power. However when the financial crisis of 2008 made itself felt fully, exports and remittances decreased in the country, unemployment increased, and so did energy prices as well as food prices. Between 2007 and 2008, the percentage of poor people grew from 34.6% to 40%. In 2009, the Salvadoran economy suffered a deflation of its GNP of 3.1% (World Bank, 2014). A product reformulation was pushed through so they would be more accessible to the medium and low income markets, therefore more adaptable to sudden shifts in its operating environment.

Such was the case of an international supermarket in the line of Accessible Markets, with a policy to provide extra shelf spaces for products valued at less than $1.75. This was when "the savings corner" products were born and the barley product was reformulated so its cost was equivalent to $1.75, which turned it into the product with the highest demand throughout the year.

However, as a competitive advantage in the market differentiation, it turns out the products are segmented as a function of the supermarket where they are found and its size, but in general it's understood that the market's targets are housewives and those persons wishing to develop their cooking, for the international supermarket as well as the national one.

For the discount club the products are meant for small and large restaurants in cheaper presentations designed to be semi-industrial.

> ***Distribution channels****:* because it's a product that's found all over the country it's necessary to have a wide-reaching distribution system, so that's why before the effects of the 2008 global financial crisis impacted El Salvador negatively (WB, 2014), THPC distributed its products directly. Later the opportunity to delegate this service to a third party presented itself, and finally it was decided to subcontract someone to provide it, distributing the product in restaurants and providing credit to their customers. When the crisis hit, the distributor's customers were driven into payment insolvency; as has been indicated previously, they couldn't pay their debts, and the distributor declared themselves bankrupt, leaving THPC with the accounts receivable of all product delivered up to that date.

Therefore, the discount club as an alternative to avoid a graver situation was turned into a collection and distribution center for imported products for large presentation, which transports the product to large and small restaurants for which this discount club became a sort of broker that might replace the product handling done by the previous distributors.

For those entities desirous of other flavors not handled by the discount club, purchase requisitions are drawn up and paid in advance to THPC, which coordinates the delivery process.

Distribution Channel Conditions

Presently there's no agreement or contract in which an established sale is maintained; all that exists is the product and effort. Occasionally promotions are carried out to increase sales under no particular term. This is done if supermarkets allow it, because if there isn't good sales performance product is taken off the shelves but they also don't support those items with the greater demand.

Products and Their Sales

Annex 6.2 refers to sales in dollars for the last four years. In Annex 6.3 sales are expressed in physical units, for the same period. Likewise, Annex 6.4 presents sales expressed in dollars for the last trimester of the last three years. Finally, Annex 6.5 indicates sales expressed in physical units for the last trimester of the past 3 years.

Star Products

By segment, the following products are handled:

Beverages: Barley and Hibiscus tea. Small packaging presentation.
Spices: Achiote and cinnamon

TABLE 6.1 Product price list in beverage variety, for supermarkets in El Salvador, according to the packaging

	Traditional beverages		
Specification	Units	International Supermarket	National Supermarket
Barley	8 oz.	8.05	8.4
Horchata and horchata with milk	1 lb.	18.9	17.43
Barley and barley with milk	1 lb.	16.45	15.4
Horchata and horchata with milk	12 oz.	14.21	13.58
Barley and barley with milk	12 oz.	12.81	13.58
Hibiscus tea	6 oz.	9.59	9.45
Tamarind natural beverage	8 oz.	10.01	9.59

TABLE 6.2 Price list for products of the beverage kind for the discount club in the semi-industrial packaging

	Traditional Beverages	
Specification	Units	Discount Club
Barley	3 lb.	40.53
Hibiscus tea	2 lb.	41.93
Tamarind natural beverage	2 lb.	37.03

All sales of these products are individual.

Criteria Used to Define Product Placement on the Supermarket Shelfs

Spices: the ground ones go first; the seeds go second and lastly those that are mixed.

Beverages: the first ones in the order are the traditional beverages and then the fruit based ones. There is a photo in Annex 6.6 to show this.

Client and Market Potential

Out of total sales 33% goes to the international supermarket chain, another 33% goes to the discount club, 33% to the national supermarket and the remaining 1% to various customers.

Guatemala and Honduras are seen as potential markets, while keeping their present portfolio of customers who will be used as a distribution channel.

This is an initiative that would be analyzed once THPC pays off its present debt and is in a better position to invest in promotion, through taste testing in the regional market. The plan is to broaden the market with the products that have the most demand, starting with barley and evolving by adding products to the company's product lineup, according to how the brand's position is seen to emerge. An advantage here is that consumers' regional tastes and preferences for this type of product are very similar among themselves.

Exports

Exports will be handled through intermediaries who function as a distribution channel. These distributors sell the products in supermarkets or stores with a segment of the nostalgic market so they will then sell to the final consumer.

These markets in the USA are located in Miami, Houston, Washington, and Los Angeles.

US Importers

One of the most important THPC product importers is Kepix Corp., which is made up of a group of Central American companies, seeking to be efficient in the international market, through market research, logistics, financial support, adaptability, creativity, and customer support. This company was founded in 2000 and began operations in October of that same year by introducing Guatemalan products into the US.

At present, Kepix exports from Guatemala containers with food products of the best Central American brands, among which is THPC, taking care of the demand from compatriots living in the US (Personal communication from Kepix Corp Trade Manager, 2014).

Volumes

Despite the product's quality, THPC faces a big problem due to the low export volumes which are a product of the lack of a direct sales offices to deal with the supermarkets that have sales in the US because at present there is a need to wait for distributors to buy the product and invest in the distribution channel but no taste tests are done or any other type of sales pitch. Instead, the brand is made known among customers residing in the US mainly by word of mouth and under a private label or white brand in which products would come in to the US under a consolidated brand and label. Nevertheless this scheme has collateral risks.

Sales to the US represent approximately 20% of sales. Annex 6.7 shows the position within the exports in the product category to which THPC'S products belong in the year 2013.

Competition

Competition can be classified by product segment:

- **Spices**. Salvadoran companies SAINSA, PROINCA and imported products Abadia, McCormick.
- **Traditional beverages**. Salvadoran companies SAINSA, PROINCA, Doña Elisa and imports Zuco Company and Tan are differentiated for being chemical formulas and shouldn't represent much competition. Nonetheless, some consumers don't consider this makes a difference when making their purchase decision.
- **Fruit beverages.** Where these are concerned, there are PROINCA, SAINSA, and PROESAL only for the tamarind product line.

Credit System to Customers

All purchasing companies receive credit. Credit to supermarkets is on a 60-day term but these are factored; THPC turns the invoices in to the bank and receives 90% of the invoiced value, an interest rate is paid while the bank collects on the invoices.

Conclusion

To this date, all kinds of offers have been received to go into partnerships with other companies seeking to increase their sales levels in the US in Miami, Houston, Washington, and Los Angeles. Mr. Barriere and his executive board are preparing a plan to attain specific objectives such as reducing the indebtedness level, improving the receivables portfolio, rehiring the San Salvador Chamber of Commerce support services, increasing production level and reorganizing the management structure starting from a clean financial situation. Considering the data of ANEP (The Private Sector National Association) in 2013, pointing out that family firms in El Salvador represent 90% of the enterprises in the country and provide the 65% of the private jobs, the relevance of THPC is tangible. What decision will the Barriere family make?

Annexes

ANNEX 6.1 Overall Balance Sheet and Income Statement of The Harvest Product Company from 2002 to 2013.

HARVEST PRODUCTS LLC
BALANCE SHEET
2002 TO 2013

Item	2013	2012	2011	2010	2009	2008	2007	2006 Jun	2006	2005	2004	2003	2002
Current assets available	$ 824.77	$ 5,759.98	$ 4,585.09	$ 9,885.01	$ 1,715.45	$ 14,244.89	$ 24,555.66	2,511.21		$ 7,774	$ 8,176		
Cash	824.77			9,885.01		14,244.89		769.95		485	286		
Banks		5,759.98	4,585.09		1,715.45			1,741.26		7,289	7,890		
Current disposable assets	$ 3,16,185.15	$ 2,99,131.13	$ 3,50,178.93	$ 3,49,647.11	$ 3,82,221.47	$ 4,08,364.25	$ 5,84,443.73	3,97,399	$ 3,20,188	$ 3,20,188	$ 2,03,024		
Inventory	52,143.68	99,049.38	99651.92	98,586.57	1,05,662.01	1,64,329.99	2,16,430.71	78,179.95	1,05,538	1,05,538	44,493		
Accounts and documents receivable	2,38,221.15	1,64,887.56	221403.28	2,15,655.97	$2,29,230.81	1,78,166.01	3,47,947.47	3,19,218.89	2,14,651	2,14,651	1,58.532		
Remain Fiscal Credit					1703.81	9,023.63	562.04						
Advance payments	25,820.32	35,194.19	29,124.33	35,404.57	45,624.84	56,844.62	19,503.51						
Total Current Assets	$ 3,17,009.92	$ 3,04,891.11	$ 3,54,764.02	$ 3,59,532.12	$ 3,83,936.92	$ 4,22,609.14	$ 6,08,999.39	3,99,910	$ 3,99,910	$ 3,27,962	$ 2,11,200	2,22,218	1,78,164.46
Fix Assets	3,79,448	3,85,478	3,69,731	3,46,466	3,48,230	3,59,733	2,97,442	3,25,742		1,72,340	1,56,585		
Furniture and office equipment	4,73,923.37	4,71,861.17	4,56,113.42	4,54,278.96	4,56,022.32	4,65,929.94	23,418.47	19,951.52		24,344	21,558		
(-) Accumulated depreciation	(96,515.01)	(96,515.01)	(96,515.01)	(1,17,924.90)	(1,17,924.90)	(1,16,328.79)	(24,876.32)	(19,686.89)		(16,459)	(13,994)		
Production machinery and equipment							69,966.30	69,633.68		61,449	52,590		
(-) Accumulated depreciation							(34,916.77)	(43,664.98)		(28,775)	(28,496)		
Sales room equipment							239.94	455.75		1,701	1,701		
Transportation equipment							1,11,226.15	1,11,226.15		83,721	68,318		
(-) Accumulated depreciation							(42,379.64)	(47,825.82)		(35,436)	(26,435)		
Facilities							81,992.24	40,246.00		12,555	12,103		
Property							1,09,239.43	1,09,239.00		69,239	69,239		
Long term investments	2,040.00	10,132.19	10,132.19	10,132.19	10,132.19	10,132.19	3,532.19	86,167.97					
Other Assets	11,383.70	41,447.30	61,453.52	59,134.81	59,133.10	60,541.02	55,519.33	9,389		11,662	10,596		
Transitory account								7,617.68			$0		
Advance payments (deposits in guaranties)	1,000.00							1,771.23					
Intangible assets							27,148.17			11,662	10,596		
Other assets	10,383.70	27,151.75	57,151.75	57,151.75	57,151.75	57,151.75	28,371.16						
		14,295.55	4,301.77	1,983.06	1,981.35	3,389.27							
TOTAL ASSETS	$ 7,07,841.98	$ 7,31,816.76	$ 7,85,948.14	$ 7,65,153.18	$ 7,91,299.63	$ 8,42,883.50	9,61,961	7,35,041	$ 7,35,041	$ 5,11,964	$ 3,78,380	3,76,293.00	3,07,200.00
Current Liabilities	2,60,835	1,86,353	1,53,209	2,71,544	3,04,791	4,39,304	6,02,849	4,40,455		2,21,689	1,16,807	1,21,313.00	80,560.45
Accounts and documents payable	38,104.13	33,672.56	17,559.80	21,965.45	26,282.54	20,509.45	90,701.13	1,31,050.89		68,259	58,885		
Short-term bank loans	83,990.32	99,347.83	71,525.81	2,05,982.29	2,17,576.40	4,13,889.45	4,71,836.90	1,66,376.09		1,44,456	47,646		
Other loans	75,564.25	19,825.67	53,572.65	41,060.43	47,907.95		35,835.05	1,15,745.25		1,362	1,177		
Forecasts and withholdings	63,176.29	35,506.84	10,550.87	2,545.77	13,023.87	4,905.09	4,475.83	27,282.27		7,612	9,100		
Long-term Liabilities	3,66,870.99	3,91,924.95	4,43,198.98	3,07,781.39	3,07,781.39	1,63,719.48	1,21,340.26	85,080.33		87,818	90,556		
Long-term bank loans	3,66,870.99	3,91,230.57	443198.98	3,07,781.39	3,07,781.39	1,20,307.54	1,21,340.26	85,080.33		87,818	90,556		
Other long-term liabilities						42,008.09							
Other Liabilities						1,403.85		5,555.53		5,488	6,186		
Labor liabilities	694.38					1,403.85		5,555.53		5,488	6,186		
TOTAL LIABILITIES	6,27,706	5,78,278	5,96,408	5,79,325	6,12,572	6,03,023	7,24,189	5,31,090		3,14,995	2,13,548	2,42,206.00	2,00,768.00
EQUITY	80,136.00	1,53,538.91	1,89,540.03	1,85,953.85	1,78,727.48	2,39,860	2,37,772	2,03,951		1,96,969	1,64,832	1,34,087.00	1,06,432.00
Share capital	84,067.03	1,59,067.03	1,89,067.03	1,89,067.03	1,89,067.03	1,89,067.03	1,89,067.03	1,48,000.00		1,24,000	1,00,000		
Profits of last year	(34,842.25)	(28,627.94)	(28,627.94)							4,264	27,729		
Profits of last year	9,400.82	9,400.82	6,307.60	(28,627.94)	(28,627.94)	16,786.06		8,205.26		27,941	535		
Utility	1,309.37	(6,214.31)	3,093.22	6,307.60	6,307.60	15,718.90	30,736.06	32,861.78		29,178	27,941		
Legal reserve	20,201.03	19,913.31	19,700.12	19,207.16	18,288.39	18,288.39	17,968.45	14,883.83		11,586	8,627		
Total	$ 7,07,841.98	$ 7,31,816.76	$ 7,85,948.14	$ 7,65,279.18	$ 7,91,299.63	$ 8,42,883.85	9,61,961	7,35,041		5,11,964	3,78,380		

ANNEX 6.2 THPC Sales in US Dollars from 2011 to 2014

PLC Code	2011	2012	2013	2014	Total Sales
Achiote	280,622	299,224	395,735	31,851	1,007,432
Sesame	405	0	0	0	405
Birdseed	62,381	38,117	28,069	11,558	140,125
Cinnamon	171,835	216,400	236,981	94,155	719,371
Barley	277,066	373,767	419,337	203,212	1,273,382
Chan 3	13,909	17,116	15,187	16,421	62,633
Chan 1	10,530	9,437	13,514	12,474	45,955
Chili	122,393	154,280	137,947	19,505	434,125
Clove	15,081	16,517	15,158	7,498	54,254
Cumin	10,142	12,671	14,706	5,071	42,590
Mix concentrade	4,883	0	0	0	4,883
Seasoning	64,430	77,026	70,255	15,856	227,567
Coriander	12,447	15,425	7,498	5,705	41,075
Chickpea	17,806	33,690	43,808	8,762	104,066
"Horchata"	140,361	166,698	194,008	94,091	595,158
Laurel	16,788	18,063	19,795	8,113	62,759
Linseed	91,974	100,973	104,631	43,832	341,410
Chamomile	12,098	13,764	12,098	5,216	43,176
Nutmeg	8,430	2,437	0	0	10,867
Oregano	27,511	27,798	28,959	10,160	94,428
Pepper	26,079	27,890	22,865	11,321	88,155
Pineapple concentrate	4,883	2,905	4,270	2,042	14,100
Refreshments	54,303	54,168	63,909	28,330	200,710
"Relajo"	48,931	60,811	44,986	14,995	169,723
Rosemary	13,830	16,705	17,434	6,665	54,634
Thyme	34,970	36,590	19,179	8,095	98,834
Total Sale	1,544,088	1,792,472	1,930,329	664,928	

ANNEX 6.3 THPC Sales in units for the past four years

PLC Code	2011	2012	2013	2014	Total Sales
Achiote	60,886	59,542	57,225	11,767	189,420
Sesame	805	0	0	0	805
Birdseed	67,648	68,222	48,482	13,104	197,456
Cinnamon	38,892	40,838	35,714	9,744	125,188
Barley	106,582	128,989	141,554	42,875	420,000
Chan 3	19,334	20,293	10,213	4,809	54,649
Chan 1	19,887	19,040	14,322	5,747	58,996
Chili	58,254	60,564	46,816	11,571	177,205
Clove	19,810	20,783	9,142	5,033	54,768
Cumin	19,894	20,867	19,411	5,075	42,590
Mix concentrade	4,151	0	0	0	4,151
Seasoning	40,040	41,909	34,573	10,129	126,651

ANNEX 6.3 (Continued)

Coriander	20,069	21,112	7,686	5,187	54,054
Chickpea	19,873	19,271	17,612	5,229	61,985
"Horchata"	64,428	79,436	98,595	29,365	271,824
Laurel	19,943	21,273	19,754	5,271	66,241
Linseed	63,028	64,323	55,601	16,065	199,017
Chamomile	20,524	21,609	19,677	5,439	67,249
Nutmeg	20,685	3,689	0	0	24,374
Oregano	20,769	21,728	20,153	5,481	68,131
Pepper	41,790	42,028	19,453	11,088	114,359
Pineapple concentrate	22,232	20,146	14,966	6,489	63,833
Refreshments	83,384	89,901	69,783	23,877	266,945
"Relajo"	19,243	20,209	18,865	4,767	63,084
Rosemary	21,154	22,113	20,496	5,663	69,426
Thyme	21,238	22,197	9,506	5,705	58,646
Total Sale	914,543	950,082	809,599	249,480	

ANNEX 6.4 THPC Sales for the last trimester of the past three years in US Dollars

PLC Code	2011	2012	2013	Total Sales
Achiote	205,284	202,860	299,027	707,171
Birdseed	15,692	10,285	6,352	32,329
Cinnamon	59,079	60,174	62,369	181,622
Barley	87,132	106,808	94,837	288,777
Chan 3	3,550	4,742	0	8,292
Chan 1	3,240	1,188	4,158	8,586
Chili	64,506	90,787	94,754	250,047
Clove	6,388	6,013	8,204	20,605
Cumin	3,227	3,912	4,854	11,993
Seasoning	34,423	42,000	37,560	113,983
Coriander	4,593	4,509	3,586	12,688
Chickpea	7,914	15,884	9,892	33,690
"Horchata"	45,438	47,737	43,156	136,331
Laurel	7,722	7,268	8,156	23,146
Linseed	26,313	25,949	22,112	74,374
Chamomile	3,767	3,767	1,956	9,490
Nutmeg	3,095	0	0	3,095
Oregano	11,163	9,399	9,508	30,070
Pepper	8,548	7,705	10,175	26,428
Pineapple concentrate	956	495	804	2,255
Refreshments	16,257	14,363	11,916	42,536
"Relajo"	21,403	28,977	18,762	69,142
Rosemary	4,171	4,829	4,685	13,685
Thyme	15,904	13,800	10,377	40,081
Total Sale	659,765	713,451	767,200	

ANNEX 6.5 THPC Sales in units for the last trimester of the past three years

PLC Code	2011	2012	2013	Total Sales
Achiote	28,784	29,288	24,003	82,075
Birdseed	29,652	30,219	18,459	78,330
Cinnamon	18,123	18,473	16,835	53,431
Barley	48,405	59,157	63,259	170,821
Chan 3	9,030	9,205	0	18,235
Chan 1	9,555	6,468	8,848	24,871
Chili	27,342	27,867	22,855	78,064
Clove	9,156	9,331	5,950	24,437
Cumin	9,177	9,352	8,519	27,048
Seasoning	18,417	18,767	17,101	54,285
Coriander	9,240	9,415	6,006	24,661
Chickpea	9,261	9,436	8,596	27,293
"Horchata"	28,791	39,018	44,555	112,364
Laurel	9,282	9,457	8,617	27,356
Linseed	27,972	28,497	25,977	82,446
Chamomile	9,366	9,541	8,701	27,608
Nutmeg	9,387	0	0	9,387
Oregano	9,408	9,562	8,722	27,692
Pepper	18,879	19,187	12,250	50,316
Pineapple concentrate	9,842	6,692	6,454	22,988
Refreshments	35,518	39,858	31,101	106,477
"Relajo"	9,009	9,184	8,386	26,579
Rosemary	9,513	9,667	8,813	27,993
Thyme	9,534	9,688	6,188	25,410
Total Sale	412,643	427,329	370,195	

ANNEX 6.6 Photograph of THPC product placement in Salvadorian supermarkets

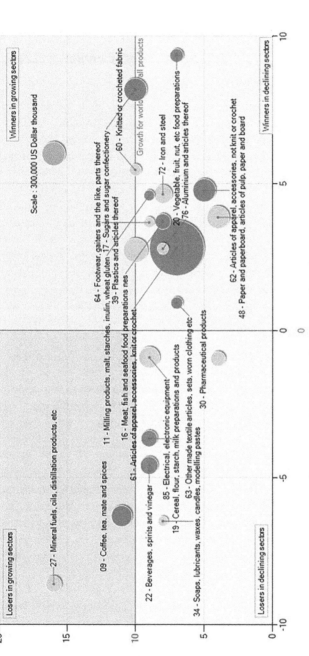

ANNEX 6.7 Specification of the products exported from El Salvador to the world, placing The Harvest Products (THCP) in 19th place

(World Trade Organization, 2009–2013)

Case 6.2 Grupo Lorsa: A Family Firm that Found Innovation from within

Héctor X. Ramírez-Pérez, Luis Jimenez-Castillo, and Salvador Rivas-Aceves

For the first time in 50 years, Lorsa lost an MXP $30 million (US$1.67 million) contract, the biggest one in its history, against a new and smaller competitor. It was November 2016, when Ernesto Ousset, the newly appointed Business Development Director of Grupo Lorsa (Lorsa), a Mexico-based supplier of laundry and dry-cleaning equipment, was trying to assimilate this unprecedented news and facing probably the biggest challenge of the family firm. For 30 years, two companies led the industry, but new competitors started emerging in an industry that used to be steady. Although Lorsa was recognized one of those main competitors because of its business knowledge and resources, it could not beat a 20% cheaper proposal offered to a new beach resort complex in Western Mexico.

The family-owned business was generally tradition-bound and resistant to change. However, in 2001, Lorsa was able to innovate the business model used since its inception and revolutionized the industry by adding value to customers through offering service components, maintenance, and repair parts, beyond only selling equipment. This was a key decision to endure the 2008 economic crisis and maintain Lorsa's leadership position. The company was founded in 1965 and by the first decade its variety of products grew 178% and sales increased 444%. According to Mexican business classification it was considered a big company since 1985 (INEGI, 2009); from that year, Lorsa's economic activities fostered the laundry and dry-cleaning machinery industry in Mexico, therefore the company gained a strong reputation among suppliers and customers. In 2016, Lorsa's sales reached almost MXP $561 million (US$30 million) and employed 165 people.

By the end of 2016, when producers of equipment (suppliers) challenged the historical entry barrier of Lorsa and started getting closer to customers through vertical integration strategies, Ernesto needed to find new ways to add value to customers and to maintain the growth of the company. Also, Lorsa was near to the second succession process when the third generation was a few years from being ready to take charge of the family firm.

Losing the contract was only the tip of the iceberg; Ernesto's main concern was the new competitive environment created by suppliers in which Lorsa was not ready to compete yet.

Mexican Economy and Industry Information

For the last 25 years, Mexico has been recognized as a dynamic and growing economy (World Bank, 2017). In 2015, Mexico and Brazil had been the countries with the highest growth rates, reaching a GDP of USD$1.21 and US$2.3 trillion respectively, versus other countries such as Argentina, Chile, and Peru (Exhibit 6.1). In the last 8 years, the constant GDP growth in Mexico had strongly depended on micro, small, and medium enterprises. According to the last Economic Census performed by the *Instituto Nacional de Estadística y Geografía* in 2014 (INEGI, 2014), in Mexico, there were around 4.2 million economic entities,[2] an average growth of 2.6% from 2008 to 2013 (see Exhibit 6.2). The more dynamic states during that same period are shown at Exhibit 6.3.

Lorsa is classified within the service sector and this sector grew on average 25.3% over the same period in the states mentioned before (INEGI, 2014). When analyzing the companies' size, only 0.8% of the 4.2 million were considered big companies, Lorsa being one of those.

The Laundry and Dry-Cleaning Industry in Mexico was officially recognized in 1941 by the creation of the Cámara Nacional de Lavanderías (CANALAVA), a business agency representing the Industrial Association of Laundries. By 2003, the industry was integrated by 19,158 entities (INEGI, 2004), where 78% were dry-cleaners and 22% laundries (CANALAVA, 2017). By 2014, there were 30,805 entities, a growth of almost 61% with respect to 2003. The industry employed 66,000 people (68.9% women and 31.1% men) and the value of total salaries reached MXP $1,297 million (US$60.4 million) (INEGI, 2014). In 2014, six out of 32 states had 57% of the total laundry and dry-cleaners entities, see Exhibit 6.4. Ernesto mentioned that in spite of the official statistics. "There are no more than 5,000 entities compared to the more than 19,000 reported. The difference is because many of those entities are not laundries or dry-cleaners, but intermediaries (drop offs) that seek small margin in every transaction."

The Heart of the Business

During the first 40 years, the main business in Lorsa consisted of selling equipment for laundries and dry-cleaners (Exhibit 6.5). In those years, there were only two main competitors in Mexico (Lorsa and Centrax) with sales exclusivity in Mexico because they could close agreements with the biggest producers of equipment in the US and Europe. The brands they handled were the most recognized in the laundry and dry-cleaner industries and therefore, they were the industry leaders. According to Ernesto, to gain contracts with laundries and dry-cleaners "was easy; since either Centrax got the contract or we did."

These exclusivity distribution agreements became main barriers for entry to the industry. Margins were almost 25%, and the commercialization process was simple once you had the exclusive contracts. The market became attractive for other competitors, but they did not last since they could not have the brands handled by Centrax or Lorsa; therefore, competitors appeared and left constantly.

In the short-term the business model was already profitable, but in 2001 Lorsa recognized a competitive advantage over Centrax by establishing, as a central focus in the strategy, the offering of immediate delivery of maintenance equipment, components, repair parts, and technical support besides selling equipment. Eventually this move created longer-term relationships with customers, but required accomplishing different business processes such as getting technicians, handling customers' service requests, and changing the inventory system because of the inclusion of supplements and accessories. Certainly, offering maintenance and repair services were not new for Lorsa, but since 2001 those activities became central in Lorsa's strategy.

Centrax did not follow Lorsa; their business model consisted only in bigger sales, bigger margins, and possible higher dividends to the stockholders in the short-term. Lorsa earned considerable resources because of its conservative dividends strategy; stockholders did not receive dividends until 2008 so all profits were reinvested during the first 40 years. Nevertheless family members received competitive salaries and agreed that business growth was a priority. Also, they were willing to make some sacrifices: they had to employ only the required family members to avoid increasing the salary base with people without a functional role. In most years, only five family members have been employed in the company.

With those resources they hired more technicians and invested in components inventory. By 2016, this division represented almost 50% of the business and its margins reached 25% as the rest of the divisions. For example, Lorsa used to sell hangers for laundries since 1999; in 2008, hangers represented the third highest product sold in the company.

The 2001 decision was not simple either to make or implement. In those years there were many discussions among family members regarding splitting the business; some family members suggested having two companies, one for selling equipment and one for selling accessories and supplements, while other family members wanted to keep the company together. It was Luis, the patriarch and founder, who forced the decision to keep the company together because of the ample knowledge they had acquired throughout the years. He knew that if they were able to learn this model, he could guarantee the future of the family firm, different to other nonfamily firm competitors who only sought profits in the short-term. After a few years, even Centrax directed its customers to Lorsa when they required repair parts.

Lorsa's performance has been outstanding. From 1965 to 2016, sales increased from MXP $1.6 million (US$81,000) to MXP $560 million (US$28.2 million), profits went from MXP $45,000 (US$2,117) to MXP $50.8 million (US$2.3 million), variety products increased from 55 to 15,100, and there were six offices that covered operations in 23 states in Mexico (Exhibit 6.6).

Brief History of the Family Firm

The first attempt of the company started in 1953 in Guadalajara (western Mexico) by its founder Luis Ousset, an entrepreneur who had worked as an employee and independent advisor in the dry-cleaning sector in Guadalajara and Mexico City for 11 years before starting his own business. In 1942 he got his first job as a delivery boy in the dry-cleaning sector. Through hard work and strong commitment, he was promoted to supervisor, and in 1952 he worked in a bigger company, Tintorerías Texas (a dry-cleaning company) in Mexico City. With all the experience and networking he acquired from those years, he returned to Guadalajara with the idea to launch a distribution company of products for dry-cleaners. At that moment, there were no similar companies in Guadalajara. He did not have the necessary resources, but with a clear vision and enthusiasm convinced a few investors and opened a business named Representaciones Parra y Ousset. Two years after, Luis Ousset continued the business by himself and in 1965 started Lorsa.

From the beginning, Luis Ousset knew he wanted a family business. He got married in 1951, and had seven children: Luis Jr., Laura Alicia, Fernando, Ana Elena, Juan Carlos, Lorena María, and Ernesto (Exhibit 6.7). The children were involved in the company since a young age, but their education was a priority. This situation prevailed for almost 20 years. In 1984, when all of them got married, only the men remained working in Lorsa.

Family values taught at home were generosity, honesty, respect, trust, and solidarity. Luis and his wife promoted love among siblings and the principle of *"being* before *having"*. The Ousset children remembered their parents as good human beings who lived their lives according to their principles and moral values. Within the family meetings, the tradition was to hear only positive news about the company.

The first two decades of the firm were stable. The authority and leadership from Luis was trustworthy. This allowed a fast decision-making process even when conflicts appeared. Cash flow and profits were increasing, and family members were becoming experts in the industry. Loyalty from customers, employees, and suppliers was strong. However, Lorsa grew without control or administrative systems. Because of the founder's desire to be involved in every detail of daily operations, the company had inefficient resource management, lack of planning, and job descriptions.

The Beginning of the Succession Process

According to Ernesto, "the first sign of the beginning of the succession process takes place in 1965 when Luis Jr. starts going to the company during school vacation time", but it was not a formal process yet. It was in 1984 when Luis recognized the need to prepare his successors by involving them in the company and increasing their experience. He knew that if they did not plan the succession correctly, Lorsa could be part of the statistics: 70% of family firms disappeared between the founder and the next generation (de Vries, 1993). In 1984, Luis named himself CEO of the company and Fernando was the General Manager; Luis Jr. was only interested in sales.

Even though all four sons were working in the company, it seemed that the first successor was going to be Luis Jr. He was in charge of key accounts for Lorsa and was the most important sales agent. However, a few conflicts arose at the end of 1999 when Luis Jr. announced to the family he had other interests additional to Lorsa.

Luis Jr. had a different perspective on the style of doing business, and requested permission to have freedom to create side agreements with third parties. Family members considered this request a conflict of interests because while other family members were working full-time in the company, Luis Jr. wanted free time to attend other activities and businesses. Furthermore, the side-businesses he was planning were with current clients, which instead of expanding Lorsa's revenues would directly go to his pocket. Luis Sr. tried to encourage his son to focus all efforts to the family firm and grow the company with the belief that in the long run the whole family was going to earn more.

Years of Uncertainty

The period between 2000 and 2005 was not easy for Lorsa. Besides the challenge of instituting the new business model, Luis Sr. and his sons had to make decisions regarding the unexpected announcement from Luis Jr., who kept working in the company without being fully convinced. The other brothers were not happy with the situation either, but Luis Sr., with his leadership, convinced his sons to accept Luis Jr. in the company. Luis Jr. was the main sales agent and future risks would be enormous if he left; therefore, to stabilize the situation Luis Sr. asked Ernesto to leave the Controller's office and to lead the new sales division of Service Components and Repair Parts. At that moment, Ernesto was probably the son with the more optimistic perspective of this new area.

Another big announcement came from Luis Sr., who was the majority shareholder: he mandated the creation of a Board of Directors composed by an external advisor and the five male family members. He left daily operations and appointed Juan Carlos as acting CEO while the Board of Directors defined a "better structure". Fernando was in charge of Equipment Sales, Ernesto of the Service Components and Repair Parts area, and Luis Jr. of Key Accounts. A "better structure" was defined in the following months: the CEO position was going to be replaced by three co-CEOs: Fernando, Juan Carlos, and Ernesto, all three in charge of the entire firm, sharing the same power over decisions. This structure remained until December 31, 2016 when the structure was going to change.

Although having three co-CEOs in any company is not the normal approach, this worked out because of the brothers' empathy and because Lorsa was a family firm. Luis Jr. agreed not to be part of this co-CEOs group because he was not convinced to remain in the company. According to Ernesto, the decision-making process with the three co-CEOs was easy and it lasted 15 years: decisions were made when two out of the three agreed on something. They had quarrels, but they always found the way to solve them. This new structure was a wise decision since power and visibility were equal between them, so they had to sacrifice their personal interests for Lorsa's sake. Besides being part of the co-CEOs group, each one had a functional responsibility: Fernando took over Key Accounts, Juan Carlos the Equipment Sales, and Ernesto the Service Components and Repair Parts. The Controller office was run by a nonfamily employee.

In 2005, Luis Jr. found a new alternative and left Lorsa. He remained working as a freelance sales agent. That same year the family firm recognized the need of having a family constitution and designed its own, in which they established some guidelines: separate family and business concerns, create rules and policies, and define a schedule for meetings, among others.

In 2008 the family firm confronted a new situation: Luis Jr. passed away. Although a freelancer, he was still the main sales representative. With this unfortunate news, the family members recognized the need to prepare the new generation. Víctor, Luis Jr's son, after a year working in Lorsa, was appointed as Equipment, Service Components, and Repair Parts Director. With this move, Ernesto returned as Controller. Víctor was a third-generation family member who might become the successor. He was not the only third-generation family member considered but was the most experienced one.

During 2016, Lorsa was getting ready for a new stage in its history. The co-CEOs group had been functioning through the second generation and it was going to be possible while they remained in the company, but preserving that structure throughout the third generation would have represented a risk in family relationships on business operation. Therefore, they established that by January 1, 2017, Lorsa was going to have a single CEO again. Through a lengthy process, Juan Carlos was chosen as the new CEO. Fernando had some health issues that made him set his priorities regarding having a full-time job, therefore, Víctor was appointed Commercial Director and Ernesto took the Business Development Director position.

Suppliers Started Switching the Strategy

During almost all its existence, Lorsa benefited from brand exclusivity from the suppliers. The exclusivity contracts' time span was undefined. However, Lorsa's suppliers had a discretionary clause stated that exclusivity could be canceled at suppliers' convenience. In 2015, suppliers were lowering the most powerful entry barrier to the industry: they started some moves to either compete directly against their own distributors or sell through other smaller distributors.

The first move consisted in following a vertical integration strategy. Many suppliers wanted to get closer to the final consumer and established sales operations in the country (i.e., Mexico City). However, Ernesto thought "they would not be successful, the experience will not be very positive for them. Nonetheless, they believe in the Mexican market, they see it as an emerging economy with a lot of potential."

The second move directed toward exclusivity contracts. Suppliers did not revoke contracts; instead, they found an alternative: exclusivity would consist in brands, not in products. Hence, other small distributors were able to compete with different brands, but the same products, in the same markets, and with lower prices; competitors did not have to maintain a big employer's structure or high levels of inventory as Lorsa did.

Concern Toward the Future

Ernesto was in his office reflecting on the future of the company. What changes would the company need to implement in order to keep the competitive advantages it had enjoyed for so many years? After all, trying to beat a competitor with 20% lower prices would take a lot of resources from the family and the company. Another concern was the suppliers' strategies that were destroying entry barriers. After spending an afternoon on long reflection, he had to go home for dinner to his wife and daughter.

References

Banco de México. (2017). *Estadísticas, crecimiento económico industrial.* Retrieved May 23, 2017 from www.banxico.org.mx
CANALAVA. (2017). Retrieved April 20, 2017, from http://canalava.org.mx/
de Vries, M. (1993). The dynamics of family controlled firms: The good and the bad news. *Organizational Dynamics,* 59–71.
Instituto Nacional de Estadística y Geografía. (2004). *Censos Económicos.* Retrieved April 20, 2017, from www.inegi.org.mx/est/contenidos/proyectos/ce/ce2004/default.aspx
Instituto Nacional de Estadística y Geografía. (2009). *Censos Económicos 2009.* Retrieved April 4, 2017, from Micro, Pequeña, Mediana y Gran Empresa www.inegi.org.mx/est/contenidos/espanol/proyectos/censos/ce2009/pdf/Mono_Micro_peque_mediana.pdf
Instituto Nacional de Estadística y Geografía. (2013). *Sistema de Clasificación Industrial de América del Norte.* Retrieved April 20, 2017, from www.inegi.org.mx/est/contenidos/proyectos/SCIAN/presentacion.aspx
Instituto Nacional de Estadística y Geografía. (2014). *Cencos Económicos.* Retrieved April 20, 2017, from www.inegi.org.mx/est/contenidos/proyectos/ce/ce2014/default.aspx
World Bank. (2014, 2017). *National accounts data, Mexico.* Retrieved April 20, 2017, from http://data.worldbank.org/indicator/NY.GDP.MKTP.KD?contextual=default&locations=MX&view=chart

Exhibits

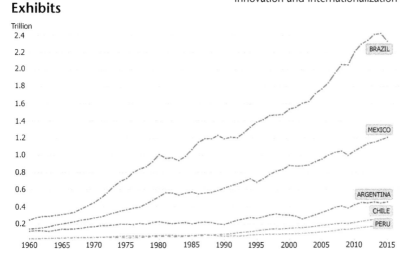

EXHIBIT 6.1 GDP (constant 2010 USD), World Bank national accounts data and OECD national accounts data files

Source: http://data.worldbank.org/indicator/NY.GDP.MKTP.KD?contextual=default&end=2015&locations=MX-CL-AR-BR-PE&start=1960&view=chart

EXHIBIT 6.2 Economic growth by industry sector in Mexico from 1993 to 2015

Source: Own elaboration with GDP data, Banxico (2017)

Estado de México	12.6%
Distrito Federal	9.8%
Jalisco	7.4%
Puebla	5.9%
Veracruz	5.7%
Guanajuato	5.3%

EXHIBIT 6.3 Averaged Economic Growth Rate of selected states, 2008–2013
Source: (INEGI, 2014)

State	%
Distrito Federal	18.6
Estado de México	16.7
Jalisco	7.4
Veracruz	5.4
Puebla	4.8
Guanajuato	4.3

EXHIBIT 6.4 Percentage of laundry and dry-cleaner entities by states in Mexico in 2014
Source: (INEGI, 2014)

EXHIBIT 6.5 Printed advertisement from 1965

Year	1965	1975	1985	1995	2000	2006	2008	2015	2016
Sales (in 000 MXP)	1,653	8,998	327,721	26,285	118,096	195,116	290,841	403,336	560,889
COGS	1,248	6,647	225,014	15,756	75,120	144,796	222,795	286,470	393,218
Gross Profit	404	2,351	102,707	10,529	42,976	50,320	68,046	116,865	167,670
Operating Expenses	371	1,997	71,632	9,329	36,789	50,175	58,233	98,162	118,368
Operating Profit	33	354	31,075	1,200	6,186	144	9,813	18,704	49,302
Other Income and Expenses	12	148	(17,745)	(394)	1,851	2,724	(3,936)	2,547	1,494
Earnings Before Taxes (in 000 MXP)	45	502	13,330	805	8,038	2,868	5,877	21,251	50,796
Earnings Before Taxes (in 000 USD)	4	40	50	122	837	260	525	1,329	2,708

EXHIBIT 6.6 Financial results from selected years

Source: Own elaboration provided by family members

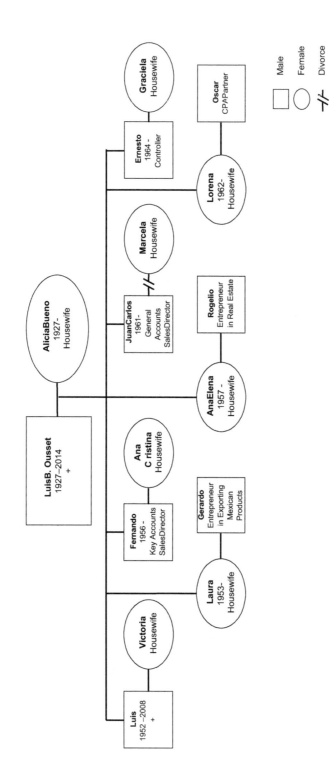

EXHIBIT 6.7 Ousset family genogram

Case 6.3 Popa Group: The International Presence of an Information Technology Family Business in Central America

Nadina Mazzoni Pizzati, Carlos R. Arias, and Allan Discua Cruz

On January 2018, Gerardo Pacheco, current CEO and main owner of POPA Group, an information technology (IT) firm in Honduras, had an important business decision to make. He needed to analyze different internationalization alternatives to decide if (whether) POPA should internationalize. Gerardo believed the new trends for automation and information systems, as well as cloud services, could provide POPA a niche to explore new opportunities within the Central American region.

After a short international experience in Nicaragua between 2013 and 2015, the Pacheco family believes that POPA can expand their operations outside of Honduras. In a meeting with the top management team, composed of the second generation members of the Pacheco family, questions about how and where POPA should establish its international presence next and who should lead such efforts were asked. Different aspects were being considered, including their previous internationalization experience, expertise, and family objectives. The final decision has to be made by the end of 2018. Failing to reach an appropriate decision may make POPA stagnant in the growing IT sector in Latin America and make the company unable to compete effectively with local and international players. The top management team realizes that the decision will impact the future of the firm and the family in business.

Industry Background

Family Businesses and Information Technology (IT)

Family businesses are present in all sectors and their participation in information technology (IT) is no exception (Forbes, 2014). According to the International Family Enterprise Research Academy (IFERA), 90% of the world's companies are family business (IFERA, 2003). While some family firms become involved in IT from their creation, others become involved over time (Guillarte, 2013). Examples include Samsung and Kaspersky Lab. Samsung, founded in 1938 in South Korea, was first a leader in consumer goods (Guillarte, 2013) before turning gradually into a worldwide IT player after it purchased Sanyo Electronics in 1969. Kaspersky Lab, an international family owned and run business, was founded in Russia in 1997 based on computer antivirus and online security software (Kaspersky, 2010). Yet, while evidence of family businesses in the IT industry is well documented in most developed economies, there is limited information about their development in the Central American region.

Honduras

Honduras, with a population of 8.6 million people (INE, 2015), is located in the Central American isthmus (Exhibit 6.9) and considered a low middle-income country (World Bank, 2016). Honduras is a stereotypical Latin American context in terms of family influence and participation in business activities over time (Discua Cruz, Ramos Rodas, Raudales, & Fortín, 2016). Family participation in business ventures is socially expected—a paternalistic culture in business is the norm (Discua & Howorth, 2008). Business is inseparable from family due to deep familial social relations and expectations of family involvement and support in business creation and development (Gupta, Levenburg, Moore, Motwani, & Schartz, 2008).

The presence of family businesses in the Honduran business landscape is widespread. A recent study suggests that approximately 90% of businesses in Honduras are family owned and controlled (Alvarez, 2013). A family business in Honduras is defined by family ownership, the involvement of family members in top management positions and their influence in the long-term strategy of the firm (Howorth, Rose, Hamilton & Westhead, 2010). Thus, decisions about business expansion, both within and outside country borders, would be influenced by the objectives, skills, and intentions of family members involved in business (Discua Cruz, 2010).

Honduras and the IT Industry Sector

Currently, Honduras is number 94 out of 139 countries evaluated in the Networked Readiness Index (NRI) of the World Economic Forum Report (Kirkman, Cornelius, Sachs, & Schab, 2016). This index assesses several factors, policies and institutions that enable a country to fully leverage information and communication technologies to increase their competitiveness and well-being. The closer to 6.0 in the NRI index, the better evaluation the country has. Countries like Singapore and Finland are ranked 6.0, with the US following close behind with a 5.8. Honduras, with 3.7 points, still needs to improve in the 10 items evaluated in the index, particularly in infrastructure, government and individual usage of technology. See Exhibits 6.1A and 6.1B of Annex. Despite its ranking in the NRI, Honduras has shown a gradual increase in high-technology exports during the last five years (World Bank,

2016). This increase in the IT market is associated with the high demand for professionals in this industry and the increase of business opportunities in software development—currently, universities only satisfy 50% of the demand for IT professionals (Arias, 2013). Such context suggests that firms engaged in the IT industry may be able to pursue diverse business opportunities both locally and overseas yet face great challenges in terms of procuring specialized local personnel.

POPA Group: The Formation of an IT Business Group

The POPA Group was founded in Tegucigalpa, the capital of Honduras, in 1992 by René Portela (Cuban American) and Gerardo Pacheco (Honduran). The name POPA emerged out of the first two letters of the founders' family names. Figure 6.1 shows a timeline of the company, including business creation and acquisitions, since its foundation. It originally started by focusing on two business sectors: Medical (managed by Portela) and Information Technology (managed by Pacheco). The first IT company founded by the partners was called OFISIS (Oficinas y Sistemas S. de R.L. or "Offices and Systems"). The company was the representative of one of the leading US personal computer companies at that time, AST Research Inc., and focused on supplying office and computer supplies for the corporate market in Honduras.

In 1993, the company expanded by starting CPM. CPM stands for Cárcamo, Pacheco, Moran—the last names of its founders. The emphasis was software development, which gradually included databases, educational consulting, and fourth generation languages (rapid application development languages that help to decrease the development time of applications) (Misra & Jalics, 1988). CPM later obtained the rights to represent several international software companies in Honduras. By 1994, as a response to the high demand for information technology in Honduras, a third firm, SASA (Sistemas Abiertos S.A or "Open Systems") was founded to represent Hewlett Packard Co. in Honduras and eventually absorbed CPM and OFISIS.

Due to the dynamism and growth of all of these companies, and because of the increasing managerial complexity, the owners decided to consolidate all business units under one holding group. In 1997, the POPA group was established; the company name was based on the last names of the owners. By the year 2000 Sistemas Abiertos S.A. absorbed OFISIS and CPM, consolidating all major business areas: hardware, software development, and international IT companies representation.

The company grew in the years afterwards and consolidated its presence as a leader in IT in Honduras. In 2008, POPA acquired Smart Solutions, which specialized in information technology and communications projects. In 2009, POPA created the International Technology Group (ITG), which led to the opening of the first Tier 2 Data Center (Uptime Institute, 2017) in Honduras. The company grew from strength to strength since, and incorporated new companies are related to the IT industry.

By 2017, POPA has more than 50 full-time employees, an "on-demand" staff, and part-time consultants. Currently POPA imports and commercializes product lines mainly from Dell, Lexmark, SAP, and Oracle. Services for Dell and Lexmark products are delivered completely with Honduran personnel. Services for SAP and Oracle are delivered with personnel from Honduras, El Salvador, Colombia, Mexico, and USA. POPA delivers data center services mainly to Honduran companies but also has several customers from the Central American region, USA, Europe, and the Middle East. See Exhibit 6.3 for detailed products offer by POPA in Annex. Notwithstanding POPA's reach of international clients, the Pacheco family is interested in establishing an international presence in the region.

In summary, the history of POPA is characterized by an outstanding entrepreneurial drive: POPA has been a risk taker and proactive investor in state-of-the-art technology systems and strategic alliances. Since its foundation, company owners showed an extraordinary ability for innovation and renewal, following closely the needs of the corporate and government market. The values of POPA are found in Exhibit 6.4.

Family Ownership and Governance

POPA is currently controlled and run by the Pacheco family. In 2002, René Portela decided to sell his ownership stake to Pacheco and leave POPA to pursue business opportunities in the medical sector in the USA and Central America. Since then, Gerardo Pacheco became the president of the POPA group and acts as CEO. In terms of ownership, Gerardo Pacheco and his family are the majority shareholders, owning the largest percentage of equity and shares. Currently, there is only one minority nonfamily shareholder controlling a small percentage of shares.

In terms of governance, Gerardo Pacheco, who is getting closer to his sixtieth birthday, is the current CEO of the company. The second generation of the Pacheco family in business is composed by his two sons, Emerson and Gerson, who lead key areas within the company. Table 6.1 shows the role of family members in the business. Emerson, who is the oldest son and is in his mid-thirties, is currently in charge of the Commercial division, including marketing, services, and sales. Gerson, who just turned thirty, oversees Operations (processes, certifications, logistics, financial, and imports). Emerson and Gerson are the only children and are expected to succeed Gerardo Pacheco when he decides to retire. Gerardo expects that the business will be run in the future by the brothers through shared leadership.

Timeline

1992	1993	1994	1997	2000	2008	2009	2013
OFISIS is founded to represent AST Research.	CPM Corporation is created to provide databases solutions and 4th generation languages.	Open Systems is created to manage the coporate line of HP.	POPA Group was founded as an integrating entity for all companies.	SASA absorbs OFISIS and CPM.	POPA group acquires Smart Solutions for Tekos solutions, and creates ITG for data center services.	ITG inaugurates the first Data Center, level 3 in Honduras.	Opening of office in Nicaragua. Honduras leader in IT services, featuring the leading companies in information technology, with special focus on HP, SAP, Oracle and Microsoft.

FIGURE 6.1 Timeline of POPA group development

Sources: www.popa.hn; Global Competitiveness Index (2015–2016). Retrieved from www.weforum.org/reports/the-global-competitiveness-report

TABLE 6.1 Family involvement in the firm

Name	Family Relation	Current Position	Years of involvement at POPA
Gerardo Pacheco	Father, Founding Generation	CEO	25 years
Emerson Pacheco	Oldest Son, 2nd Generation	Commercial Manager	11 years
Gerson Pacheco	Youngest Son, 2nd Generation	Operations Manager	4 years

Source: Interviews with the Pacheco family in business (2017)

The Family Management Team

The current top management team at POPA is composed of members of the founding and second generation of the Pacheco family. Gerardo Pacheco, a founding generation member, is a visionary who is still active in the business and is well known in the Honduran business landscape and community. He studied computer science at Purdue University in the USA and has developed POPA to the leading position it occupies today in the Honduras IT industry. His current focus is to transform the family team into a highly specialized unit. To do so, he aims to concentrate on the strategic and networking function of the business for the corporate market while empowering his sons to lead the operational and administrative side of POPA.

Emerson and Gerson represent the second generation of the Pacheco family in the business. Following his father's footsteps, Emerson studied overseas at Purdue University. He specialized in business management with a minor in marketing and business psychology and joined POPA in 2005. He worked from the bottom up and has been involved in several areas of the firm. He started in marketing, eventually moving to sales and then to services, and now he oversees the areas of marketing, sales, and services. Gerson is about to finish his bachelor degree in Business Administration from UNITEC (Universidad Tecnológica Centroamericana), the leading private university in Honduras. He joined the firm in 2011 combining his studies with involvement in the firm. Gerson became involved in the operational side of the business. He has been a key player in the certification ISO 9000 process of the business group. He currently oversees the finances and logistics aspects of the firm and has been leading the imports aspects of the business (see Exhibit 6.3 for a complete list of POPA's products and services).

A shared "from the bottom up" approach among the second-generation family members, with each member of the second generation leading a specific division of the business, is considered a key managerial career progression at POPA. Although there is no formal succession plan and they were not formally expected to join the family firm, both sons decided to do so voluntarily and expect to lead the firm in the future. In line with cultural expectations, involvement in

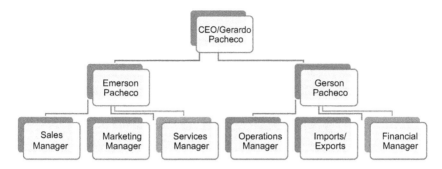

FIGURE 6.2 POPA's organizational chart
Source: Interviews with Pacheco family (2017).

existing businesses, tenure, and experience acquired by family members of the second generation will be key factors in determining the future leader of the firm (see Figure 6.2 for POPA's organizational chart).

The First Internationalization Experience: Nicaragua

In 2013, POPA decided to expand its operations internationally. Nicaragua, a neighboring country, was chosen due to a growing client base outside of Honduras and the awareness that POPA needed to keep up with the globalization of technological trends. The decision to expand operations in Nicaragua was supported by establishing a satellite office and appointing a Honduran manager to oversee operations in promoting POPA's core information technology products.

Unfortunately, in 2015, POPA decided to exit the Nicaraguan IT market. In recalling the experience, Gerardo Pacheco expressed:

> the [Nicaraguan] industry wasn't interested in investing in technology during those years.

POPA's top management team realized that while Nicaraguan clients demanded a variety of products, the market for their core products: SAP and/or Oracle software services, or hardware, or even Data Center Services was limited. In addition, they suspect that a committed member of the top management team might be better suited to oversee initial operations. Withdrawing from the Nicaraguan market provided key experiences for POPA. The Pacheco family acknowledged the lessons learned and perceived that they were ready to consider again their international expansion and increase their presence in the Central American region.

A New Internationalization Trial?

The Pacheco family is considering expanding its operations outside of Honduras again. After their first experience in Nicaragua, the top management team is debating whether and how they should internationalize again. They believe that expansion to either Nicaragua or El Salvador is feasible for their internationalization objectives (Exhibits 6.1A and 6.1B). POPA has already sold some of its products to clients in both countries yet further formal steps may be needed to establish the international presence of the company and push its products and services forward.

The top management team is currently debating on which country to consider first. Should it be in a country like Nicaragua or El Salvador? The discussion will revolve around the analysis of every country considered. Such analysis would include political, commercial, and legal stability of both countries and the easiness to do business (Exhibits 6.1A and 6.1B).

Nicaragua is the second safest country in Latin America, with a strong growing economy (IMF, 2017) (PNUD, 2014). POPA had already experienced working in this country for two years before withdrawing. Its current socialist government is committed to attract foreign investment in the technology sector and create partnership opportunities with foreign firms.

El Salvador, being the smallest and most densely populated country in Central America, has a lot of potential. El Salvador has the third-largest economy in Central America, behind Costa Rica and Panama (IMF, 2016). Under recent Investment Act reforms, which guarantees free movement of capital in and out of the country for foreign investors, POPA could have solid financial incentives. Also, since 2001, their currency is the US Dollar, which could facilitate transactions in imports/exports. The Salvadorian market also offers prospects in terms of other products and services that could be offered such as 50 public and private higher education institutions, as well as technical centers, where technology courses and products appear to be in growing demand (Doing Business, 2014).

Finally, regardless of the country selected, POPA's top management team has to consider the fact that its main competitor, the GBM Group, also has a strong presence in the region. As Mr. Pacheco suggests:

> POPA has to differentiate its products by personalizing them to meet industry specific business needs. POPA's products have to become so customized to the specific business sector in a way that they provide built-in added value, providing an incentive for *our customers to establish a long term commercial relationship with POPA in a way that differentiates our offerings from those of our competitors, even if we are technically offering the same base product.*

The top management team realizes that POPA's advantage lies on the hard earned reputation forged over the years. POPA's services have been in the region for over 25 years. Such a length of time has allowed their top management team to understand the similarities and differences in clientele demand within the region. Gerardo Pacheco believes the new trends for automatization and information systems, as well cloud services, could provide POPA a niche to explore new opportunities within the region. This could be an opportunity to expand the firm into new businesses.

For the top management team the questions were clear: Should POPA expand regionally? If so, should it be within the Central American region? Should a Pacheco family member in business lead and manage the office in the selected country? Or should a committed nonfamily member become involved in leading the new trial? Different aspects are being considered including the previous internationalization experience, existing skills, and family motivations. The answers to these questions will have an impact on the future of the firm for years to come.

References

Alvarez, S. (2013). *La empresa familiar en Honduras y su vinculación con el desarrollo.* (ResearchGate, Ed.). Universidad Nacional Católica de Honduras.

Arias, C. (2013). *Talento para el Desarrollo: Internal report about students in computer science.* Tegucigalpa: UNITEC, Computer Science Department.

Discua, C., & Howorth, C. (2008). Family business in Honduras: Applicability of agency and stewardship theories. In V. Gupta, N. Levenburg, L. Moore, J. Mowtwani, & T. Schwarz (Eds.), *Culturally-sensitive models of family busines in Latin America* (pp. 222–243). Cheltenham, UK: H. I. Press, Ed.

Discua Cruz, A. (2010). Collective perspectives in portfolio entrepreneurship: A study of Honduran family business groups. *EDAMBA Journal, 8*, 91–105.

Discua Cruz, A., Ramos Rodas, C., Raudales, R., & Fortín, L. (2016). Large family businesses in Honduras: State intervention and immigration. In P. Fernandez Perez & A. Lluch (Eds.), *Evolution of family business: Continuity and change in Latin America and Spain.* Cheltenham, UK: Edward Elgar Publishing.

Doing Business, A. G. (2014). *pwc.com.* Obtenido de Doing Business. Retrieved from www.pwc.com/interamericas

Forbes. (2014). Family Businessess: The Power of Resilience by Carrie Hall. Retrieved, April 21, 2018 from https://www.forbes.com/sites/ey/2014/05/01/family-businesses-the-power-of-resilience/#68d2619c2a92

Guillarte, M. (22 de Julio de 2013). *Samsung.* Retrieved from www.muycomputerpro.com/2013/07/22/samsung-historia

Gupta, V., Levenburg, N., Moore, N., Motwani, J., & Schartz, T. (2008). *A culturally sensitive analysis of Latin American family businesses: A compendium on the family business model around the world.* Hyderabad, India: ICFAI University Press, Ed., pp. 244–264.

Howorth, C., Rose, M., Hamilton, E., & Westhead, P. (2010). Family firm diversity and development: An introduction. *International Small Business Journal, 28*(5), 437–451.

IFERA. (2003). Family business dominates. *International Family Enterprise Reseach Academy,* (16), 235–241.

INE. (2015). Recuperado el 2016, de Instituto Nacional de Estadística (INE). *Proyecciones de Población de Honduras 2015.* Retrieved from www.ine.gob.hn

International Monetary Fund. (2016). *El Salvador, selected issues*, October 10. Retrieved from www.imf.org/external/pubs/ft/scr/2016/cr16209.pdf

International Monetary Fund. (2017). *Nicaragua, selected issues*, October 10. Retrieved from www.imf.org/en/Publications/CR/Issues/2017/06/27/Nicaragua-Selected-Issues-45009

Kaspersky, J. (2010). *Jem Kaspersky*. Obtenido de, de Junio de 5. Retrieved from http://jem-kaspersky.blogspot.com/2010/06/historia.html

Kirkman, G., Cornelius, P., Sachs, J., & Schab, K. (2016). *Global information technological report* (O. U. Press, Ed.). New York, USA: World Economic Forum.

Misra, S., & Jalics, P. (1988). Third-generation versus fourth-generation software development. *IEEE Software, 5*(4), 8–14.

Pacheco, G. (2017). Personal Interview. (N. Mazzoni, Interviewer), de March de 24.

PNUD. (2014). *Programa de las Naciones Unidas para el Desarrollo (PNUD)*, Mayo. Retrieved from ni.undp.org

Uptime Institute. (2017). Tier Standar Topology. Retrieved April 30, 2018 from https://es.uptimeinstitute.com/resources/asset/tier-standard-topology

World Bank. (2016). *The World Bank*. Retrieved from worldbank.org

Annex

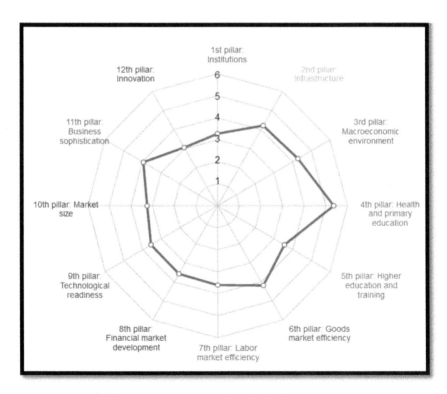

EXHIBIT 6.1A Global Competitive Index for El Salvador (2015–2016)

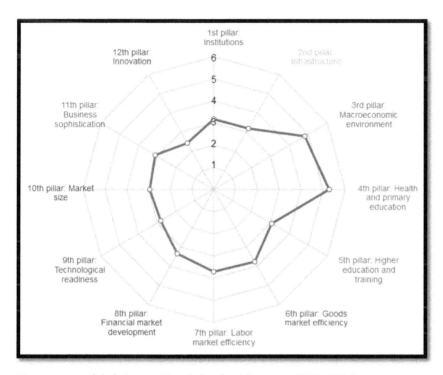

EXHIBIT 6.1B Global Competitive Index for Nicaragua (2015–2016)

Source: Global Competitiveness Index (2015–2016). Retrieved from www.weforum.org/reports/the-global-competitiveness-report

Population	Honduras	Nicaragua	El Salvador
Population (World Bank, 2016)	8.075.060	6,082,032	6,126,582
GDP per capita in US$ (World Economy Forum, 2016,)	2406.61	1949.23	4040.32
Doing Business Ranking of 190 global economies (World Bank, 2016)	105/190	127/190	95/190
Human Development Index (HDI) United Nations, 2015)	0,606	0,631	0,666
Country Risk Ratings:, Fitch Ratings, Moody's Investor Service, Standard & Poor's	N.C.,B2, B+	B+, B2, B+	B-, B3, B-
Global Competitiveness Index. Global Rank of 140 countries.	88 global 3 place in Central America	108 global 5 place in Central America	95 global 4 place in Central America
GINI coefficient World Bank (2014)	50.6	47.70	41.8

EXHIBIT 6.2 Summary of Indicators for Honduras, Nicaragua, and El Salvador

Global Readiness Index (Networked)	3.24	3.08	3.63
Level of Schooling Finish 6th grade, UNDP (2016)	86.5%	84.3%	97.14%

Source: World Bank (2016), World Economic Forum (2016), United Nations (2015), Fitch, Moody's & Standard Ratings (2016)

Indicators used:

- Human Development Index (HDI). Score 0 is the lowest and 1 as the highest in human development.
- GINI Coefficient: is a measure of statistical dispersion intended to represent the income or wealth distribution of a nation's residents, and is the most commonly used measure of inequality.
- Doing Business: provides information of how well a country is for opening and running businesses.
- Global Readiness Index: score from zero as the lowest, and the six as the highest score in the Networked Readiness Index.
- Country Risk Ratings: gives information about the risk involved in investing in a given country considering the economic aspect.

EXHIBIT 6.2 *(Continued)*

A. Software Solutions:
• SAP Business One
• SAP Success Factors HCM Suite
• SAP All-in-One
• SAP HANA
• SAP Business Objects
• Oracle Database
• Oracle Middleware
• ACL Anti-Money Laundering
• ASEINFO Human Resources
• Virtualization Solutions
B. Hardware Solutions:
• Servers and Storage Systems
• Printing Solutions
• Personal Computing Solutions
• Communication and Networking
C. Services:
• Managed printing solutions
• Installation and Maintenance of Computer Equipment
• SAP and ORACLE implementations
D. Data Center Services.
• Collocation
• Hosting
• Business Continuity
• Custody of Magnetic Media
• Online Backups
• Storage on Demand
• Software as a Service (SaaS)

EXHIBIT 6.3 Summary of POPA's main products and Services

- **Ethic:** We care about doing things well, accomplishing with honesty our commitments, without going against our values, and without affecting the benefit of our customers, employees, providers, and our own company.

- **Innovation:** We aim to innovate persistently, to anticipate the requirements of the market, setting the pattern for our customers to get the most out of the new products and services from IT to help them become more efficient organizations.

- **Profitability:** Gain the appropriate profitability by accomplishing a consistent increase on the base of austerity and efficiency in the usage of the available resources, as well as the distribution of products and services of high quality from IT, benefitting our internal and external customers.

- **Responsibility:** We pledge to do what we promise, assuming the consequences of our actions and decisions, fulfilling our duty in every sense, and trying to ensure that our actions are carried out with justice, so that they preserve and increment the confidence deposited in us.

EXHIBIT 6.4 POPA's Institutional Values.

EXHIBIT 6.5 Map of Central America

Source: www.americacentral.info

Case 6.4 The Pérez Díaz Family Business Group: At a Crossroad in Venezuela

Cristina Alvarado and Maria José Parada

> *'We had never imagined that the [company] situation could arrive to this point. Two years of losses, the closing of businesses, some of our children leaving the country. Even though it is impossible to predict what will be our future, we cannot imagine a life away. Here we have our family, our houses, the businesses founded by our father and we must be prepared when all of this has passed"*
>
> *(Elisa, 50 years old, second generation)*

At the end of 2017, the Pérez Diaz Group[3] was at a crossroad: Continue business as usual or close the leading company in the group? The Pérez Díaz siblings are gathered to decide if they close Company "O," which have been addressed to egg production and represented one of the most important businesses of the Family Agribusiness Group located in the north-central area of Venezuela, which was founded by their father more than 60 years ago when he had immigrated.

The six siblings must make this difficult decision, and very quickly because the animals have not been fed for several days, the posture index is decreasing, and it is impossible to run a production plan.

The reality is dramatic: The production cost structure is unsustainable due to the scarce and costly raw materials to produce feed. Besides, in the last weeks some food distribution establishments have been forced to sell some food products at half price because of new official regulations government. There is a high risk of closing the doors of main chain supermarkets. With the hyperinflation rates, it is complicated to cover the production costs.

The Decision

They are considering two scenarios:

1. *Continuing the Group's operations:* If they decide to maintain the business activity, it will be financed by personal assets with the uncertainty whether these efforts will serve to survive efficiently or to postpone the closing in the short-term.

2. *Partially close the business:* If they decide to close it will be according to a plan which prioritizes the continuity of Company "B" and Company "S." In this scenario, animals of Companies "O," "A" & "D" are going to be sold. Consequently, they must negotiate with the workforce to leave the company and only some workers will continue to take care of the facilities while economic conditions change. They would have to restructure Company "S" with a

new business plan which facilitates the Company's operations with new eggs producers because Company "O" would not supply eggs after its closing. Company "B" would follow producing feed to supply its own needs.

The atmosphere in which the meeting takes place is very tense. The siblings need to face the most important and maybe the most difficult decision as owners. Each sibling has its own worries and thoughts about the situation: Sara is very concerned about the future of her children who are currently working in the Group. Eva is regretting the decisions done in the past—why other family businesses have survived, and they have not—Carmen and Elisa see the situation from a more optimistic perspective: now they are struggling with the crisis, but when the economy recovers, they will have the opportunity to rebuild the Group. Maria is shocked. José thinks it could be only the beginning of many family and business changes. They must be prepared to start again.

They must find the road to survive or maybe start again. Perhaps if they answer some questions that are in their heads it would be easier:

- Are we on time to explore new business projects out of Venezuela?
- How could we have prepared for these adverse conditions in the past?
- The founder's strategy of establishing alliances with other families was successful to create a big company group. However, in the present it is complicating things. Could it be reasonable to restructure the Family Business Group in these intense moments?

About the Pérez Díaz Family Group

A European immigrant in Venezuela who had arrived at the end of 1940 founded the Pérez Díaz Family Group. Twenty years afterward, he became one of the first entrepreneurs to industrialize the poultry business in Venezuela. This group is composed of a group of agricultural companies located in the north-central zone of Venezuela. Currently, the company is managed by the second generation with the support of the founder playing an advisory role.

The family group is vertically integrated, controlling a group of companies dedicated to animal production, feed manufacturing, and egg processing. Most of these companies are owned by several families not linked by blood ties— mainly immigrants like him—but by a long-term relationship as partners and friendship. The Pérez Diaz family owns between 30% and 40% of the shares in participating companies (with the major percentage concentrated in one owner in capital's companies). Although Mr. Pérez did not have the 51% of shares, as president of these companies, he has enjoyed the trust, loyalty (he had invited the other partners to engage these businesses) and respect of the rest of the founding partners and he has led most of the companies' Group, especially Companies "S", "A" and "D". In Company "B" he governed by alliances forged with another family who owns 37% of shares, until 2014 when a conflict started with a minority partner who was managing the company beside his children. Mr. Pérez enjoyed a high prestige, credibility, and confidence in his relationship with suppliers, customers, and banks, which reinforced his position as a leader in the companies.

Nowadays, like most family businesses in Venezuela which are privately owned, they are suffering due to the devastating economic crisis which threats the continuity of the group. The consumption of eggs is decreasing at a break-neck pace, and the costs of production are increasing and becoming very high due to high prices of raw material to produce feed. Also, prices are fixed and controlled by the government. Many factors are constellated to jeopardize the survival of the family group.

One of the most relevant (concerning market share and visibility) companies of the group, which processes, classifies, and distributes eggs, has been working on an internationalization plan. One of the challenges they must face is convincing all owners that internationalization is needed to survive.

These conversations about exporting processed eggs started in 2014 but suddenly the crisis arrived, and all the plans were interrupted. Besides, the difficulty to make decisions with other families, the economic crisis, and the hostile environment for private companies could wreak havoc.

At the moment the second generation is worried about the future of the family business group, and they must deal with the economic crisis at the same time they must consolidate their power in all companies they are sharing with other families. The founding generation is observing how their dream of being a great family business group is fading.

The Venezuelan Context

Venezuela is located on the north coast of South America, with a privileged place to enter in South America. Traditionally Venezuela has been "the door" to this part of the continent. For these reasons, many international companies established their operations and headquarters in the 1980s and 1990s. This situation changed dramatically after Hugo Chavez was elected in 1999 when Venezuela found a different regime where private companies were less welcome and nationalizations where the everyday news. Around 2007 the government started a very aggressive policy to expropriate private enterprises.[4]

Venezuela is an upper middle-income country[5] with a population of over 31 million people. Venezuela has been a traditional oil producer with one of the most important reserves of oil in the world. However, Venezuela is facing a crisis never lived before, generated by the fall of oil prices and inefficient management of country resources, combined with a radical shift of political orientation. It is close to collapse, succumbing to hyperinflation, food scarcity, violence, and health crisis.[6]

According to recent studies, the accumulated inflation since September 2016 is 1,083% and the estimations to end of the year 2017 reach 1,400%. The fall in GDP will be between 12% and 14% due to political crisis and contraction of importations. The last four years, the Venezuelan economy has reduced by 36% to 40%. The purchasing power of families has fallen by 50%, and they are investing around 80% of their earnings in buying food. Government controls the foreign exchange, and most private companies must buy dollars to operate in the black market which has a value around eight times more than the official price.[7]

The answer of the Venezuelan Government to the crisis has been to adopt even more restrictive policies to control private companies through limiting the access to foreign exchange and fixing prices of essential products, notably, food producers. Consequently, food is scarce, and the economy of families is hugely affected by higher costs of it. Also, the impairment of the conditions in the exercise of democratic rights and the economic conditions of the society is a tendency in last two years.[8]

Other conditions are also very averse to business families like higher rates of crime like abductions, frequent robberies of products and company's supplies. Also the talent is leaving the country and corporations have many difficulties in retaining the human capital.[9]

Besides, private companies must deal with a hostile environment characterized by frequent threatens to the reputation of firms through published information about companies which in many cases is false. In the last two years, private companies have been defined as the perpetrators of "economic war" in the words of the government. The government considers private enterprises an opponent as they showcase the causes of lower levels of productions in some private companies, due to government mismanagement. Yet, the government fights back accusing private companies of being the cause of the problem.

The Poultry Industry in Venezuela

Poultry plays a relevant role in food security and nutrition, especially in developing countries. This sector provides energy, protein, and nutrients to humans through short production cycles and converting many agricultural products into subproducts like meat and eggs.[10]

Traditionally, Venezuela has been considered as the sixth largest *producer* in Latin America.[11] Now the industry is facing many difficulties to maintain this position due to the intense economic crisis that has been prolonged for many years. The consumption of eggs has fallen by 63.8%. Moreover, the sector of egg production has decreased around 40.7% between 2016 and 2017.[12]

Additionally, price production is reaching maximum historical levels due to higher prices of feeding animals. These factors are producing a "perfect storm" which threatens the continuity and survival of many companies of the sector, which not are linked to the government. Most of the egg production and

Indicators (thousands)	2005	2010	2015	2016
Number of laying poultry	48553	115337	115316	169785
Number of pullet for Egg's production	12265	25020	22480	13409
Egg's production (Box 360 units)	8990	11753	15706	7854

FIGURE 6.3 Main indicators of the poultry industry in Venezuela
Source: FENAVI (2017)

poultry laying industries are concentrated in the hands of few groups.[13] Company "S" has been positioned in the first three places of the ranking published by the specialized press in the sector. Due to the current conjuncture of the industry, the distance between the first positions has been reduced. Currently, they are concentrating a laying poultry population around 3.4 million of producing laying poultry[14] in contrast with statistics of 2015 when companies in the first three places generated 9.17 million of laying chicken[15] in 2015, the first company was also in the ranking of ten most relevant producers in Latin America (see Figure 6.3).

Family firms have to face the challenge of high investment to support the development of such business where fixed assets are needed, while the crisis reduces the production dramatically and in consequence, revenues drop.

Egg Production Industry

The egg production industry involves several processes as is displayed in Figure 6.4. Pérez Diaz Family Group is vertically integrated into all these phases of the process. The referred process starts with the production of feed in the mill to provide the animal with the necessary balanced nutrients for proper growth, development, and maintenance.[16] Second, with some selection genetic procedures chicks are born and raised in a controlled environment. Third, pullets are moved to farms to mature for use in the poultry process. Fourth, egg production itself is developed in a controlled environment where activities of laying, collecting, washing, handling, grading, sorting, and packing will take place.[17] Finally, eggs will be suitable to sell and to store in markets, shops, etc.

Associations' Activity in the Poultry Industry

The family business group participates in relevant associations of the poultry industry. One of these associations called "Inprohuevos" plays an essential role in promoting egg consumption. It was created in 2001 in association with four family businesses of the industry. Besides, the Latin American Poultry Association[18] has recognized the founder's labor with the individual prize to be part of the Latin American Poultry Industry Hall of Fame.

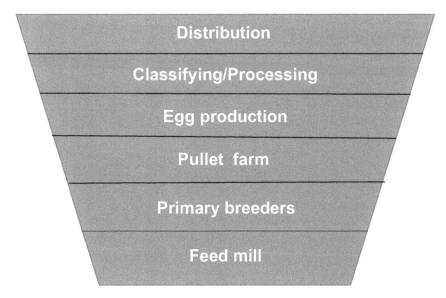

FIGURE 6.4 Egg production industry process

History of the Family Group

The history of the family group started in 1949 when the founder began to work in agriculture. As many entrepreneurs of this period he had migrated from Europe escaping from poverty and seeking new opportunities for his family. Mr. José Pérez is a self-made man who hasworked hard to create a big company to sustain his family. He arrived at Caracas in 1948 and one year later moved to Aragua to work in agriculture with other immigrants given the opportunity to work on a small farm. A couple of years later, Mr. Pérez started his project. Since the starts of the business, his wife has been very supportive and patient with his efforts to create the Group. Mrs. Laura Perez even prepared food for the first employees of the farms. She has been an example of austerity, the family unit, respect to the founder and hard work. Many family members recognize Mrs. Laura as a critical factor in the success of the family business group.

Mr. José Pérez has been a great entrepreneur and visionary in the Venezuelan poultry industry. His entrepreneurial spirit took him to create several companies with other partners. In this way, he was able to grow fast and to overcome the entry barriers of starting this kind of business, which demands a necessary amount of financial resources to begin the operations. Starting a poultry business requires high investments in purchasing or renting land, constructing and equipping the farm, hiring laborers/staff, feeding the animals and providing health care for birds. In 1960 he founded Company "A" dedicated to the poultry industry in alliance with two brothers-in-law. This company was focused on egg production and commercialization. The company is currently managed by members of two second-generation founding families. Later, Company "S" was founded to commercialize the production from company "A". However, due to the crisis in the country affecting levels of production negatively, the family decided to concentrate production and commercialization in Company "A".

In 1974 the founder created a new company (called Company "D") with one of the brothers-in-law and two additional partners. This new company was also in the poultry laying industry.

In 1978, Mr. Pérez constituted a feed production company with other nonfamily partners. Company "B" which is also the owner of a large-scale poultry integration with a capacity of 1.5 million laying poultry ("Company "E"). The Pérez family holds around one third of the shares. During the last three years, the family had to deal with corporate conflicts to recover control of the management of the company which had been delegated since its foundation to one of the partners who was a professional in the feed mill sector. Last year before conflict erupted, this owner— also director of the company—has been managing the business with nepotism and a lack of transparency. Indeed, he decided unilaterally to change the policy of selling feed to the rest of the owners who gave them special payment conditions.

In 1985, Company "C" was created focusing on incubating fertile eggs, which are sold to owners of the company and other national producers who are primary breeders. It places third on the national scale. Recently, it was acquired by Company "B." In 1989, in alliance with other poultry producers (some of them also were previously partners in the other companies), Mr. Perez created a new Company "S" which had the mission of processing, classifying, and distributing eggs and derived products. It is the only company in Venezuela which distributes eggs at a national scale, provides all supermarket chains and additionally supplies liquid egg products to the mayonnaise industry, bread factories, and pasta manufacturers.

In 1991, Mr. Perez founded the first company participated in only by family members without other nonfamily partners. This was a critical step in the history of the group. Later, a group of companies was created aligned with the mission of having an one's *own* production's holding. This group is called "Company O." The capacity of production is around 600,000 laying poultry. Besides, there are two farms intended to breed chickens which contribute to maintaining the productive cycle of laying poultry farms.

In 2014, all the members of the second generation decided to create a feed production company in the context of societal conflicts in Company "C" to assure the feed supply to their own farms. Due to the economic crisis and the high price of foreign exchange the project has been interrupted.

Pérez Díaz Family Group is vertically integrated into all stages of the egg production industry. All the companies are interrelated regarding their activities, suppliers, and synergies. The founder had the vision of creating one of the most relevant poultry industry groups in Venezuela. For these reasons, his strategy was founding companies with other partners to seize the opportunities based on joining financial, workforce and professional efforts (see Figure 6.5).

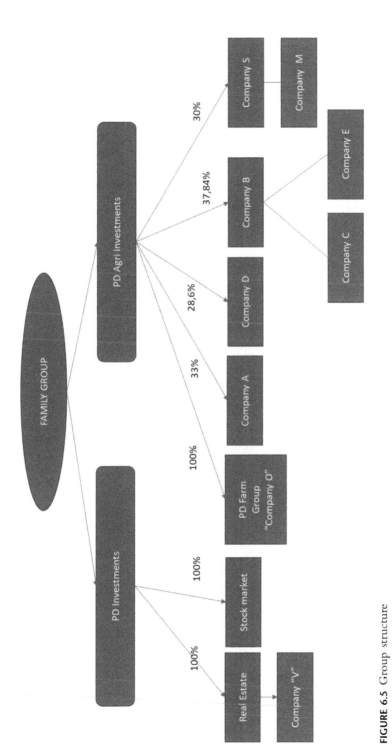

FIGURE 6.5 Group structure

Source: Information provided by family CEO (2017)

Company	Main activity	Family involvement
Company "O"	Egg production	Founder: Honorific Chairman 2nd Gen: 2 members (CEO & Administration Chief) 3rd Gen: 1 member (Animal Production Manager)
Company "A"	Egg production	2nd Gen: 2 members (Non Executive Director & Executive Director)
Company "D"	Egg production	2nd Gen: 1 member (Executive Director)
Company "B"	Feed mill	2nd Gen: 2 members (Non Executive Directors) 3rd Gen: 1 member (Executive Director)
Company "E"	Egg production	2nd Gen: 1 member (Chairman) 3rd Gen: 1 member (Non Executive Director)
Company "C"	Incubating fertile eggs	2nd Gen: 1 member (Executive Director) 3rd Gen: 1 member (Non Executive Director)
Company "S"	Classifying, distributing & processing eggs and derived products	2nd Gen: 2 members (Executive Chairwoman & Non Executive Director) 3rd Gen: 1 member (Non Executive Director)
Company "M"	Medicines, animal health care & poultry supplies	2nd Gen: 2 members (Executive Chairwoman & Non Executive Director)

FIGURE 6.6 Summary of activity's companies and family involvement

Source: Information provided by Family CEO

Nowadays most of the shares of the companies have been transmitted to the second generation who have several responsibilities in governance and management. Two of them have assigned chair roles in some organizations where the family partially participates. Additionally, this family group can be considered as a sort of entrepreneurial family because most of all family branches (4 of 6) have their own business in the poultry sector and other areas like real estate (see Figure 6.6).

Family Structure

Four generations integrate Perez Díaz Family. Both first-generation members are around their late 80s and the second generation are between 40s and 60s. Fifteen members join the third generation, whose ages are between 10 and 40. The fourth generation is composed of six members aged between 1 and 8 (see Figure 6.7).

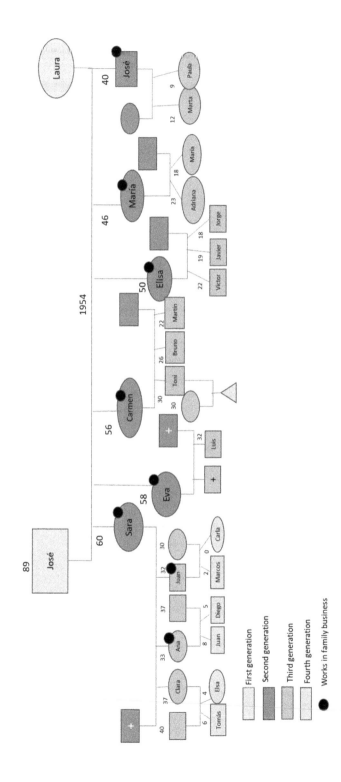

FIGURE 6.7 Family Genogram

Source: Information provided by Family CEO

The Pérez Díaz family is very proud of their values of honesty, unity, and hard work. Along the history, they have overcome difficulties together. In general, family members feel a big loyalty and sense of gratefulness to the founders. During the last years, family circumstances like divorces, the death of the husbands of two of the founder's children, have generated instability and uncertainty in the family. In addition, between 2002 and 2010 some family members have left the country and the family unity has been affected. They are looking for job opportunities and a better quality of life, especially in terms of personal security.

Family Involvement in the Business Group

Regarding the participation of the family in the business, all the second-generation members are working in several areas but with different levels of responsibility. Some of these differences have been produced by age difference and traditional family culture. The older sisters have joined the group in the last fifteen years to assume roles in real estate or controlling some business units. In the past, the participation in the company was limited to their husbands according to unwritten rules. For instance, because of the early death of one son-in-law, the oldest daughter started to work in the group.

Elisa, María, and José have been working for the last twenty years in the group, and they have assumed duties of governance and management of several companies in the group. Elisa and José are representatives in participating firms. Regarding the third generation, two of them are working in the family business group. Juan (32 years old) is leading animal department production in his own companies' division. He studied at a prestigious Panamerican Agricultural University. Ana (33 years old) is working in Company "B" as a director. Both are motivated by their jobs in the family group, but they also are afraid of the future. They have worked in the family enterprise for the last ten years. Clara, Toni, Martín, Marta y Paula are living outside Venezuela. Luis and Bruno are local entrepreneurs in industries other than poultry. The rest of third-generation members are studying at the university or in school.

This family group is a sort of multigenerational family because there are three generations involved in management. Also, in the second generation, there is a gap of 20 years between the eldest and the youngest sibling. The family has plenty of human capital to flourish the family business and to internationalize it. Both José Perez Jr. and Juan had their internships in a US company related to animal production. Most of the third generation speak English fluently and have been living in the US or England for academic reasons.

Leadership and Governance Model

The leadership and governance model is differentiated depending on whether companies are family owned or participated with other families (see Figure 6.8). In their own companies, siblings are constituted in a committee (a sort of board

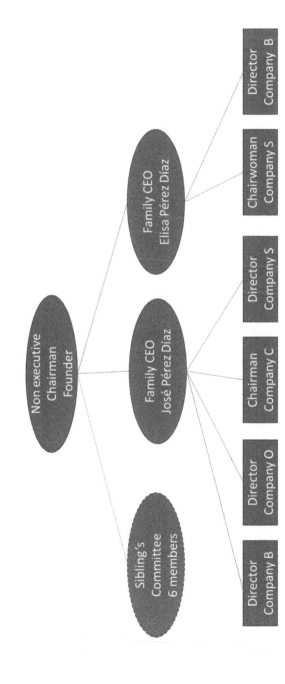

FIGURE 6.8 Leadership model

of directors) which hold meetings when they must make decisions. Because of that, the meeting frequency is variable and there is not a regular program of reunions. The decisions are made in most cases through consensus, although in some circumstances they are impeded by the difficulty of separating family and business roles. Many times, it is difficult to separate the discussions of family history and family relationships to professionally make the required decisions. All the agreements are informed to parents, but they do not participate in the siblings debate. However, in meetings the respect and loyalty to the founder are "the elephant in the room". Because of that, decision-making process is hard, especially, when some decisions can be contrary to the father's expectations or legacy.

Regarding the leadership model, Elisa and José Pérez Díaz have been delegated the representatives in participating companies, and they are succeeding to the founder in the Chair role in Company "S" and Company "C", respectively. Besides, both are members of the board of directors of Companies "S" and "M". Since the last semester of 2015, the second generation started to have a regular meeting to share information about companies, to discuss the strategy to face the societal conflict in society "B", and to work in some rules of family business relationships, among other issues.

Diversification of the Family Business Activities

Even though the primary event has focused on the poultry industry, the family business group has also invested in real estate. In 1975, the family developed the first project in this sector with partners of Company "A" addressed to construct a building with more than 20 apartments and commercial places to rent. In the 1990s, the family business group acquired several properties to rent. In 1992, all owners of Company "S" created another company (Company "M") to commercialize medicines, animal health products, and supplies to farms. That company represents an advantage for the partners because they obtain better conditions to acquire these types of supplies. In 1998, the second generation created company "V" which aimed to build houses for middle-class people given the housing deficit that the country was facing.

The Family's Dilemma

The results of the companies are getting worse (see Figure 6.9) in 2017, and it is impossible to predict the future of the family business group. Some siblings are questioning if they had to leave the country before this crisis. Eva (58 years old) said at the last meeting: "Other families have left the country. Maybe we had to do the same when the business was in best conditions. If we started a new business in the past, now they would have more chance to survive."

	Year			
Results	**2000**	**2005**	**2010**	**2015**
Revenues (Thousand $)				
Eggs production	41656	39310	31208	7396
Baby chicks	2900	1500	879	650
Feed	50545	40000	43326	2325
Total revenues	95101	80810	75413	10371
Earnings (%)	7.2	6.5	6	-2

FIGURE 6.9 Division's Group performance results

Notes

1. This case is a second version of the original written by Monica Zavala Espinoza in 2014 as her final graduation project under the supervision and advice from Marcos A. Vega Solano, associate professor from Zamorano University and is to be used as a tool for discussion in class of relevant management aspects, and not as a guideline of tactics to be used to develop a successful business. Most of the names and figures have been altered to maintain the company's confidentiality.
2. An economic entity is a public or private company, establishment, home or person that produces or provides services (INEGI, 2013).
3. This case was written with information provided by family members and secondary sources like web pages and industry sources. For confidentiality reasons, all the names have been changed.
4. (Paullier, 2012).
5. (The World Bank, 2017).
6. (Serbin, 2016).
7. (El Universal, 2017).
8. (Llenderrozas, 2016).
9. (Vilchez, 2015).
10. (Mottet & Tempio, 2017).
11. (Ruiz, 2012).
12. (Gutiérrez, 2017).
13. (Industria Avícola, 2017).
14. (Industria Avícola, 2017).
15. (Industria Avícola, 2015).
16. (American Feed Industry Association, 2017).
17. (The American Egg Board, 2017).
18. (ALA; www.avicolatina.com/).

References

The American Egg Board. (2017). *Production process.* Retrieved from www.aeb.org/farmers-and-marketers/ftip

American Feed Industry Association. (2017). *How feed is made.* Retrieved from www.afia.org/howmade

El Universal. (2017). *Ecoanalítica: Inflación en Venezuela podría cerrar en 1.400% este año.* Retrieved from www.eluniversal.com/noticias/economia/ecoanalitica-inflacion-venezuela-podria-cerrar-1400-este-ano_672821

FENAVI. (2017). Retrieved from http://fenavi.com.ve/categoria/cifras-y-estadisticas/

Gutiérrez, M. A. (2017). *Venezuela: caída del consumo de huevos en 63, 8%*. Retrieved from https://avicultura.info/venezuela-caida-del-consumo-de-huevos-en-638/

Industria Avícola. (2015). Edición Marzo. *Watt Global Media*. Retrieved from www.wattglobalmedia.com/publications/industria-avicola/

Industria Avícola. (2017). Volumen 64, 10. *Watt Global Media*. Retrieved from www.wattglobalmedia.com/publications/industria-avicola/

Llenderrozas, E. (2016). América Latina y fin de ciclo y transición regional. En A. Serbin (Ed.), *¿Fin de ciclo y reconfiguración regional? América Latina y las relaciones entre Cuba y los Estados Unidos*. Buenos Aires: Coordinadora Regional de Investigaciones Económicas y Sociales (CRIES).

Mottet, A., & Tempio, G. (2017). Global poultry production: Current state and future outlook and challenges. *World's Poultry Science Journal*, *73*(2), 245–256. doi: 10.1017/S0043933917000071

Paullier, J. (2012). Lo que se sabe de las expropiaciones de Chávez. *BBC Mundo*. Retrieved from www.bbc.com/mundo/noticias/2012/01/111207_venezuela_economia_expropiaciones_chavez_jp

Ruiz, B. (2012). *Venezuela: sexto productor avícola de Latinoamérica*. Retrieved from www.wattagnet.com/articles/11422-venezuela-sexto-productor-avicola-de-latinoamerica

Serbin, A. (2016). ¿Aliados incómodos? Venezuela y el impacto de la normalización de las relaciones Cuba-EE.UU. En A. Serbin (Ed.), *¿Fin de ciclo y reconfiguración regional? América Latina y las relaciones entre Cuba y los Estados Unidos*. Buenos Aires: Coordinadora Regional de Investigaciones Económicas y Sociales (CRIES).

Vilchez, H. (2015). *Muchos quieren regresar si cambian condiciones*. Retrieved from www.analitica.com/emprendimiento/fuga-de-talento-venezolano-por-que-emigraron-i-parte/

The World Bank. (2017). *Doing business: Venezuela RB*. Washington: The World Bank. Retrieved from www.doingbusiness.org/data/exploreeconomies/venezuela

INDEX